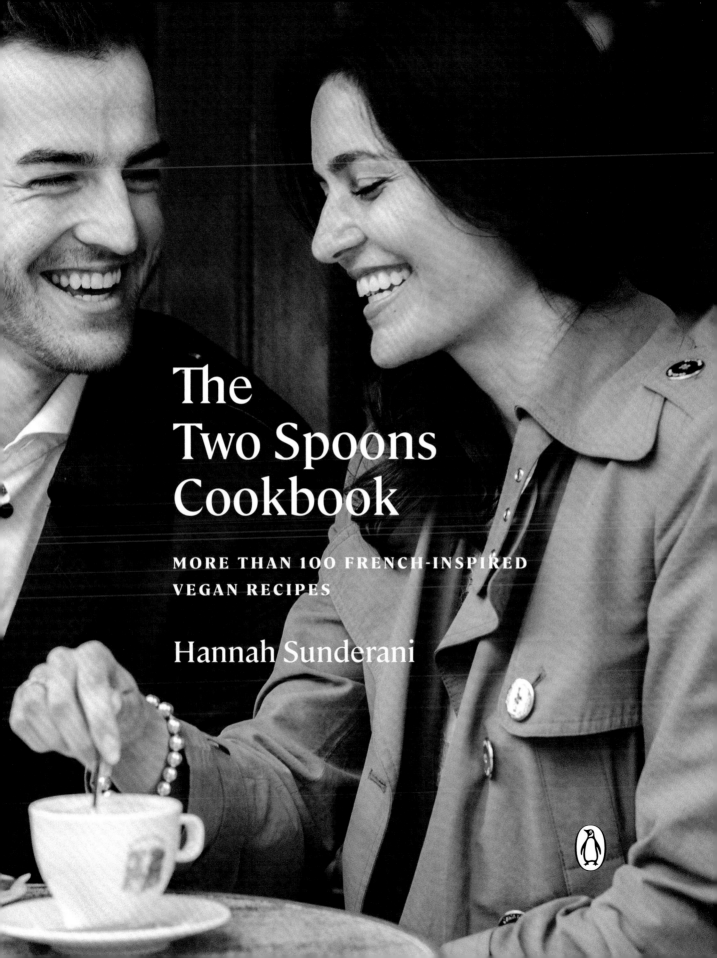

The Two Spoons Cookbook

MORE THAN 100 FRENCH-INSPIRED
VEGAN RECIPES

Hannah Sunderani

PENGUIN

an imprint of Penguin Canada,
a division of Penguin Random House Canada Limited

Canada • USA • UK • Ireland • Australia • New Zealand • India • South Africa • China

First published 2022

www.penguinrandomhouse.ca

LIBRARY AND ARCHIVES CANADA CATALOGUING IN PUBLICATION
Title: The Two Spoons cookbook : More Than 100 French-Inspired
Vegan Recipes / Hannah Sunderani.
Other titles: More Than 100 French-Inspired Vegan Recipes
Names: Sunderani, Hannah, author.
Identifiers: Canadiana (print) 20210211229 | Canadiana (ebook) 20210211385 |
ISBN 9780735241282 (softcover) | ISBN 9780735241299 (EPUB)
Subjects: LCSH: Vegan cooking. | LCSH: Cooking, French. | LCGFT: Cookbooks.
Classification: LCC TX837 .S86 2022 | DDC 641.5/6362—dc23

Cover and interior design by Lisa Jager
Cover photography by Hannah Sunderani
Food Photography by Hannah Sunderani
Lifestyle Photography by Lauren Miller
Photographs on pages i, ii–iii, v, viii, 23, 302, and 305 by Craig George

Printed in China

10 9 8 7 6 5 4 3 2 1

Penguin
Random House
PENGUIN CANADA

For my husband, Mitch:
In a noisy world, you are
my symphony. Thank you
for seeing my light, and
giving me the courage
to let it shine.

Contents

LES SOUPES ET SALADES   SOUPS AND SALADS

ENTRÉES   DELICIOUS MAINS, SHARING PLATES, AND WHOLESOME BOWLS

LE DESSERT   DARLING DESSERTS

Introduction

I would first like to take you back to the beginning, to when I started my blog, *Two Spoons*, in a quintessential French city called Lille, in 2016. My husband, Mitch, was offered a work transfer that uprooted our life from downtown Toronto and into la vie en France.

It is during these major changes in life, when we are pushed outside our comfort zone, that we realize our true desires. This was the push I needed to pursue my passion for sharing plant-based recipes—a diet that was so successful in my struggle with gut health issues and irritable bowel syndrome.

What better place to pursue my passion for cooking than in France? With its daily farmers' markets teeming with vendors calling out "Les pêches délicieuses!" for "deux euros!," endless cafés and clanking verres de vins, and the smell of freshly baked bread on every street corner, it is no secret that the French way of life revolves around good food and drink at every occasion.

And what better place to pursue my passion for plant-based cooking than in France? Surely I could have chosen a better location. In a culture where fromage, foie gras, and charcuterie are everyday staples, a plant-based diet was not always celebrated. Calling ahead to restaurants to inform them of my diet was often met with displeasure, and one time resulted in being served half a cooked carrot as my main course. What they did with the other half, I will never know.

It is no surprise that the world of plant-based eating has exploded over the past few years, and during my time in France I watched it unfold. I made friends with the early adopters, the movers and shakers of this small plant-based community, from chefs and café owners to cashiers at petits magasins. I witnessed their twists on French classics, like cashew-based cheeses and vegan mousse au chocolat, and discovered their trendy new recipes for the more adventurous.

We would chat about their changing menus, new products of theirs that I had tried and liked, and everyday things like which market vendors had the freshest produce, which boulangerie baked the best bread, and where to buy decently priced coconut yogurt.

I got to know them well. Of course, my poor French accent made me an unforgettable étrangère (foreigner). "Combien ça coûte?" (how much does that cost?) has a much different meaning than "combien ça cul?" (how much is that butt?). I also exasperated a baker once by mispronouncing "plus" when wanting more bread. I repeatedly pronounced it "*plu*" (without the "s"), interpreted as wanting less of their bread, instead of "*plus*" (pronounced with the "s"), meaning more. It was a rough go dividing the tiniest piece of bread between four friends later that day.

However, over time I understood better la vie en France. Here are some takeaways for you to nibble at:

* Any limb on the body that can bend is prime real estate for holding a baguette. Most popularly tucked under the armpit.
* Potatoes grow from the ground, so expect to buy them dirty. A vegetable scrubber will soon become your most used kitchen accessory.
* There is no hope of finding berries in October, so pick from the endless supply of apples and bake a tart.
* There is nothing more insulting to the French than adding orange juice to Champagne … oops.
* There is no occasion that cannot be improved with a glass of wine, a baguette, and fauxmage.

About this Book

This cookbook is meant to be taken lightly. By no means should it intimidate you. It is not a cookbook for French cooking enthusiasts or masterful chefs. It is a cookbook for the everyday home cook, one who wants to add more plant-based recipes into their diet without compromising taste. In addition, it is populated with recipes that pay tribute to my time in France and that are now on regular rotation in my kitchen, as well as lots of healthy and wholesome dishes that you can always expect from me.

I encourage you to adopt the elements that are special to the French way of life—enjoy your dishes as an occasion to be celebrated no matter how big or small, even if just for a moment. Even if it is a tiny piece of bread cut four ways.

In addition, I encourage you to enjoy the process from beginning to end. Start by taking joy in gathering your ingredients, whether by visiting your local farmers' markets or simply making a connection with the cashier at your grocery store. Maybe it is growing some simple vegetables in your garden if that is available for you or herbs on your windowsill if it is not. Giving a story to our ingredients makes cooking more pleasurable.

Finally, I encourage you to cook what is in season—a mantra that the French strongly live by but one that is less adhered to by North Americans. It was a great lesson for me in expanding my range of recipes. Savour fresh berries in the summer, and bake with apples in the fall. Cook with sweet potatoes in the winter and asparagus in the spring. Eating seasonally will open doors to more recipes that you might not otherwise try. It will make your shopping experience so much more enjoyable, and less expensive, and your food will taste better.

I have organized my book to take you through the day from beginning to end, to give you a real taste of what to eat in a day, starting with breakfast and ending with dessert.

Enjoy a vegan Classic Flaky Croissant (page 33) for breakfast, savoury Buckwheat Crepes with Cashew Cream Cheese and Greens (page 55) for brunch, a healthy Chickpea Salad Niçoise (page 207) for lunch, Madeleines (page 117) for an afternoon snack, and my Balsamic Mushroom Risotto (page 251) for dinner. These are recipes I enjoy cooking for friends and take pleasure indulging in at local restaurants. As for dessert, choose from your favourite flavours: Mousse au Chocolat (page 281) if you are a chocolate lover, or Pear Tarte Tatin (page 267) if you love fruit.

You will also find dishes inspired by the younger generation of French plant-based foodies, which I treasured at the trendy cafés. Enjoy tucking into wellness lattes like a Golden Turmeric Latte (page 86) and wholesome bowls like a Winter Bliss Bowl (page 233). Sink your teeth into gourmet toasts (pages 70 to 77) and devour Wally's Chocolate Coffee Freakshake (page 93), inspired by my friend Wally's café hyper chouette (super-cool café).

You will find recipes for some of my favourite healthy dishes, some inspired by Moroccan and Lebanese cuisine, such as my Hearty Moroccan Lentil Soup (page 203) and Oven-Baked Falafels (page 231), and wholesome bliss bowls and curry. A blend of traditional recipes, modern plant-based ones, and flavours from nearby cultures so perfectly captures what I enjoyed as a plant-based foodie in France.

I have also included recipes for dairy-free basics done right. My recipes for quality plant-based milks are great go-tos if you cannot find those ingredients at your grocery store. Or perhaps they are too expensive, or do not measure up to the quality you are hoping for. Whether you need it quick (try my Super-Quick Oat Milk, page 82) or you have ten minutes to spare for Creamy Dreamy Almond Milk (page 81) to sip like a fine wine, you'll find them here. In addition, there are recipes to make an array of easy vegan cheeses (starting on page 155) to share at l'apéritif (cocktail hour).

I have provided a selection of menu ideas for breakfast or brunch, afternoon tea, l'apéritif, and dinner to tie together tastes, textures, colours and sensations for a well-balanced meal. This is something that the French consider for every meal to give a complete experience from beginning to end. A Sunday brunch is served with at least three courses, whether at a café or a friend's house, all carefully selected so that you get the full dégustation (tasting). Even busy morning bakeries offer a small menu of fresh orange juice, coffee, and a pastry.

Perhaps it is not common in North America to think through a menu so carefully for each meal, but it is certainly something to consider for special occasions. Whether you're entertaining a crowd, having brunch with your besties, or serving a romantic dinner for two, let my menu ideas be an example of what you can pair together for a memorable meal. Use them as inspiration to create your own.

In offering a taste of my life in France as a plant-based foodie, I hope you enjoy these recipes as much as I have enjoyed creating them. I hope this cookbook will transform your experience of cooking, and that these recipes will bring stories to your ingredients and help turn monotonous tasks, like scrubbing a dirty potato, into a thankful moment. It is a lesson I am so grateful to have learned from my time in France.

Most of all, I hope you enjoy these plant-based recipes to the fullest and that you are proud of what you create—a delicious dish or meal worth sharing. Whether you are making a simple smoothie or a bubbling ratatouille, it is time to be cherished.

Bon appétit!

Hannah
xx

I love hearing from you!
Show me the dishes you make on social media
using the hashtag #twospoonscookbook.
Nothing makes me happier than to see your pictures.

Cooking Tips

Here are some helpful tips to help you achieve the best results. I will admit, when I first started cooking I did not abide by many of these suggestions—but lesson learned! Following these simple tips should make pulling a dish together much easier and more enjoyable. Trust me when I say that I speak from experience!

I am a huge advocate of modifying recipes to suit your personal taste, to use what you have on hand, or to meet dietary or allergy restrictions, especially when you are a comfortable cook. When it comes to baking, however, recipes can be a little more finicky, so I encourage you to follow the recipe for the perfect outcome.

1. Read the Entire Recipe Before Starting

I used to be notorious for embarking on recipes without reading them first, which sometimes led to unwelcome surprises, such as realizing that I hadn't soaked the nuts in advance, or discovering that a recipe needed to chill for two hours—not ideal when you have offered to bring dessert to your friend's dinner party in one hour.

I encourage you to read the recipe all the way through before starting. It will help you to know exactly what to expect from the recipe. To help you feel a little prepared even before reading, I have included a call-out at the top when a recipe requires soak time, chill time, or proof time, and when recipes are one-pot or one-bowl.

The notes section provides helpful tips, and I encourage you to give them a read before starting a recipe. This is especially useful for some of my more involved recipes, such as the Classic Flaky Croissants (page 33) and Chocolate Macarons (page 113). I include storage instructions so that at a glance you will know how long a recipe will keep, how to store it, and whether it is refrigerator or freezer friendly. In addition, you'll find a "Do Ahead" note when the recipe (or a part of it) can be prepared in advance to save you time.

2. Pre-Cut and Pre-Measure Ingredients

It is helpful to prepare your ingredients and measure them before starting to make the recipe, so that you have everything ready as you follow along. (For teaspoon and tablespoon measures, I find these are quick enough to do on the spot. Just make sure you have the ingredients and measuring spoons handy.) A little prep work will mean the cooking itself flows more smoothly and is less hectic and stressful, which in turn will boost your confidence as you cook.

3. Allergy/Dietary Restrictions

I do not have food allergies myself and enjoy using an abundance of ingredients. Before moving to France, I was an advocate of elimination-style recipes, for example, gluten-free, sugar-free, low-fat, and so on. However, in Europe I witnessed what a tiny part dietary restrictions played in a healthy diet, while obesity was much less prevalent than in North America. My belief now follows that of Michael Pollan: "Eat food, not too much, mostly plants." I find that with this mentality, my relationship with food is much healthier.

However, when you, a loved one, or a guest has a food allergy or medical dietary restriction, it's important to take it seriously. Many of my recipes are gluten-free, sugar-free, nut-free, and more. You will find call-outs to these at the beginning of each recipe:

* Vegan: The recipe contains no animal products or animal by-products. Lucky for us, all the recipes in this cookbook are vegan!
* Gluten-free: The recipe is free of gluten. If you are celiac or cooking for someone with celiac disease, check package labels to ensure they are certified gluten-free, such as looking for certified gluten-free oats.
* Grain-free: The recipe contains no grains, such as wheat, rice, or oats, or grain pasta.
* Nut-free: The recipe contains no tree nuts, such as almonds, cashews, or walnuts. If you have a nut allergy or are cooking for someone who does, check package labels to ensure they are certified nut-free.
* Oil-free: The recipe contains no liquid oils, such as olive, coconut, or avocado oil, and no vegan butter products. The recipe may contain naturally occurring oils from whole foods such as avocados or almonds.

- Soy-free: The recipe contains no soy-based ingredients, such as tofu, tamari, miso, edamame, or tempeh. Note that recipes that use tamari can be made soy-free by substituting coconut aminos. I prefer using tamari in recipes, however, because it is less expensive and easier to find.
- No added sugar: The recipe contains no added sugar, be it refined or natural.
- Refined sugar-free: The recipe contains no refined sugars, such as organic cane sugar. The recipe may contain natural sweeteners, such as maple syrup, molasses, dates, or coconut sugar.
- Raw/no-bake: The recipe does not require cooking or baking.

I have added call-outs for optional dietary modifications, such as "oil-free option," at the top of the recipe when possible, with instructions in the note section on how to modify the recipe.

Lastly, if an ingredient can easily be substituted with another that you might have handy, I have noted that below the recipe, such as swapping the sweet potato for butternut squash in my Ultra-Cozy Sweet Potato, Chickpea, and Spinach Curry (page 242).

Kitchen Tools and Equipment

When it comes to kitchen tools and equipment, I do my best to keep it minimal. I do not have a ton of storage space, so I love tools that do multiple tasks, like my 3-in-1 food processor. I am not a big fan of single-use items, unless they are used often (like my citrus juicer). As my cooking has evolved, I have naturally come to rely on a few more essentials. Here are the ones that I use often, some inexpensive and others more of an investment, and highly recommended to make cooking a breeze. These items are certainly helpful for making the recipes in this cookbook.

Knives

If you are new to cooking, my top recommendation is to invest in a couple of quality sharp knives. Forgo the fancy knife set and buy the following two knives for all your chopping, slicing, and dicing. My favourite brands are Sabatier and Miyabi.

* 8-inch chef's knife
* 4-inch paring knife

Baking Sheets, Baking Dishes, and Pots and Pans

Baking Sheets: Quality baking sheets have so many uses, from roasting vegetables like my Maple Spiced Roasted Carrots (page 228) to baking like My Darling Flourless Chocolate Chip Cookies (page 118). A half sheet pan (18 x 13 inches) fits most home ovens perfectly and meets all my needs. Quality aluminium pans with rims are important because cheap pans will warp when they get too hot. This is not good when you are baking a Blueberry

Ginger Galette (page 291) and all the juices start to spill out because the baking sheet warped halfway through! I use the Nordic Ware Natural Aluminum Commercial Baker's Half Sheet. You can buy it online.

Tart Pans: Tart pans are used a lot in this cookbook for such dishes as Mushroom and Spinach Quiche (page 57) and the many tarts in the dessert chapter. The two tart pans I use are 9-inch and 11-inch non-stick tart pans with removable bottoms. The removable bottom makes it so easy to lift out the tart and serve your gorgeous creations.

Baking Pans and Dishes: The following pans will be handy for the recipes in this cookbook.
* 8-inch square baking pan to make Brookies (page 135), Pumpkin Chickpea Blondies (page 139), and Healthier Millionaire Bars (page 133)
* 8½ x 4½-inch and 9 x 5-inch loaf pans to make Buttery Brioche (page 39), Chocolate Chip Banana Bread (page 143), and Sneaky Zucchini and Walnut Bread (page 144)
* 12-cup non-stick muffin pan, for Feel-Good Raspberry Muffins (page 146), Chocolate Hazelnut Swirl Muffins (page 149), and Chickpea Eggy Muffins (page 61)
* 8 x 11-inch baking dish to make Spinach and Ricotta Stuffed Shells (page 257), and 8 x 11-inch oval baking dish to make Cauliflower au Gratin (page 258)
* 7½-inch round baking dish, such as a brie baking dish, for recipes like Luxurious Baked Brie (page 160) and Raspberry Clafoutis (page 285)
* 9-inch round cake pan to make Chocolate Almond Torte (page 140)
* Set of four 4-ounce ramekins to make Blue Cheese (page 156), Kryptonite Chocolate Lava Cakes (page 278), Classic Crème Brûlée (page 293), and Crème Caramel (page 297)

Pots and Pans: Over the years I have collected a range of pots and pans for various dishes. Here are the ones I found the most helpful for the recipes in this cookbook:
* Skillets in small, medium, and large. Although not necessary, a large non-stick skillet is particularly helpful for recipes like Parisian Crepes (page 43), Buckwheat Crepes (page 55), and Oaty Banana Pancakes (page 30). I particularly like granite-stone-coated non-stick skillets.
* Medium (8-inch) cast-iron skillet for Ooey Gooey Cheesy Fondue (page 163), and large (10-inch) cast-iron skillet for Summer Rainbow Ratatouille (page 253), Green Beans Amandine (page 223), and Grilled Asparagus with Cherry Tomatoes and Parmesan (page 224)
* Small and medium stainless steel saucepans for heating sauces and liquids, melting chocolate, and making hot drinks like Golden Turmeric Latte (page 86) and Chocolat Chaud (page 90)

* Large stainless steel or cast-iron pot for making soups recipes like Hearty Moroccan Lentil Soup (page 203) and Gourmet French Onion Soup (page 199)

Small Appliances

Hand Mixer: For many years I have used my trusty hand mixer to whip together delicious baked goods, from Ginger Snap or Chewy Cookies (page 122) to Chocolate Macarons (page 113), to Pain d'Épices (page 129) to Chantilly (page 298). You can do pretty much everything with an affordable $50 hand mixer. I like the brands Cuisinart and KitchenAid.

Stand Mixer: As I have become more of a baker, I found it advantageous to invest in a stand mixer. The ease and convenience of being able to step away, or to use two hands to add ingredients, is a welcome luxury. Stand mixers do come at a high price. I use the Precision Master 5.5-Quart Stand Mixer by Cuisinart. I absolutely love it, and it is less expensive than other brands. Although not necessary for this book, I highly recommend a stand mixer for my bread recipes: Classic Flaky Croissants (page 33) and especially Buttery Brioche (page 39).

High-Speed Blender: If you are going to invest in one high-performance appliance, my recommendation is always a high-speed blender. They are so versatile and will make your cooking much easier. I use my Vitamix blender daily. It is my kitchen baby and I adore this little sous-chef. Use it in this book to make everything from my refreshing Supreme Blueberry Smoothie (page 94) to Oaty Banana Pancakes (page 30), my vegan milks, including Barista Cashew Coconut Oat Milk (page 85), and my vegan cheeses like Dreamy Cashew Cream Cheese (page 155). Use it to purée sauces and soups for velvety smooth texture and to make silky desserts like my Lemon Tart filling (page 265), Crème Caramel (page 297), and Classic Crème Brûlée (page 293).

3-in-1 Food Processor: I love my 3-in-1 food processor because it is so versatile. I use it for many recipes, including making pastry dough and puréeing my Pink Beet Hummus (page 168). Most often, I use the S-blade for chopping and mixing, but the machine is also useful for grating and shredding vegetables at lightning speed, which is handy for my Shaved Brussels Sprouts Salad (page 215). My 3-in-1 food processor also comes with blender and juicer units. I'll use the blender as a backup if I'm in the middle of a recipe and my Vitamix is preoccupied (as in, the blender jar is in the dishwasher because I couldn't be bothered to clean it), and I love the juicer to make my Immunity Boost Juice (page 98) and Energizing Green Tonic (page 101). The food processor I have is the Cuisinart Kitchen Central 3-in-1 with blender, juicer, and 8-cup food processor.

Kitchen Scale: Another kitchen essential is my digital kitchen scale. They are so affordable and an essential tool for precision in baking recipes, like my Chocolate Macarons (page 113). A scale is also helpful for weighing fruits and veggies. In this book, I have included measurements in grams, ounces, or pounds when it is helpful to know the weight of an ingredient or when they are purchased by weight. Take out all the guesswork and get yourself one of these treasured kitchen staples.

Storage

Reusable Wrap: I absolutely love to use my reusable wraps in the kitchen! They are easy to clean and hold their shape for wrapping. Use them to wrap everything from pastry dough for chilling to half a lemon and other half-used fruits and veggies. Use them to cover bowls like Creamy Chia Pudding (page 47) and Blueberry Muffin Overnight Oats (page 48) until you're ready to eat, and wrap up Feel-Good Raspberry Muffins (page 146) or Sneaky Zucchini and Walnut Bread (page 144) to enjoy on the go. My favourite brand is Bee's Wrap.

Glass Mason Jars, Bottles, and Airtight Containers: My glass jars and bottles are a collection of reused tomato sauce and jam jars. Whenever I finish a jar of interesting shape or size, I reuse it! They are so helpful for storing things like Raspberry Chia Jam (page 66) and Chocolate Hazelnut Spread (page 69) as well as for bottling my many vegan milk recipes (starting on page 79) and juices (pages 98 and 101).

As for airtight containers, my bottom kitchen drawer is far from orderly. It is more an amalgamation of random containers that I have adopted over the years. My favourites are the freezer-safe glass containers, like Pyrex. It really helps to be able to see the leftovers in your refrigerator and freezer, so you remember you have them!

Other Useful Equipment

Nut Milk Bag: I swear by a nut milk bag to make the creamiest and dreamiest vegan milks. Yes, you can also do it with a thin kitchen towel, but trust me—it is so much easier with a nut milk bag. Use a nut milk bag to make my milk recipes (starting on page 79). If you do not have a juicer, use it to make my juices (pages 98 and 101). A nut milk bag costs less than $15. Opt for nylon mesh material for a strong, unbreakable bag.

Measuring Tape: You may not think of measuring tape as a kitchen essential, but it is a helpful little item. Use it to measure baking dishes and cake and loaf pans so that you use the size specified in the recipe. As well, it's very helpful in baking recipes that require a little precision, such as my Classic Flaky Croissants (page 33) and Baked Beignets (page 127). I like to use a flexible tape measure because it shrinks right down and is easy to store in my drawer.

Microplane Grater: I really like this tool for grating ginger and zesting citrus. This will be helpful in recipes that call for grated ginger, such as my Creamy Carrot and Ginger Soup (page 194) or Blueberry Ginger Galette (page 291), and recipes with lemon zest, like my Madeleines (page 117) and Lemon Tart (page 265).

Stainless Steel Mesh Sieves: A large mesh sieve is great for straining soaked nuts or chickpeas and cooked pasta. It is also wonderful for sifting flour, which helps baked goods to be light and fluffy. I also like a small mesh sieve for straining Golden Turmeric Latte (page 86) and for lightly dusting desserts with icing sugar.

A Few More Basics: Some other must-have basics worth mentioning, which you likely already have in your kitchen, are mixing bowls, measuring cups, measuring spoons, wooden spoons, silicon spatulas, pastry brush, stainless steel whisk, rolling pin (wood and/or marble), wire cooling racks, garlic press, bread knife, citrus juicer, kitchen twine, parchment paper, plastic wrap and tin foil, paper muffin tin liners, and vegetable scrubber.

Specialty Items: A few recipes in this book call for specialty items, such as special moulds that will help you make beautiful sweet treats like Madeleines (page 117) and Cannelés (page 125). Here are the special tools I love using. They are available at most kitchen stores or online.

* Non-stick madeleine pan, 16 moulds
* Non-stick cannelé pan, 6-cavity or 12-cavity
* Aluminum Bundt pan, 12-cup
* Cookie cutter, 2½-inch
* Bamboo matcha whisk
* Piping bags
* No. 12 small round piping tip (for making Chocolate Macarons, page 113)
* No. 32 large star piping tip (for making Pretty Petites Meringues, page 110)
* Ramekins: three 6-ounce (optional for making Classic Crème Brûlée, page 293, or you can use four 4-ounce ramekins)
* Kitchen torch, for making the crackle caramel top in Classic Crème Brûlée (page 293)

Pantry Staples

irst, let me assure you that I am not the type of person who has a Pinterest-perfect pantry with everything labelled and alphabetized. Not even slightly. Open up my pantry cupboard and you will get a direct insight into my chaotic brain! Frankly, it is an explosion that only I know how to navigate, and it drives my husband, Mitch, bonkers. However, it has everything I need for making flavourful, wholesome meals.

On the following pages is a list of pantry staples that I like to keep on hand and that will be helpful in making the recipes in this book. You will see a range from classic flours (like all-purpose flour) to less common ones (like chickpea flour), from classic sweeteners (like organic cane sugar) to natural ones (like maple syrup).

I am a firm believer that life is not about restriction but about celebrating all types of foods—sometimes healthy and sometimes a little more indulgent. Being open-minded about ingredient types allows me to not fixate on diet or restrictions, and I believe this has allowed me to have a good relationship with food. You will see this translated in the recipes throughout this book.

Most of the following staples can be purchased at your local grocery store, while you can find some specialty items, such as spirulina or matcha powder, at specialty grocers like Whole Foods or online from retailers such as Amazon or Well.ca. In some instances, I specify a favourite brand to help you with your shopping. Of course, it is not necessary to seek out these specific brands, but my blog readers often find it helpful to know what I am using in my kitchen.

Salts

* Fine black salt: also known as Himalayan black salt or kala namak; it can be pink in colour. Black salt has a sulphurous eggy smell. Great for recipes like Chickpea Eggy Muffins (page 61) and Chickpea Omelette (page 62). I like the brand Lumière de Sel found at Whole Foods and Well.ca.
* Fine sea salt
* Flaky sea salt: Great for sprinkling on toast and finished dishes.

Sweeteners

* Agave
* Coconut sugar
* Dark brown sugar
* Demerara sugar
* Granulated sugar: also known as white sugar or table sugar. Not all granulated sugar is vegan. You can make granulated sugar for my recipes by pulsing organic cane sugar in a high-speed blender a few times to create a finer texture. I like to do this in batches and store in an airtight container for later use.
* Organic cane sugar: Not all cane sugar is vegan, but certified organic cane sugar is. I like brands such as Kirkland, Whole Foods 365, and Wholesome.
* Organic icing sugar: I like the brand Wholesome.
* Molasses, fancy
* Pure maple syrup
* Medjool dates

Flours and Grains

* All-purpose flour: When measuring flour (all types), I use the "spoon and sweep method." Spoon the flour into the measuring cup until very full. Turn a kitchen knife upside down and sweep the knife over the measuring cup to remove any excess flour. (Scooping the flour directly into the container or bag packs down the flour and will result in too much).
* Almond flour: made from ground blanched almonds
* Buckwheat flour
* Whole wheat flour
* Chickpea flour
* Gluten-free baking flour: I like Bob's Red Mill Gluten-Free 1-to-1 Baking Flour.

- Gluten-free old-fashioned rolled oats: Oats are naturally gluten-free, but often manufactured in the same facility as gluten-containing grains. Check the packaging for a certified gluten-free label if you are celiac. I like Bob's Red Mill Gluten-Free Old-Fashioned Rolled Oats, and Only Oats Gluten-Free Rolled Oats.
- Bread crumbs
- Rice: wild rice blend, whole-grain basmati, arborio, brown
- White quinoa

Oils and Vegan Butters

- Vegan butter: For my Classic Flaky Croissants (page 33), I recommend using the quality brand Miyoko's Organic Cultured Vegan Butter. It is firm when cold, just like dairy butter, and the ingredient list is minimal and wholesome. It is more expensive, but highly recommended for this recipe. For my other recipes, vegan butter like the brands Earth Balance or Melt Organic work very well, either for melting or in baking. They are also great for using in pastry dough as their butter consistency results in a more flexible dough.
- Avocado oil: This is a great neutral-flavour liquid oil for cooking with high heat. I like the brand Chosen Foods.
- Cold-pressed extra-virgin olive oil: Great for salads or cooking and baking at lower heat.

Coconut

- Canned coconut milk, full-fat: I like Thai Kitchen and Whole Foods 365 brands.
- Coconut cream
- Coconut flakes (long, wide flakes)
- Shredded coconut, unsweetened
- Coconut oil, virgin, unrefined
- Coconut yogurt, unsweetened: My favourite brand is Riviera.

Raw Nuts, Seeds, and Butters

- Almonds, whole, slivered, and natural almond butter
- Almond flour: Fine ground blanched almonds (not to be confused with almond meal, which contains skins and has a coarser grind)
- Cashews
- Dry-roasted hazelnuts: If using raw hazelnuts, toast them on a baking sheet in a 350°F (180°C) oven for 12 to 15 minutes or until fragrant and blistered. Wrap the hazelnuts in a kitchen towel and vigorously rub to remove most of the skins.

* Peanuts, whole, and natural peanut butter
* Pecans
* Pine nuts
* Pistachios
* Walnuts
* Chia seeds, whole and ground: To make ground chia seeds, pulse ½ cup chia seeds in a high-speed blender to a flour-like consistency. Store in an airtight container at room temperature for up to 3 months. Chia seed mixed with water is a great vegan substitute for eggs in cooking and baking.
* Flaxseeds, whole and ground: To make ground flaxseed, pulse ½ cup flaxseeds in a high-speed blender to a flour-like consistency. Store in an airtight container at room temperature for up to 3 months. Ground flaxseed mixed with water is a great vegan substitute for eggs in cooking and baking.
* Hemp hearts
* Pumpkin seeds
* Sesame seeds
* Tahini
* Unsweetened almond milk (or try my Creamy Dreamy Almond Milk, page 81)

Acids

* Apple cider vinegar: Buy a good-quality vinegar in a glass bottle. The vinegar should look a little murky. Choose brands labelled "unfiltered" or "unpasteurized."
* Balsamic vinegar
* Lemon juice and zest
* Lime juice
* Wine, dry white and full-bodied red. Les Jamelles brand is vegan and well priced.

Beans and Legumes

* Chickpeas: Reserve the liquid, called aquafaba, from canned chickpeas and store in the refrigerator or freezer. It is a great egg replacement for cooking, baking, and making Chantilly (page 298) and Pretty Petite Meringues (page 110).
* Edamame beans
* French green lentils (du Puy lentils)

Herbs and Spices

* Allspice
* Bay leaves, dried
* Cardamom, pods and ground
* Chili powder
* Cilantro, fresh and dried
* Cinnamon, ground and sticks
* Cloves, ground and whole
* Cumin, ground
* Curry powder
* Garlic powder
* Ginger, fresh and ground
* Herbes de Provence
* Italian seasoning
* Lemon dill seasoning, or dried dill
* Mint, fresh
* Nutmeg, ground
* Nutritional yeast
* Onion powder
* Oregano, dried
* Paprika, sweet and smoked
* Parsley, fresh flat-leaf
* Pepper, black, peppercorns and ground
* Pumpkin spice
* Red chili flakes
* Rosemary, fresh
* Sage, fresh
* Star anise
* Thyme, fresh
* Turmeric, fresh and ground

Powders and Starches

* Agar agar powder: A natural vegetable gelatin used for thickening fillings like in my Lemon Tart (page 265), Classic Crème Brûlée (page 293), and Crème Caramel (page 297). Agar agar can be found at speciality stores like Whole Foods and on Amazon. I use the brand Everland.

- Arrowroot powder
- Baking powder
- Baking soda
- Blue spirulina powder: I like the brand Rawnice, available online.
- Cream of tartar
- Matcha powder, premium ceremonial grade: My favourite brand is From the Reserve, available online.
- Tapioca powder

Soy

- Gluten-free low-sodium tamari
- Organic non-GMO tofu, extra-firm, firm, and silken
- White miso

Dairy-free Chocolate

- 70% dark chocolate: Most dark chocolate is naturally vegan, but check the ingredient list.
- Semi-sweet chocolate bars and chips
- Cacao nibs
- Cocoa powder

Miscellaneous

- Apricot jam
- Canned tomatoes, diced
- Capers
- Dijon mustard
- Dry pasta
- Greek olives
- Pumpkin purée
- Pure vanilla extract
- Pure almond extract
- Sun-dried tomatoes, oil-packed
- Tomato paste
- Vegetable broth
- Whole-grain tortillas

Petit Déjeuner

Breakfast and Brunch

asily my favourite meal of the day is breakfast. From the moment
I go to bed, I am counting down the hours to my next meal.
Therefore, to break the fast, it has to be delicious!

This chapter has all the sweet and savoury basics covered from quick
and easy weekday breakfasts like Blueberry Muffin Overnight Oats (page 48)
to recipes that are a little more gourmet to enjoy on weekends, like my
Cinnamony French Toast with Apple Compote (page 29). Here is a beautiful
collection of my favourite plant-based breakfast recipes that I am sure you
will love.

Brunch Menus

I love bringing people together over brunch, be it brunch with my besties or a sweet brunch for two while we are still in our jammies. There is something so special about sitting down to your first meal of the day after having put a little thought and care into it.

I particularly love to throw a brunch party in the summertime. It is my favourite way to entertain and the perfect opportunity to gather friends in my backyard on a warm, sunny Sunday. People arrive bursting with energy and ready to eat! (The best party guests, if you ask me.)

Be inspired by these menus carefully crafted for an unforgettable feast.

Brunch with Besties

Green Detox Smoothie (page 97)

Creamy Chia Pudding with Red Fruits
(page 47)

Classic Flaky Croissants (page 33)

Avocado Toast with Pink Beet Hummus
and Granola (page 70)

Matcha Latte (page 89) or
Golden Turmeric Latte (page 86)

Brunch for Two

Immunity Boost Juice (page 98) or
Energizing Green Tonic (page 101)

Cinnamony French Toast with Apple
Compote (page 29) or
Savoury French Toast (page 52)

Wally's Chocolate Coffee Freakshake
(page 93)

Family Fun

Supreme Blueberry Smoothie (page 94)

Parisian Crepes with Chocolate Hazelnut
Spread and Banana (page 43) or
Oaty Banana Pancakes (page 30)

Veggie Tofu Scramble with
Roasted Baby Potatoes (page 65)

Chocolat Chaud (page 90)

Brunch for Entertaining

Immunity Boost Juice (page 98) and/or
Energizing Green Tonic (page 101)

Maple Pecan Granola (page 44; serve
with coconut yogurt and fresh fruits)

Mushroom and Spinach Quiche (page 57)

Buttery Brioche (page 39) with
Raspberry Chia Jam (page 66)

Tea and Coffee

Quick and Easy

Blueberry Muffin Overnight Oats (page 48)

PB&J with Fried Banana Toast (page 73) or Chickpea Eggy Muffins (page 61)

Matcha Latte (page 89) or Golden Turmeric Latte (page 86)

Serves 3 or 4

Cinnamony French Toast with Apple Compote

Vegan • Refined Sugar-free

In France they call French toast le pain perdu, which means "forgotten bread." And making French toast is exactly how you should be repurposing your slightly stale loaf. This is how you turn your bread from forgotten to famed! Pan-fried until golden, this classic French toast is made vegan by using silken tofu for the egg mixture. Here I pair it with a simple, sweet, and cinnamony apple compote topping. Do not underestimate the power of thick bread when making French toast. A thick slice is twice as nice!

1. Make the Apple Compote: In a medium pot, mix together the apples, water, maple syrup, cinnamon, vanilla, and sea salt. Cover the pot with a lid and bring to a boil, then reduce the heat to medium-low and simmer the apples, stirring occasionally, for 10 minutes. Remove the lid and continue cooking, stirring frequently, until the liquid has evaporated almost entirely and the apples are very soft. Taste, and add more maple syrup to sweeten, if desired. Keep warm until ready to use.

2. Make the French Toast: In a high-speed blender, combine the almond milk, tofu, flour, ground flaxseed, maple syrup, cinnamon, vanilla, and black salt. Blend on low speed until smooth. Transfer the eggy mixture to a shallow medium bowl.

3. Heat a large non-stick skillet over medium heat. Add 1 teaspoon of the coconut oil and swirl it around to evenly coat the bottom of the skillet. Soak the bread slices, one at a time, in the eggy mixture for 10 to 15 seconds, coating both sides. Cook the French toast in batches of 2 or 3 slices until golden on both sides, 2 to 3 minutes per side. Add more coconut oil as needed so the bread does not stick to the skillet.

4. Serve the French toast topped with the Apple Compote and maple syrup. Sprinkle with coconut flakes, if desired.

APPLE COMPOTE

1½ pounds (675 g) Pink Lady or Honeycrisp apples, peeled, cored, and chopped into 1-inch pieces (4 cups/4 medium apples)

6 tablespoons water

2 tablespoons pure maple syrup, more if needed

1 teaspoon cinnamon

½ teaspoon pure vanilla extract

Pinch of fine sea salt

FRENCH TOAST

1 cup unsweetened almond milk

½ block (5½ ounces/150 g) silken tofu

¼ cup all-purpose flour

1 tablespoon ground flaxseed or ground chia seeds

1 tablespoon pure maple syrup, more for serving

1 teaspoon cinnamon

½ teaspoon pure vanilla extract

¼ teaspoon fine black salt or sea salt

1 to 2 teaspoons coconut oil, for frying

6 slices (each 1 inch thick) French or Italian loaf, or day-old Buttery Brioche (page 39), or bread of choice

Coconut flakes, for sprinkling (optional)

STORAGE

Store leftover French Toast and Apple Compote in separate airtight containers in the refrigerator for up to 2 days. Reheat before serving.

Oaty Banana Pancakes

Vegan   ∗   Gluten-free   ∗   Soy-free   ∗   Refined Sugar-free

1 cup gluten-free old-fashioned
    rolled oats

1 very ripe medium banana

2 tablespoons coconut sugar

1 tablespoon arrowroot powder

½ teaspoon baking powder

¼ teaspoon baking soda

½ teaspoon cinnamon

Pinch of fine sea salt

1¼ cups unsweetened almond milk

1 tablespoon avocado oil,
    more for frying

½ teaspoon pure vanilla extract

FOR SERVING

1 to 2 bananas, sliced into rounds

Pure maple syrup

Puffed quinoa or coconut flakes,
    for sprinkling (optional)

STORAGE

Store leftover pancakes in an airtight container in the refrigerator for up to 2 days. Reheat before serving.

I love these pancakes because they are a healthful spin on the classic, using blitzed gluten-free oats in place of wheat flour and banana to sweeten. I have been making these pancakes for years and never tire of them. They are comforting and wholesome, sweet and utterly crowd-pleasing. From now on, let this be your go-to pancake recipe.

1. Preheat the oven to 200°F (100°C). Line a baking sheet with parchment paper.

2. In a high-speed blender, combine the oats, banana, coconut sugar, arrowroot powder, baking powder, baking soda, cinnamon, salt, almond milk, avocado oil, and vanilla. Blend until smooth. Let the batter sit for 15 to 20 minutes to thicken.

3. Lightly grease a large non-stick skillet with avocado oil and set over medium heat. Give the batter a good stir, then pour 2 heaping tablespoons of batter for each pancake into the skillet, making 2 or 3 pancakes at a time. Cook until tiny bubbles cover the surface of the pancake and the bottom is golden brown, about 2 minutes. Flip and continue to cook until golden brown on the bottom, about 2 minutes more. Transfer the pancakes to the prepared baking sheet and keep warm in the oven while you cook the remaining pancakes. Add more avocado oil to the pan as needed to prevent the pancakes from sticking.

4. Serve the pancakes with sliced bananas on top and maple syrup. Sprinkle with puffed quinoa or coconut flakes, if desired.

Makes 12 croissants * Requires: proof time + chill time

Classic Flaky Croissants

Vegan * Soy-free

If I was up early enough, I would see the boulangers in Lille filling their storefront windows with trays of flaky golden croissants. Their uniform shape and sheer quantity made it look as if it were an effortless task, but I knew the bakers had risen in the early hours of the morning to shape and bake them. I fondly remember passing by on morning runs and inhaling that yeasty, buttery smell before the daily rush began.

These vegan croissants are flaky and golden, light and buttery. Making croissants is a bit involved, but well worth the effort. There is nothing more gratifying than the glorious moment of removing freshly baked homemade croissants from your oven. Take pride in earning your status as a master baker!

Like many pastry recipes, time, precision, care, and composure will be key to your success. Before starting this recipe, I encourage you to read through the Tips section, as it provides helpful pointers for making these croissants with ease.

1. Make the Dough: In a small saucepan, heat the almond milk over medium heat until warm. (Be sure that the milk is not too hot or it will deactivate the yeast.) Add the sugar and vanilla and whisk to melt the sugar. Remove the pot from the heat and add the yeast. Whisk to remove any lumps. Let sit for at least 10 minutes, until tiny bubbles have formed on the surface of the milk.

2. Sift the flour into the bowl of a stand mixer. Add the salt and stir to combine. Attach the dough hook. Gently pour in the yeast mixture and mix on low speed until the dough is well combined, smooth, and soft, 7 to 8 minutes. (If you do not have a stand mixer, you can knead the dough in a large bowl with a wooden spoon.)

3. Form the dough into a ball using your hands and transfer to a work surface. Wash out and dry the mixer bowl and put the dough back in it. Cover the bowl with reusable wrap and let chill in the refrigerator overnight (at least 8 hours, but no longer than 16 hours).

1½ cups unsweetened almond milk

¼ cup (54 g) organic cane sugar

1 teaspoon pure vanilla extract

1 tablespoon + ¼ teaspoon (½ ounce/13 g) active dry yeast

3¾ cups (488 g) all-purpose flour, more for dusting

1 tablespoon fine sea salt

1½ cups (12 ounces/340 g) vegan butter, cold (see Tip)

Recipe continues

1. I recommend taking the full hour of chill time between folds, to ensure the dough stays as cold as possible while rolling. This will help to keep the butter contained between the layers of dough, without oozing out.

2. It is helpful to use a chilled marble rolling pin to keep the dough cold while rolling. Keep the rolling pin in the refrigerator during chill times.

3. If the rolling pin gets buttery while rolling, simply wipe clean with a kitchen towel and continue.

4. You can make only the first batch of 6 croissants, instead of all 12, and leave the second piece of dough in step 8 in the refrigerator to make the following day. Be sure the dough is wrapped well in reusable wrap so there is no air exposure. The croissants might taste more yeasty, but they're still delicious.

5. I have the most success baking these croissants with Miyoko's Organic Vegan Butter. See Pantry Staples (page 17) for more information about this vegan butter and other recommendations for successful vegan baking.

4. Shape the Butter Layer: Cut the butter lengthwise into ½-inch thick strips and arrange them on a large sheet of parchment paper to form an 8 x 5-inch rectangle. (It helps to draw the rectangle onto the paper with a pencil first. Flip over the paper to prevent pencil marks transferring to the butter.) Fold the parchment paper over the butter to cover. Using a heavy rolling pin, gently tap and roll to make a solid, even sheet of butter ½ inch thick, maintaining an 8 x 5-inch rectangle. Chill in the refrigerator for 1 hour.

5. Combine the Dough and Butter: Lightly sprinkle the work surface and rolling pin with flour. Roll out the dough into a 16 x 10-inch rectangle with a short side facing you. Remove the parchment paper from the sheet of butter and place the butter across the centre of the dough with the long side of the butter parallel to the short side of the dough. Fold both ends of the dough over the butter. Pinch together the sides of the dough so that the butter is well enclosed. Wrap the dough in parchment paper to cover and chill in the refrigerator for 1 hour.

6. Roll Out the Dough and Make the First Fold: Lightly sprinkle the work surface and rolling pin with flour. Remove the parchment paper and turn the dough seam side down so a short side is facing you. Gently pat the dough with the rolling pin from top to bottom (this helps to solidify the layers together before rolling). Roll out the dough into a 15 x 10-inch rectangle. (Take your time rolling out the dough to ensure that the dough does not break open and that the butter remains contained between the layers of dough. Do not worry if some butter surfaces during rolling. Simply sprinkle the area with a bit of flour, then brush the excess flour away with a pastry brush.) Fold the top half down to the centre, fold the bottom half up to meet it, then fold one half over the other at the join. Wrap the dough in parchment paper and chill in the refrigerator for 1 hour.

7. Roll Out the Dough and Make the Second Fold: Lightly sprinkle the work surface and rolling pin with flour. Remove the parchment paper and turn the dough seam side down so a short side is facing you. Pat gently with the rolling pin from top to bottom, and gently roll out the dough again into a 15 x 10-inch rectangle. (Again, take your time rolling out the dough. Dust with flour if sticking. Wipe down the rolling pin if it gets buttery.) This time, fold the dough like a letter: fold the top third down, then fold the bottom third over the dough. Wrap the dough in parchment paper and chill in the refrigerator for 1 hour.

Recipe continues

Combine the Dough and Butter

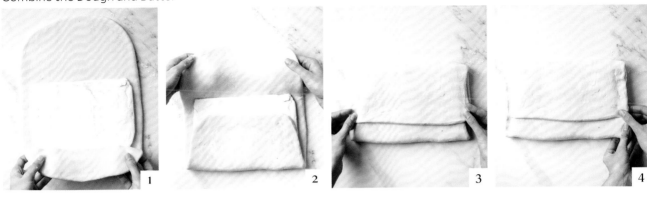

Roll Out the Dough and Make the First Fold

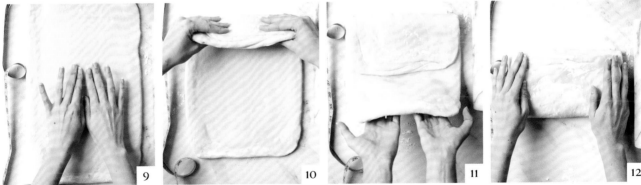

Roll Out the Dough and Make the Second Fold

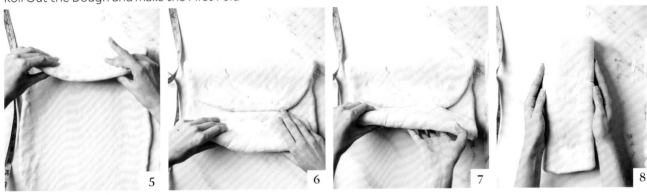

Prepare the Croissants

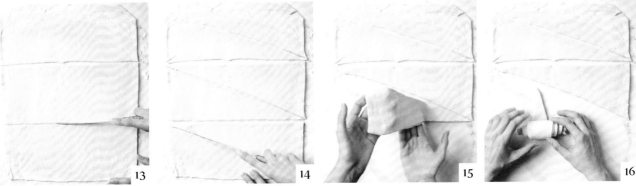

Although these croissants are best the day they are made, you can cool them completely and store them in an airtight container in the freezer for up to 1 month. When ready to eat, preheat the oven to 350°F (180°C) and warm the croissants from frozen for 3 to 5 minutes.

8. Prepare the Croissants: Remove the parchment paper and turn the dough so a short side is facing you. Cut the dough in half crosswise. Cover one half of the dough with reusable wrap and chill in the refrigerator until ready to use. Lightly sprinkle the work surface and rolling pin with flour and gently roll out the first piece of dough, with the cut end facing away from you, into a rectangle slightly larger than 15 x 12 inches. (Again, take your time rolling out the dough. Dust with flour if sticking. Wipe down the rolling pin if buttery.) Trim the wobbly ends of the dough with a sharp knife to make straight edges. Cut the rectangle crosswise into thirds to make three smaller rectangles, each 12 inches long by 5 inches wide. Cut each rectangle in half diagonally to make 6 triangles in all.

9. Line a baking sheet with parchment paper. Working with one triangle at a time, gently lift and flip the triangle (you can use a spatula to gently lift the dough if it's easier). Place the triangle with the short side facing you. Gently stretch out each corner of the short side to shape it from a right angle triangle into more of an isosceles (for a more symmetrical triangle for rolling). Gently roll the dough towards the tip to make a croissant shape. The roll should overlap three times. Place the croissant on the baking sheet with the tip side down, and press down gently.

10. Continue rolling croissants until you have rolled all 6 triangles. Work as quickly as possible so the butter stays cold. Proof the croissants by placing the baking sheet in the oven with the light on and the door closed for 1 hour, or until the croissants double (or nearly double) in size. When proofed, remove the croissants from the oven and, using a pastry brush, brush the tops with any of the oily juices that released while proofing.

11. Place the oven rack in the middle of the oven. Preheat the oven to 400°F (200°C).

12. Bake the croissants until golden brown on top, 10 to 12 minutes. Using a spatula, transfer the croissants to a wire rack.

13. Let the oven cool, then repeat steps 8 through 12 with the second batch of dough to make 6 more croissants. The croissants are best served the day they are made.

Buttery Brioche

Vegan ✳ Soy-free

This homemade buttery brioche is light, pillowy, and sweet. Tearing open a slice is like parting clouds. This sweet bread can be served on its own or is delicious smeared with vegan butter and Raspberry Chia Jam (page 66). I recommend using a stand mixer for this recipe. The longer you knead the dough, the fluffier your brioche will be, and kneading the dough by hand is far too onerous, if you ask me. Your stand mixer is an excellent sous-chef, so work it hard!

1. Make the Sponge: Combine the flour and yeast in the bowl of a stand mixer fitted with the dough hook.

2. In a small saucepan, heat the almond milk over medium heat until lukewarm. Pour the almond milk over the flour mixture and mix on medium-low speed until combined. Remove the bowl from the stand, cover with reusable wrap, and let sit at room temperature for 1 hour. Tiny bubbles will form on the surface.

3. Make the Dough: Return the bowl to the stand mixer fitted with the dough hook. Add the sugar and salt and begin mixing on medium speed. With the mixer running, gradually add the flour so as not to overwhelm the stand mixer. When all the flour has been added, pour in the coconut cream and vanilla and mix on medium speed until well combined, 3 to 5 minutes. You might have to occasionally stop and scrape down the sides of the bowl to ensure everything is mixing together. Increase the speed to medium-high and continue mixing until the dough starts to form a plush, shiny ball and smacks the sides of the bowl, about 10 minutes.

4. With the mixer running, begin adding the butter a tablespoon at a time, mixing after each addition until you can no longer see the butter. Continue to knead the dough until it is elastic, slightly sticky to the touch, and passes the "window pane test," 15 to 20 minutes. (To perform the window pane test, stop the mixer. With slightly damp hands, gently stretch a handful of dough with your fingers and thumb into a thin,

SPONGE

1 cup (130 g) all-purpose flour

2¼ teaspoons (8 g) active dry yeast

1 cup unsweetened almond milk

DOUGH

¼ cup (54 g) organic cane sugar

½ teaspoon fine sea salt

2 cups (260 g) all-purpose flour,
    more for dusting

¼ cup coconut cream, more for brushing

1 teaspoon pure vanilla extract

⅓ cup (70 g) vegan butter, softened,
    more for the pan

1 teaspoon demerara sugar
    (optional for sprinkling)

TIPS

1. To keep the mixer stable while mixing on higher speeds, dampen a kitchen towel and place it underneath the mixer.

2. Do not let your day-old brioche go to waste. Use it to make my Cinnamony French Toast with Apple Compote (page 29).

Recipe continues

translucent membrane—or a window pane. If the dough tears easily, knead the dough for a few more minutes and try again.) The longer you knead, the softer and stretchier the dough becomes. Cover the bowl with reusable wrap and let proof at room temperature for 1 hour or until the dough has doubled in size. (At this point you can choose to continue or make the brioche the next day. For next-day baking, punch down the dough to deflate, cover the bowl with reusable wrap, and store in the refrigerator. When ready to use, remove the dough from the refrigerator and proof it again until it has doubled in size, 1 to 1½ hours.)

5. Sprinkle the work surface with a bit of flour. Turn out the dough onto the work surface and shape and pat down the dough to form a rectangle. (The size and thickness of the rectangle does not matter, but the rectangle shape will make it easier to cut equal pieces.) Cut the dough into 6 equal pieces. It's okay if they're not entirely uniform.

6. Using your hands or a rolling pin, flatten one piece of dough into a 7 x 5-inch rectangle (The rectangle doesn't need to be perfect.) With the shortest side facing you, fold the dough like a letter: fold the top third down, then fold the bottom third over the dough. Turn the dough so a short side is facing you and gently flatten it down again. Tightly roll the dough into a log. Repeat to roll the remaining pieces of dough.

7. Lightly grease a 9 x 5-inch loaf pan with vegan butter. Arrange the dough logs in a row, placing the biggest logs on the outside and the smallest logs in the middle (so they bake evenly). Snugly fit the arranged logs in the pan, seam side down, in the same order, with the biggest logs at each end of the pan. (If the rolls are a bit short for the pan, gently tug their ends to lengthen before popping them in the pan. They will also lengthen as they proof, so don't worry if they're a bit short.) Cover the loaf pan with reusable wrap and let proof at room temperature for at least 1 hour or until doubled in size.

8. Meanwhile, preheat the oven to 375°F (190°C).

9. Lightly brush the top of the proofed brioche with some coconut cream and sprinkle with demerara sugar (if using). Bake until golden brown, about 25 minutes. Remove from the oven and let the brioche cool slightly in the pan for 5 minutes, then transfer to a wire rack to cool completely.

10. To serve, slice the brioche with a bread knife or simply tear apart the sections with your hands. Best enjoyed the day it is made.

Make the Sponge

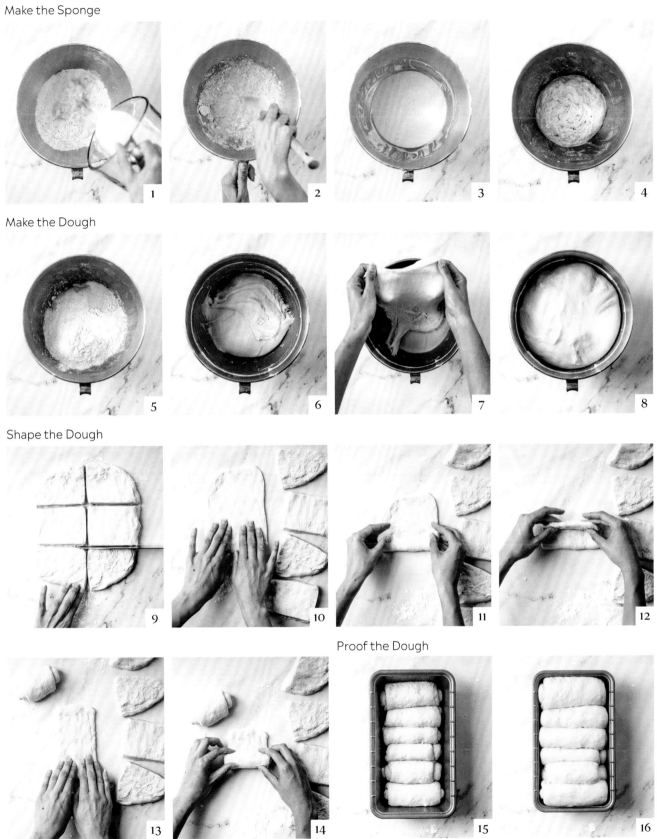

Make the Dough

Shape the Dough

Proof the Dough

Parisian Crepes with Chocolate Hazelnut Spread and Banana

Vegan * Soy-free

A trip to Paris is incomplete without a crepe in hand from a crêperie stand. It is mesmerizing to watch them swish the crepe with a T-shaped spreader on an oversized hot plate. Biting into a warm crepe stuffed with melty chocolate hazelnut spread and chopped banana is heavenly.

So why not bring the Parisian crepe into our kitchens? These crepes taste just like those from Montmartre. They are light, chewy, delicately sweet, and a playful brunch to share with your family. Forgo the special gadgets and let your wrists dance with the pan to "La Vie en Rose."

1. Preheat the oven to 200°F (100°C). Line a baking sheet with parchment paper.
2. In a medium bowl, whisk together the flour and salt. Pour in the almond milk, avocado oil, maple syrup, and vanilla and whisk together until smooth with no lumps. Cover the bowl with a kitchen towel and refrigerate for 1 hour.
3. Heat a medium nonstick skillet over medium heat and add a small amount of avocado oil to coat the bottom of the pan. Pour ¼ cup of the batter into the skillet and swirl to evenly coat the bottom of the pan. Cook until the edges of the crepe start to pull away from the pan and the bottom is lightly golden, 1 to 2 minutes. Carefully flip and continue to cook until lightly golden on the other side, about 30 seconds. Slide the crepe onto the prepared baking sheet and keep warm in the oven while you cook the remaining crepes. If the batter is a bit too thick, add a splash more almond milk (up to 1 tablespoon should do). Repeat to use the remaining batter, lightly coating the pan with more avocado oil if needed.
4. Spread a thin layer of the Chocolate Hazelnut Spread over one half of each crepe and layer banana rounds on top. Fold the other half over and then fold again to form a triangle. Top the crepe with more banana rounds and more Chocolate Hazelnut Spread. Serve the crepes topped with maple syrup, chocolate chips, and coconut flakes, if desired.

CREPES

1 cup (130 g) all-purpose flour

¼ teaspoon fine sea salt

1½ cups unsweetened almond milk, more if needed

3 tablespoons avocado oil, more for the pan

4 teaspoons pure maple syrup

1 teaspoon pure vanilla extract

FILLING

1 batch Chocolate Hazelnut Spread (page 69)

2 bananas, sliced into rounds

FOR SERVING (OPTIONAL)

Pure maple syrup

Dairy-free chocolate chips

Coconut flakes

STORAGE

Store leftover crepes in an airtight container in the refrigerator for up to 2 days. Reheat before serving. Store any leftover Chocolate Hazelnut Spread in a jar at room temperature for up to 10 days.

Maple Pecan Granola

Vegan ✳ Gluten-free ✳ Soy-free ✳ Refined Sugar-free ✳ One-bowl

3½ cups gluten-free old-fashioned
    rolled oats

1 cup raw pecans, chopped

½ cup unsweetened shredded coconut

½ cup unsweetened dried cranberries

¼ cup raw pumpkin seeds

¼ cup sesame seeds

1 tablespoon cinnamon

½ teaspoon ground cardamom

½ teaspoon fine sea salt

½ cup coconut oil, melted

½ cup pure maple syrup

STORAGE

Store the granola in mason jars at
room temperature for up to 1 month
or in the refrigerator for up to 3 months.

Naturally sweetened with maple syrup, this healthy granola is crunchy, nutty, sweet, and lightly spiced. It's a wholesome yet simple granola that I like to gift in jars for my loved ones. Sprinkle it over smoothie bowls, Creamy Chia Pudding with Red Fruits (page 47), Blueberry Muffin Overnight Oats (page 48), Heavenly Coconut Quinoa Porridge (page 51), or Avocado Toast with Pink Beet Hummus and Granola (page 70) or enjoy by the handful.

1. Preheat the oven to 300°F (150°C). Line 2 baking sheets with parchment paper.

2. In a large bowl, mix together the oats, pecans, shredded coconut, cranberries, pumpkin seeds, sesame seeds, cinnamon, cardamom, and salt. Pour in the melted coconut oil and maple syrup and mix to ensure the mixture is well coated.

3. Divide the granola between the 2 prepared baking sheets, spreading out to make an even layer. Bake the granola until golden, 25 to 30 minutes, giving it a quick stir with a wooden spoon every 10 minutes to ensure it is evenly toasted. Let cool completely, about 30 minutes.

Serves 2

Creamy Chia Pudding with Red Fruits

Vegan * Gluten-free * Grain-free * Oil-free * Soy-free * Refined Sugar-free * Raw/No-bake * One-bowl

If you are looking for lighter fare, then this creamy chia pudding is a great choice. This recipe is ultra-creamy and refreshing. I like to top mine with fresh red fruits, but feel free to swap the summer fruits for seasonal fruits depending on the time of year. Mixed berries are perfect for summer, and figs or plums in the fall. It's also delicious served with my Winter Poached Pears with Spiced Syrup to drizzle (page 289). To make it extra lush, use my Creamy Dreamy Almond Milk instead of store-bought. You will notice a big difference in the thickness and creaminess.

1. Make the Creamy Dreamy Almond Milk, if using.
2. In a small bowl, whisk together the chia seeds, almond milk, and maple syrup (if using). Let sit for 5 minutes. Whisk again to break up any clumps. Cover with reusable wrap and place in the refrigerator to thicken for at least 30 minutes or preferably overnight (see Tip).
3. Whisk the chia pudding one more time for a pudding-like texture with no clumps. Divide the pudding between cups or bowls and top with the mixed red fruits. Sprinkle with shredded coconut, if desired.

TIPS
1. If using store-bought almond milk, I recommend using 1½ cups for this recipe. If using Creamy Dreamy Almond Milk, I recommend using 1¾ cups. Store-bought almond milk is much more watery, so you won't need as much liquid to achieve the right pudding texture. Using homemade almond milk in this recipe will result in a premium lush and creamy chia pudding. My Super-Quick Oat Milk (page 82) is a lovely substitute for almond milk; use 1¾ cups.
2. The longer you allow the chia to soak, the thicker it will become. Typically, it takes at least 30 minutes to thicken, but I recommend letting it sit longer, preferably overnight. Prepare it the night before for a quick and simple morning breakfast.
3. Maple syrup to sweeten is optional. I find a splash of maple syrup is needed when using store-bought almond milk instead of homemade.

1½ to 1¾ cups Creamy Dreamy Almond Milk (page 81) or unsweetened store-bought (see Tip)
¼ cup chia seeds
1 tablespoon pure maple syrup (optional; see Tip)
½ cup fresh or thawed frozen red fruits (combination of raspberries, strawberries and/or pitted cherries)
Unsweetened shredded coconut, for sprinkling (optional)

DO AHEAD
The chia pudding can be made up to 3 days in advance. Store in an airtight container in the refrigerator.

Blueberry Muffin Overnight Oats

Vegan ✳ Gluten-free ✳ Oil-free ✳ Soy-free ✳ Refined Sugar-free ✳ Raw/No-bake ✳ One-bowl

½ cup Creamy Dreamy Almond Milk
(page 81) or unsweetened
store-bought

⅓ cup gluten-free old-fashioned
rolled oats

2 teaspoons chia seeds

Pinch of cinnamon

Pinch of fine sea salt

¼ cup plain coconut yogurt

2 teaspoons pure maple syrup

¼ cup fresh or thawed frozen blueberries

1 tablespoon natural peanut butter or
almond butter

1 teaspoon coconut flakes

TIP
My Super-Quick Oat Milk (page 82) is
a lovely substitute for the almond milk.

DO AHEAD
The overnight oats can be made up to
3 days in advance. Store in an airtight
container in the refrigerator.

Unlike classic oatmeal, overnight oats are served cold without cooking. The result is a light and refreshing breakfast that is especially welcome during the warmer months. Overnight oats make for a delicious quick breakfast that you can prep the night before. It has become one of my husband's favourite on-the-go breakfasts for busy work mornings. We both eat a late breakfast, and this is a perfect desk brekkie to enjoy while sifting through emails. I top these cinnamony oats with blueberries and peanut butter. It tastes like a delicious oat muffin! But let your imagination run wild! It is also delicious with strawberries, banana, or chocolate chips.

1. Make the Creamy Dreamy Almond Milk, if using.

2. In a small bowl, combine the oats, chia seeds, cinnamon, and salt. Whisk in the almond milk, coconut yogurt, and maple syrup with a fork, ensuring no clumps form. Let sit for 5 minutes, then whisk again. Cover with reusable wrap and chill in the refrigerator for at least 1 hour or overnight.

3. When ready to serve, top the overnight oats with the blueberries, peanut butter, and coconut flakes.

Serves 2

Heavenly Coconut Quinoa Porridge

Vegan * Gluten-free * Nut-free * Oil-free * Soy-free * Refined Sugar-free * One-pot

We do not typically think of quinoa in sweet recipes, but we absolutely should. Swap out your usual breakfast oatmeal for this heavenly quinoa porridge bowl. It is naturally gluten-free, protein-packed, and just as warm and comforting as a bowl of oatmeal. Top with your favourite fresh fruits; I like fresh cherries, raspberries, or mango, and during the winter months I like to top it with thawed frozen berries.

1. In a medium saucepan, stir together the quinoa, coconut milk, water, maple syrup, vanilla, and salt. Bring to a boil, then reduce the heat to medium-low and simmer the quinoa, stirring often, until it is soft and the coconut milk is almost entirely absorbed, 10 to 15 minutes. Add a splash or two more water if the mixture is too thick.

2. Divide the quinoa porridge between bowls and top with your favourite fruits. Sprinkle with coconut flakes.

½ cup white quinoa

1 can (14 ounces/400 mL) full-fat
     coconut milk

¼ cup water, more if needed

1 tablespoon pure maple syrup or agave

½ teaspoon pure vanilla extract

Pinch of fine sea salt

½ cup fruits of choice

2 teaspoons coconut flakes

STORAGE

Store leftover coconut quinoa porridge in an airtight container in the refrigerator for up to 3 days. Reheat before serving and thin with splashes of water or unsweetened almond milk.

TIP

This quinoa porridge is also delicious sprinkled with Maple Pecan Granola (page 44) and topped with Raspberry Chia Jam (page 66).

DO AHEAD

The quinoa porridge can be made up to 3 days in advance (see Storage).

Serves 3

Savoury French Toast

Vegan * Nut-free * Soy-free * Refined Sugar-free * No Added Sugar

FRENCH TOAST

¾ cup unsweetened almond milk

1 tablespoon all-purpose flour

1 tablespoon ground flaxseed or
    ground chia seeds

¼ teaspoon ground cardamom

Pinch of ground cumin

Pinch of fine black salt or sea salt

2 teaspoons olive oil, more if needed

6 slices (each 1 inch thick) French or
    Italian loaf, or sourdough bread

FOR TOPPING

½ cup plain coconut yogurt

½ cup cooked edamame beans

1 avocado, pitted, peeled, and sliced

Olive oil, for drizzling

1 tablespoon fresh thyme leaves

Fine sea salt and freshly ground
    black pepper

STORAGE

Store the French toast in an airtight
container in the refrigerator for up to
2 days. Reheat before serving.

This recipe turns classic sweet French toast into a savoury delight. Lightly spiced with cardamom and cumin and topped with creamy avocado, edamame, and tart coconut yogurt, it's a perfect treat for you savoury breakfast lovers. I love to make this French toast when I am feeling in more of a savoury mood than sweet.

1. In a small shallow bowl, whisk together the almond milk, flour, ground flaxseed, cardamom, cumin, and black salt. Let the eggy mixture sit for 5 to 10 minutes to thicken.

2. Heat a large non-stick skillet over medium heat. Add the olive oil and swirl to evenly coat the bottom of the skillet. One at a time, soak the bread slices in the eggy mixture for 10 to 15 seconds, coating both sides. Cook the French toast in batches of 2 or 3 slices until golden on both sides, 2 to 3 minutes per side. Add more olive oil as needed so the bread does not stick to the skillet.

3. Serve the French toast with a dollop of coconut yogurt, then top with edamame beans and sliced avocado. Lightly drizzle with olive oil. Sprinkle with thyme, sea salt, and pepper.

Buckwheat Crepes with Cashew Cream Cheese and Greens

Vegan * Gluten-free * Soy-free * No Added Sugar * Refined Sugar-free

These savoury crepes are naturally gluten-free when made with buckwheat flour. The taste is wholesome, earthy, and satisfying. In France, buckwheat crepes are called galettes de sarrasin and originated in Brittany. Crêperies in the small coastal towns are as abundant as boulangeries in Paris. Crepes are enjoyed at any time of day, be it breakfast, lunch, or dinner. I have fond memories of tucking into these savoury crepes while vacationing with our family, including our pup Penny, who was always welcome inside the local restaurants! For this recipe, I stuff the crepes with my Dreamy Cashew Cream Cheese (page 155) and fill with arugula and avocado, a simple combination that is bright and refreshing. Enjoy these gorgeous nutty crepes for a lazy Sunday brunch with family.

1. Make the Dreamy Cashew Cream Cheese.

2. Preheat the oven to 200°F (100°C). Line a baking sheet with parchment paper.

3. Make the flax egg: In a small bowl, whisk together the ground flaxseed and 3 tablespoons of the water. Let sit for at least 10 minutes to thicken into an eggy consistency.

4. In a medium bowl, mix together the buckwheat flour, baking soda, and salt. Add the flax egg mixture, the remaining 2½ cups water, and the apple cider vinegar. Whisk well to make a smooth batter. Cover and let sit for at least 15 minutes, until the batter has resembled the consistency of melted ice cream.

5. Heat a medium non-stick skillet over medium heat and add a small amount of olive oil to coat the bottom of the pan. Pour ½ cup of the batter into the pan and swirl to evenly coat the bottom. Cook until the edges of the crepe start to pull away from the pan and the bottom is lightly brown, 1 to 2 minutes. Carefully flip and continue to cook until lightly brown on the other side, about 30 seconds. Slide the crepe onto the prepared baking sheet and keep warm in the oven while you cook the remaining crepes. If the batter is a bit too thick,

1 batch Dreamy Cashew Cream Cheese
    (page 155)

CREPES

1 tablespoon ground flaxseed

2½ cups + 3 tablespoons water, divided

1½ cups buckwheat flour

½ teaspoon baking soda

½ teaspoon fine sea salt

1 teaspoon apple cider vinegar

1 teaspoon olive oil, for frying,
    more if needed

FILLING

2 cups tightly packed arugula

2 or 3 avocados, pitted, peeled, and sliced

¼ cup chopped fresh chives

¼ cup tightly packed microgreens
    (optional)

Flaky sea salt

Freshly ground black pepper

Recipe continues

Store leftover buckwheat crepes in an airtight container in the refrigerator for up to 2 days. Reheat before serving.

TIP
Try swapping out the filling for Balsamic Roasted Beets with Toasted Pine Nuts and Blue Cheese (page 227). Or swap the cream cheese for Herb and Garlic Cheese (page 159).

DO AHEAD
1. The crepe batter can be made 1 day in advance. Store, covered, in the refrigerator and stir well before using.
2. The Dreamy Cashew Cream Cheese can be prepared up to 5 days in advance. Store in an airtight container in the refrigerator. The cream cheese can also be frozen for up to 3 months.

add a splash more water (up to 1 tablespoon should do). Repeat to use the remaining batter, lightly coating the pan with more olive oil if needed.

6. Spread a thin layer of the Dreamy Cashew Cream Cheese on each crepe. Layer one half of each crepe with the arugula and avocado, then sprinkle with chives, microgreens (if using), and a pinch each of flaky sea salt and pepper. Fold the other half of the crepe over top to close. Serve with the remaining cashew cream cheese on the side.

Serves 8 ✳ Requires: 1 hour chill time

Mushroom and Spinach Quiche

Vegan ✳ Nut-free ✳ Refined Sugar-free ✳ No Added Sugar

This savoury tart is made with a flaky pastry and flavourful mushroom and spinach filling, and will please even non-vegans with its cheesy taste and eggy consistency. I love to serve this for brunch or a gourmet breakfast with friends.

I first tried vegan quiche at a little plant-based restaurant called La Clairière within walking distance of our apartment. It was a welcome dish, especially for my husband, Mitch, who used to love the quiches and frittatas that I made before going vegan. This recipe is inspired by the quiches from that go-to restaurant, the mushroom and spinach combo being my favourite.

1. Prepare the Pastry Crust: In a food processor, combine the flour and salt. Cut the vegan butter into small chunks and add to the bowl. Pulse a few times to lightly mix the ingredients. Add the water and apple cider vinegar and pulse a few more times to form a crumbly dough. (You can also combine all the ingredients in a large bowl, except the water, and massage with your hands to form a crumbly dough. Add the water and massage to form a shaggy dough.) Do not over-knead the dough (see Tip).

2. Transfer the dough to a work surface and bring together to form a ball. Cover with reusable wrap and chill in the refrigerator for 1 hour.

3. Preheat the oven to 425°F (220°C).

4. Lightly sprinkle the work surface with flour. Using a rolling pin, roll out the dough into a 12-inch circle. If needed, lightly sprinkle the dough with flour to stop the rolling pin from sticking.

5. Roll the dough around the rolling pin. Gently lift the dough and unroll over an 11-inch tart pan with removable bottom. Press into the bottom and up the sides of the pan. For a clean edge, trim excess dough with a knife. Patch any cracks with excess dough. Poke a few holes in the base with a fork. (This will stop the base from lifting as it cooks. There's no need to use pie weights with this crust.) Transfer the

PASTRY CRUST

1½ cups (195 g) all-purpose flour

¼ teaspoon fine sea salt

½ cup (4 ounces/115 g) + 1 tablespoon vegan butter, cold (see Tip)

¼ cup cold water

1 teaspoon apple cider vinegar

FILLING

1 tablespoon coconut oil

2 cloves garlic, finely chopped

1 yellow onion, finely chopped

8 ounces (225 g) cremini mushrooms, thinly sliced

4 cups (5 ounces/140 g) tightly packed baby spinach

1 block (12 ounces/340 g) silken tofu

¼ cup unsweetened almond milk

¼ cup nutritional yeast

1 tablespoon arrowroot powder

¼ teaspoon ground turmeric

¼ teaspoon onion powder

¼ teaspoon garlic powder

¼ teaspoon fine sea salt

¼ teaspoon fine black salt (or more sea salt)

¼ teaspoon freshly ground black pepper

Recipe continues

Store the quiche, covered with reusable wrap or in an airtight container, in the refrigerator for up to 4 days.

TIPS

1. The pastry dough can be prepared by hand or in a food processor. I like to use the food processor to ensure the ingredients are evenly distributed. Do not over-knead the dough. Pulse or massage the ingredients together until just combined, and then form together with your hands.

2. Different vegan butters have different water contents. If your pastry dough is too crumbly as you roll, it's too dry. Bring the dough back together, rinse your hands with water, and lightly flick over the dough to add a few water droplets. Work the water in gently and roll again. If the dough gets too warm, cover it with reusable wrap and transfer to the refrigerator to let it chill. Once chilled, it should roll more easily.

3. I recommend using a softer vegan butter for this recipe, such as Earth Balance, for a more flexible pastry dough. See Pantry Staples (page 17) for more information about this vegan butter and other recommendations for successful vegan baking.

DO AHEAD

The pastry dough can be prepared up to 2 days in advance. Cover well and store in the refrigerator until ready to use.

tart pan to a baking sheet and blind-bake for 15 minutes. Remove from the oven and let cool. Reduce the oven temperature to 350°F (180°C).

6. Make the Filling: Heat the coconut oil in a large skillet over medium heat. Add the garlic and onion and cook, stirring frequently, until the onion is softened, about 10 minutes. Add the mushrooms and cook until the juices they release have evaporated and the mushrooms have softened and browned, about 10 minutes. Add the spinach, cover with a lid, and let the spinach wilt, 2 to 3 minutes. Remove from the heat.

7. In a food processor or high-speed blender, combine the silken tofu, almond milk, nutritional yeast, arrowroot powder, turmeric, onion powder, garlic powder, sea salt, black salt, and pepper. Pulse until smooth.

8. Pour the tofu mixture into the skillet and mix together with the cooked vegetables to combine. Pour the filling into the pre-baked crust in a smooth and even layer. Bake until the filling is golden and firm, about 40 minutes. Let cool slightly before slicing.

Makes 12 muffins

Chickpea Eggy Muffins

Vegan ＊ Gluten-free ＊ Grain-free ＊ Soy-free

These savoury eggy muffins make a delicious on-the-go breakfast. They are protein-packed, veggie-packed, herby, and savoury. I absolutely love to make a batch to last us through the week. Not only are they great for breakfast but they are also a tasty savoury snack to replenish. In addition, they are the perfect accompaniment to my Chunky Vegetable Soup (page 193) or Butternut Squash, Apple, and Sage Soup (page 197). You will love the versatility of these eggy muffins.

1. Preheat the oven to 375°F (190°C). Lightly grease a 12-cup non-stick muffin pan with avocado oil. Make sure the sides and bottoms of the cups are greased.

2. In a medium non-stick skillet, heat the avocado oil over medium heat. Add the spinach and cook, stirring occasionally, until wilted, 3 to 5 minutes. Remove from the heat and set aside.

3. Rinse and pat dry the sun-dried tomatoes. Chop into small chunks and add to the wilted spinach.

4. In a medium bowl, combine the chickpea flour, nutritional yeast, garlic powder, baking powder, sea salt, and black salt. Stir to combine. Pour in the almond milk and whisk together until smooth with no clumps.

5. Add the spinach and sun-dried tomatoes, shallot, and parsley and stir to combine.

6. Scoop the mixture into the muffin cups, filling each to the rim. Bake until the tops are golden brown and a toothpick inserted into the centre comes out clean, 20 to 25 minutes. Let the muffins cool in the pan for 10 to 15 minutes, then turn out onto a wire rack to cool completely.

2 teaspoons avocado oil, more for the pan

4 cups (5 ounces/140 g) tightly packed baby spinach

1 cup oil-packed sun-dried tomatoes, drained

1¾ cups chickpea flour

¼ cup nutritional yeast

1 teaspoon garlic powder

1 teaspoon baking powder

½ teaspoon fine sea salt

¼ teaspoon fine black salt (or more sea salt)

2 cups unsweetened almond milk

1 shallot, finely chopped

½ cup fresh flat-leaf parsley leaves, finely chopped

STORAGE

Store the eggy muffins in an airtight container in the refrigerator for up to 5 days or in the freezer for up to 2 months.

Chickpea Omelette with Ricotta, Grilled Asparagus, and Tomato

Vegan * Gluten-free * Grain-free * No Added Sugar * Refined Sugar-free

¾ cup Refreshing Ricotta Cheese
  (page 164)

1 batch Grilled Asparagus with Cherry
  Tomatoes (made without parmesan;
  see page 224 and Tip)

CHICKPEA OMELETTE

1 cup chickpea flour

2 tablespoons nutritional yeast

½ teaspoon onion powder

½ teaspoon garlic powder

½ teaspoon baking soda

½ teaspoon fine sea salt

¼ teaspoon fine black salt (or more sea salt)

¼ teaspoon freshly ground black pepper

1⅓ cups unsweetened almond milk

1 teaspoon apple cider vinegar

1 teaspoon olive oil, for frying, more
  if needed

STORAGE

Store leftover chickpea omelettes in
an airtight container in the refrigerator
for up to 2 days. Reheat before serving.

TIP

This recipe does not include the
parmesan cheese in the grilled asparagus
recipe. However, if you want to include
it, follow the recipe on page 224. Make
the Sprinkle-on-Everything Parmesan
(page 167) in advance.

This savoury chickpea omelette is satiating and packed with protein. Chickpea flour and almond milk is a simple swap for the traditional eggs. The omelette itself is loaded with flavour, but stuffing it with ricotta, grilled asparagus, and cherry tomatoes lifts the calibre to that of a high-end café in the chicest of neighbourhoods. Best of all, it is quick to whip together. I often serve it as an easy lunch or dinner. All-day-breakfast lovers, you are going to adore this chickpea omelette!

1. Make the Refreshing Ricotta Cheese.

2. Preheat the oven to 250°F (120°C). Make the Grilled Asparagus with Cherry Tomatoes. Cover with an oven-safe lid or foil and keep warm in the oven until ready to use.

3. Make the Chickpea Omelette: Sift the chickpea flour into a medium bowl. Add the nutritional yeast, onion powder, garlic powder, baking soda, sea salt, black salt, and pepper. Mix together.

4. Pour in the almond milk and apple cider vinegar and whisk until the batter is smooth with no clumps.

5. Heat a drizzle of olive oil in a medium non-stick skillet over medium-high heat. When the oil is hot, pour ½ cup of the batter into the pan and cook until bubbles begin to form on the surface and the bottom is lightly golden brown, 5 to 6 minutes. Flip and cook until lightly golden brown on the other side, 1 to 2 minutes. Transfer to a parchment-lined baking sheet and place in the oven to keep warm. Repeat to use the remaining batter, adding more olive oil to the pan as needed so the batter does not stick to the skillet.

6. Transfer each omelette to a plate. Slather one half of each omelette with Refreshing Ricotta Cheese. Top with the grilled asparagus and tomatoes. Fold the other half of the omelette over top.

DO AHEAD

The Refreshing Ricotta Cheese can be made up to 5 days in advance. Store in an airtight container in the refrigerator.

Serves 4

Veggie Tofu Scramble with Roasted Baby Potatoes

Vegan * Gluten-free * Grain-free * Nut-free * No Added Sugar * Refined Sugar-free

This veggie tofu scramble makes for a scrumptious savoury breakfast or brunch. Packed with protein, it is perfect to enjoy when you need to fuel up. I often cook up this scramble to sustain me for a day out on the ski hills or after a long morning run. Roasted baby potatoes make this dish extra comforting. It reminds me so much of the old-time diners that my parents used to take us to for Sunday brunch as kids—now made vegan, healthier, and tastier too.

1. Make the Roasted Baby Potatoes: Preheat the oven to 400°F (200°C). Line a baking sheet with parchment paper.

2. Cut the potatoes into bite-size pieces and toss them into a medium bowl. Drizzle the potatoes with the avocado oil and sprinkle with the sea salt and pepper. Mix to combine. Spread the potatoes evenly on the prepared baking sheet and roast until golden and sizzling, about 40 minutes. Stir at the 30-minute mark for more even roasting.

3. Make the Veggie Tofu Scramble: Heat 1 tablespoon of the coconut oil in a large, deep skillet over medium-high heat. Add the red onion and bell pepper and cook, stirring often, until the vegetables have softened, about 10 minutes.

4. Drain and rinse the tofu, then gently pat dry with a kitchen towel. (You do not need to press the tofu.) Using your hands, break apart the tofu into small, rough chunks directly over the skillet. Add the remaining 1 teaspoon coconut oil, the nutritional yeast, turmeric, cumin, garlic powder, chili powder, sea salt, black salt, and black pepper. Stir to combine and continue to cook over medium-high heat, stirring often, until the excess water has evaporated and the desired "eggy" consistency is reached, 5 to 7 minutes.

5. Add the baby spinach. Cover with a lid and let the spinach wilt, 2 to 3 minutes. Stir to combine.

6. Serve the tofu scramble alongside the roasted potatoes. If desired, top with chives, cilantro, and chili flakes for a bit of spice.

ROASTED BABY POTATOES

1½ pounds (675 g) baby potatoes, colour of choice

2 tablespoons avocado oil

½ teaspoon fine sea salt

Pinch of freshly ground black pepper

VEGGIE TOFU SCRAMBLE

1 tablespoon + 1 teaspoon coconut oil, divided

1 small red onion, finely chopped

1 red bell pepper, finely chopped

1 block (14 ounces/398 g) firm tofu

1 tablespoon nutritional yeast

¾ teaspoon ground turmeric

½ teaspoon ground cumin

½ teaspoon garlic powder

¼ teaspoon chili powder

½ teaspoon fine sea salt

¼ teaspoon fine black salt (or more sea salt)

Pinch of freshly ground black pepper

1½ cups tightly packed baby spinach

FOR SERVING (OPTIONAL)

1 to 2 tablespoons finely chopped chives

A handful of fresh cilantro leaves, chopped

Pinch of red chili flakes

STORAGE

Store leftover Veggie Tofu Scramble in an airtight container in the refrigerator for up to 3 days. The Roasted Baby Potatoes are best enjoyed the same day.

Raspberry Chia Jam

Vegan ✳ Nut-free ✳ Gluten-free ✳ Grain-free ✳ Oil-free ✳ Soy-free ✳ Refined Sugar-free ✳ One-pot

1 heaping cup fresh or frozen raspberries

2 tablespoons pure maple syrup,
    more as needed

1 teaspoon chia seeds

Pinch of fine sea salt

STORAGE

Store the jam in an airtight container in the refrigerator for up to 1 week or in the freezer for up to 2 months. If frozen, thaw before using.

This healthy spin on classic jam makes it so easy to say goodbye to the sugary store-bought versions. Sweet, fruity, and oh so jammy, this delicious jam is made with nothing more than raspberries, chia, and maple syrup.

I love making a big batch of this jam to start the week. Enjoy it slathered on PB&J with Fried Banana Toast (page 73), serve with Buttery Brioche (page 39), or use it to make grain-free Raspberry Jam Thumbprint Cookies (page 121). It is also delicious spooned onto Heavenly Coconut Quinoa Porridge (page 51).

1. In a small saucepan, heat the raspberries over medium-high heat. Stir and muddle the fruit so that the raspberries break down and bubble, about 5 minutes.

2. Reduce the heat to low, maintaining a gentle simmer, and add the maple syrup, chia seeds, and a pinch of salt. Stir to combine. Continue simmering for 10 to 12 minutes, stirring often, until the water has mostly evaporated and the mixture has become thick and jammy. Remove from the heat and let cool completely. (The jam will continue to thicken as it cools.)

Makes 1 cup

Chocolate Hazelnut Spread

Vegan ＊ Gluten-free ＊ Grain-free ＊ Oil-free ＊ Soy-free ＊ Raw/No-bake

This vegan Chocolate Hazelnut Spread tastes just like Nutella, but is so much healthier. It is sweet, thick, and smooth, with the perfect balance of hazelnut to chocolate for that familiar Nutella taste. In France, Nutella is a beloved household staple, and one of the only things I ever actually saw available in Costco-sized packaging! Enjoy this vegan version in recipes such as my Chocolate Hazelnut Spread and Strawberry Toast (page 74), Parisian Crepes with Chocolate Hazelnut Spread and Banana (page 43), Chocolate Hazelnut Swirl Muffins (page 149), and Chocolate Macarons (page 113).

1. In a food processor, blend the hazelnuts until smooth and creamy, 10 to 12 minutes. Stop as needed to scrape down the sides of the bowl.
2. In a small saucepan, bring 2 inches of water to a low simmer over low heat. Place a small heatproof bowl on top of the pot, making sure the bottom of the bowl is not touching the water. Add the chocolate chips and melt, stirring often, until completely smooth. (Alternatively, you can melt the chocolate in the microwave in 30-second intervals.)
3. Transfer the melted chocolate to the food processor along with the maple syrup and salt. Process until smooth, about 5 minutes. (If the hazelnut mixture firms up when you add the melted chocolate, it's likely that the hazelnuts weren't blended for long enough. Process on high speed until the mixture softens and smoothens, about 10 minutes.)

1 cup unsalted dry-roasted hazelnuts
1 cup semi-sweet dairy-free chocolate chips
2 teaspoons pure maple syrup
Pinch of fine sea salt

STORAGE
Store the Chocolate Hazelnut Spread in a jar at room temperature for up to 10 days.

TIPS
1. This recipe calls for dry-roasted hazelnuts with the skins removed. If using raw hazelnuts, you will have to toast and skin them first. To do this, toast the hazelnuts on a baking sheet in a 350°F (180°C) oven for 12 to 15 minutes, until fragrant and blistered. Wrap the hazelnuts in a kitchen towel while warm and vigorously rub to remove most of the skins. Let cool completely.
2. The Chocolate Hazelnut Spread should be kept at room temperature. If it is too cool, it will harden. If your spread does harden, heat the jar in the microwave in 15- to 30-second intervals, until you have reached a silky smooth consistency.

Serves 2

Avocado Toast with Pink Beet Hummus and Granola

Vegan ✳ Gluten-free Option ✳ Nut-free ✳ Soy-free ✳ Refined Sugar-free

¼ cup Pink Beet Hummus (page 168)

2 tablespoons Maple Pecan Granola
(page 44) or store-bought

2 slices whole wheat bread, toasted

1 avocado, pitted, peeled, and thinly sliced

Freshly chopped fresh basil leaves,
for sprinkling (optional)

STORAGE

1. The Pink Beet Hummus can be stored
in an airtight container in the refrigerator
for up to 1 week or in the freezer for up
to 2 months. If frozen, thaw before using.

2. The Maple Pecan Granola can be
stored in mason jars at room temperature
for up to 1 month or in the refrigerator for
up to 3 months.

GLUTEN-FREE

Swap the toast for some Super-Seedy
Crackers (page 183) or your favourite
gluten-free bread.

This beautiful gourmet toast is a showstopper for brunch with your besties or just your special other. It is scrumptious and picture-perfect made with smooth beet hummus, creamy avocado, and crunchy granola. Relish the taste and beauty of this simple savoury toast—after snapping a photo or two, of course!

1. Make the Pink Beet Hummus.

2. Make the Maple Pecan Granola, if using.

3. Spread a thick layer of Pink Beet Hummus on each slice of whole wheat toast. Top with sliced avocado and sprinkle with the Maple Pecan Granola. Sprinkle with basil, if desired.

Serves 2

PB&J with Fried Banana Toast

Vegan ＊ Refined Sugar-free ＊ Soy-free

If you have not tasted fried bananas before then you are in for a real treat! Fried banana is sweet and caramelized; it is like having dessert for breakfast. This simple pairing of peanut butter, raspberry jam, and caramelized banana is a truly decadent combo.

1. Make the Raspberry Chia Jam.
2. In a medium non-stick skillet, heat the coconut oil over medium heat. Add the banana rounds and cook until golden and caramelized, 2 to 3 minutes per side. Transfer to a plate.
3. Spread a layer of peanut butter and Raspberry Chia Jam on the slices of whole wheat toast. Top with the caramelized bananas. Sprinkle with puffed quinoa or coconut flakes, if desired.

¼ cup Raspberry Chia Jam (page 66)

2 teaspoons coconut oil

1 ripe banana, sliced into ¾-inch rounds

2 tablespoons natural peanut butter

2 slices whole wheat bread, toasted

Puffed quinoa or coconut flakes,
      for sprinkling (optional)

STORAGE

The Raspberry Chia Jam can be stored in an airtight container in the refrigerator for up to 1 week or in the freezer for up to 2 months. If frozen, thaw before using.

Serves 2

Chocolate Hazelnut Spread and Strawberry Toast

Vegan ＊ Soy-free

¼ cup Chocolate Hazelnut Spread
(page 69)

2 slices whole wheat bread, toasted

½ cup fresh strawberries, hulled
and sliced

1 teaspoon coconut flakes

1 teaspoon cacao nibs (optional)

STORAGE

The Chocolate Hazelnut Spread can
be stored in a jar at room temperature
for up to 10 days.

This gourmet toast combines two favourites—strawberries and chocolate—for a rich, decadent, sweet, and juicy toast. The combo of sweet, chocolatey, and tart is a heavenly pairing.

1. Make the Chocolate Hazelnut Spread.
2. Slather the slices of whole wheat toast with the Chocolate Hazelnut Spread. Top with strawberry slices and sprinkle with coconut flakes and cacao nibs.

Serves 4

Tofu Eggy Scramble on Whole Wheat Toast

Vegan ✳ Nut-free ✳ Refined Sugar-free ✳ No Added Sugar

This is a great recipe for when you want a flavourful savoury breakfast tout de suite! This speedy tofu scramble comes together quickly and effortlessly for a mouth-watering, protein-packed eggy scramble.

1. Drain and rinse the tofu, then gently pat dry with a kitchen towel. (You do not need to press the tofu.)

2. In a large skillet, heat the coconut oil over medium-high heat. Using your hands, break apart the tofu into small, rough chunks over the skillet. Add the nutritional yeast, turmeric, cumin, garlic powder, chili powder, sea salt, black salt, and pepper. Stir to combine and cook, stirring often, until excess water has evaporated and the desired eggy consistency is reached, 5 to 7 minutes.

3. Spread coconut oil on each piece of whole wheat toast. Scoop the tofu scramble onto the toast and top with chopped tomatoes and chives. Sprinkle with flaky sea salt and more pepper, if desired.

1 block (14 ounces/396 g) firm tofu

1 tablespoon coconut oil, more for
    the toast

1 tablespoon nutritional yeast

¾ teaspoon ground turmeric

½ teaspoon ground cumin

½ teaspoon garlic powder

¼ teaspoon chili powder

½ teaspoon fine sea salt

¼ teaspoon fine black salt
    (or more sea salt)

Pinch of freshly ground black pepper

FOR SERVING

4 slices whole wheat bread, toasted

½ cup grape tomatoes, chopped

¼ cup chopped fresh chives

Flaky sea salt (optional)

TIP

If you like this recipe, then I encourage you to take it to the next level with my Veggie Tofu Scramble with Roasted Baby Potatoes (page 65).

Du Lait et des Boissons

Milks and Other Drinks

Trust me when I say that you are going to find this chapter very helpful. Crack the spine of this book and start folding the corners of the pages! Although drinks might seem like a casual purchase from the grocery store, this chapter takes your basics to a quality that store-bought versions can never match.

I like to think of this chapter as "the basics done right." These easy drink recipes will teach you how to make the creamiest, most luscious vegan milks you've ever had—ones that froth beautifully for velvety barista-approved lattes. In addition, you will learn how to make simple wellness smoothies that you can't stop sipping on, delicious juices at a fraction of the cost of store-bought, and the best Matcha Latte (page 89).

Creamy Dreamy Almond Milk

Vegan * Gluten-free * Grain-free * Oil-free * Soy-free * Refined Sugar-free * Raw/No-bake

Once you try this almond milk, there is no turning back. It is creamy, rich, and velvety smooth. Homemade almond milk is like a fine wine: you want to sip and savour it and let the gorgeous flavours dance on your palate.

I like to use this almond milk for my frothy Golden Turmeric Latte (page 86) and Matcha Latte (page 89). In addition, it is lovely in recipes like my Creamy Chia Pudding with Red Fruits (page 47) and Blueberry Muffin Overnight Oats (page 48) where its almond flavour really takes centre stage. Leave the store-bought version for cooking and baking, and keep a batch of this quality milk in your refrigerator at all times.

1. Place the almonds in a small bowl and cover with room-temperature water. Soak for at least 6 hours or overnight, then drain. Alternatively, you can shorten the soak time to 2 hours by pouring boiling water over the almonds to cover, then drain.

2. In a high-speed blender, combine the almonds, date, water, vanilla, cinnamon, and salt. Blend on high speed until smooth, about 1 minute. (If using a standard blender, blend for 2 minutes.)

3. Place an open nut milk bag over a medium bowl. Pour the almond milk blend into the bag. Squeeze the bag to strain all the milk into the bowl. (If you do not have a nut milk bag, you can use a thin kitchen towel. Linen towels, with their loose weave, work great for this. You can also use a couple of layers of cheesecloth.) Taste, and if you prefer a less creamy almond milk, add a splash more water. (Save the pulp; see Tip.)

4. Return the almond milk to the blender (so it's easier to pour), then pour into a glass bottle or jar and place the lid on tightly.

1 cup raw almonds

1 Medjool date, pitted

3 cups water, more as needed

½ teaspoon pure vanilla extract

½ teaspoon cinnamon

Pinch of fine sea salt

STORAGE

Store the almond milk in a glass bottle or jar in the refrigerator for up to 5 days. It's normal for the almond milk to separate as it stands. Shake well before using.

TIP

Use the leftover almond pulp to make almond meal for baked goods. Preheat the oven to 200°F (100°C) and spread the pulp onto a baking sheet lined with parchment paper. Bake for 1½ to 2 hours, stirring every 20 minutes, until the pulp is dry. Let cool. Pulse in a high-speed blender or food processor to break up any clumps. Store in an airtight container in the freezer for up to 3 months.

Super-Quick Oat Milk

Vegan * Gluten-free * Nut-free * Oil-free Option * Soy-free * Refined Sugar-free * Raw/No-bake

1 cup gluten-free old-fashioned
    rolled oats
4 cups cold water (see Tip)
2 tablespoons pure maple syrup
4 teaspoons avocado oil
    (optional; see Tip)
1 teaspoon pure vanilla extract
Pinch of fine sea salt

STORAGE

Store the oat milk in a glass bottle or
jar in the refrigerator for up to 5 days.
It's normal for the oat milk to separate
as it stands. Shake well before using.

OIL-FREE

Omit the avocado oil.

Making your own oat milk is quick, easy, and much more cost-effective than store-bought brands. This oat milk is ready in 30 seconds and satisfies with a delicious oaty and sweet flavour. Most homemade oat milks run into the problem of being too slimy in texture, but my recipe, with a touch of fat and just a short blend, yields a gorgeously silky smooth consistency every time. Enjoy this oat milk cold; use it to make smoothies, overnight oats, and chia puddings, or splash it into your tea or coffee.

1. In a high-speed blender, combine the oats, water, maple syrup, avocado oil (if using), vanilla, and salt. Blend on high speed for just 30 seconds. (Blending for longer may cause the milk to heat and thicken, which can result in a slimy texture. If using a standard blender, blend for no more than 45 seconds.)
2. Place an open nut milk bag over a medium bowl. Pour the oat milk blend into the bag. Squeeze the bag to strain all the milk into the bowl. (If you do not have a nut milk bag, you can use a thin kitchen towel. Linen towels, with their loose weave, work great for this. You can also use a couple of layers of cheesecloth.)
3. Return the oat milk to the blender (so it's easier to pour), then pour into a glass bottle or jar and place the lid on tightly.

TIPS

1. It is important to use cold water to avoid heating the oat milk. This will result in a less slimy texture.
2. The avocado oil helps to create a very smooth, silky, and creamy oat milk. For the same reason, store-bought brands often use sunflower oil.
3. This oat milk is not suitable for heating. Heating it will give it a thick, soupy consistency as the oats cook. If you prefer an oat milk that can be heated for lattes and other warm recipes, try my Barista Cashew Coconut Oat Milk (page 85) or my Creamy Dreamy Almond Milk (page 81).
4. It's normal for oat milk to have more sediment fall to the bottom of the bottle than other plant-based milks. It washes away easily when you clean the bottle.

Makes 2⅔ cups ✳ Requires: soak time

Barista Cashew Coconut Oat Milk

Vegan ✳ Gluten-free ✳ Oil-free ✳ Soy-free ✳ Refined Sugar-free ✳ Raw/No-bake

In the past few years, oat milk has truly won over the hearts of coffeehouses. This homemade barista blend offers the same irresistible rich and creamy flavour, but it's made with healthy fats from cashews and shredded coconut to achieve a drink that surpasses your favourite store-bought brands. Froth and pour into dreamy lattes and bring the coffeehouse to your home.

1. Place the cashews in a small bowl and cover with boiling water. Soak for 1 hour, then drain. (Alternatively, soak the cashews in room-temperature water to cover for at least 6 hours or overnight, then drain.)

2. In a high-speed blender, combine the cashews, shredded coconut, oats, date, sea salt, water, and vanilla. Blend on high speed for 1 minute. (If using a standard blender, blend for 2 minutes.)

3. Place an open nut milk bag over a medium bowl. Pour the oat milk blend into the bag. Squeeze the bag to strain all the milk into the bowl. (If you do not have a nut milk bag, you can use a thin kitchen towel. Linen towels, with their loose weave, work great for this. You can also use a couple of layers of cheesecloth.)

4. Return the cashew coconut oat milk to the blender (so it's easier to pour), then pour into a glass bottle or jar and place the lid on tightly.

½ cup raw cashews

½ cup unsweetened shredded coconut

¼ cup gluten-free old-fashioned
    rolled oats

1 Medjool date, pitted

Pinch of fine sea salt

3 cups water

1 teaspoon pure vanilla extract

STORAGE

Store the cashew coconut oat milk in a glass bottle or jar in the refrigerator for up to 5 days. It's normal for the oat milk to separate as it stands. Shake well before using.

Serves 2

Golden Turmeric Latte

Vegan ＊ Gluten-free ＊ Grain-free ＊ Soy-free ＊ Refined Sugar-free

2 cups Creamy Dreamy Almond Milk
    (page 81) or unsweetened
    store-bought

½ cup water

1 tablespoon agave

1¼ teaspoons ground turmeric

½ teaspoon ground ginger

½ teaspoon coconut oil

3 black peppercorns

2 cardamom pods (see Tip)

1 (3-inch) cinnamon stick

TIPS

1. If you cannot find cardamom pods,
replace with a pinch of ground cardamom.

2. I recommend using Creamy Dreamy
Almond Milk (page 81) for this recipe for
an ultra-creamy latte. However, you can
use store-bought almond milk.

3. Save the black peppercorns, cardamom
pods, and cinnamon stick to remake this
recipe. Rinse and let air-dry. The spices
can be reused four or five times.

4. Power up by adding ¼ to ½ teaspoon
more ground turmeric when making
this latte. I prefer to use 1½ teaspoons
of turmeric, but my family and friends
prefer the recipe amount listed above.

This is a wonderful spiced latte that you can enjoy in the colder months at any time of day, morning, noon, or night. It is spicy, creamy, caffeine-free, and so cozy. Full of antioxidants and immunity-boosting spices, this sweet cup of wellness will have you glowing as bright as this latte.

1. Make the Creamy Dreamy Almond Milk, if using.

2. In a small saucepan, combine the almond milk, water, agave, turmeric, and ginger. Whisk to combine. Bring to a low simmer over medium heat. Add the coconut oil, peppercorns, cardamom pods, and cinnamon stick and simmer for 5 to 7 minutes for the flavours to incorporate and for the latte to develop a rich orange hue.

3. Pour the latte through a fine-mesh sieve or strainer into cups.

Serves 1

Matcha Latte

Vegan ❋ Gluten-free ❋ Grain-free ❋ Oil-free ❋ Soy-free ❋ Refined Sugar-free

Not a day goes by without my indulging in a cozy matcha latte. This latte is my hot beverage of choice, and I have made it enough times now to have landed on the perfect blend. Warm, earthy, lightly nutty, with notes of bitter and sweet, it is the ideal drink for that peaceful moment in your day.

1. Make the Creamy Dreamy Almond Milk, if using.

2. Add the matcha powder to a small flat-bottomed bowl. Gently swirl the matcha powder across the bottom of the bowl using a matcha whisk (or a regular whisk) to reduce clumping.

3. Pour in the hot water and whisk together using the matcha whisk in a W shape until smooth and foamy. (You can also use a regular or electric hand whisk.) Pour the matcha mixture into a cup.

4. Using a milk frother or electric hand whisk, froth the almond milk until warm and velvety. (Alternatively, warm the milk in a small saucepan or the microwave.) Pour the heated milk over the matcha mixture to fill the cup. Add the maple syrup (if using) and stir to combine.

½ cup Creamy Dreamy Almond Milk (page 81) or unsweetened store-bought

1 teaspoon premium ceremonial-grade matcha powder

¾ cup hot water

1 teaspoon pure maple syrup, or to taste (optional)

TIPS

1. You can make this recipe without a flat-bottomed bowl and a matcha whisk, but they do help achieve a smooth matcha with no clumps.

2. A quality matcha will ensure your matcha is smooth and creamy and not bitter in taste. In fact, a quality matcha needs little or no sweetener. See Pantry Staples (page 17) for my brand recommendation.

3. For an ultra-creamy latte, I recommend using Creamy Dreamy Almond Milk (page 81) or my Barista Cashew Coconut Oat Milk (page 85) for this recipe. You can use store-bought almond or oat milk, but the taste and frothiness will vary depending on the brand. When it comes to store-bought milk, I prefer oat milk in this latte.

Serves 2

Chocolat Chaud

Vegan ※ Gluten-free ※ Grain-free ※ Oil-free ※ Soy-free ※ Refined Sugar-free

1¼ cups unsweetened almond milk

7 ounces full-fat coconut milk
    (half a 14-ounce/400 mL can)

2 tablespoons cocoa powder

1 tablespoon natural almond butter

1 tablespoon pure maple syrup

½ teaspoon pure vanilla extract

Pinch of fine sea salt

1 (3-inch) cinnamon stick

Chantilly (page 298) or vegan whipped
    cream, for topping (optional)

Shaved dairy-free dark chocolate,
    for sprinkling (optional)

TIPS

1. This hot chocolate is also delicious
with a little heat. Add a pinch of red
chili flakes to spice up the drink.

2. Save the cinnamon stick to remake
this recipe. Rinse and let air-dry. It can
be reused four or five times. Use it in
my Golden Turmeric Latte (page 86)
or Winter Poached Pears with Spiced
Syrup (page 289).

On cold winter days, this chocolat chaud (hot chocolate) is just the thing to warm my body and soul. I absolutely love to make this hot chocolate after a snowy hike in the woods with our sweet dog Penny, or to snuggle up with for a movie during the holidays. It is the perfect blend of creamy, chocolatey, and sweet with a hint of cinnamon. My secret ingredient for the lushest hot chocolate? Almond butter! It adds gorgeous richness and depth to the drink.

1. In a small saucepan, combine the almond milk, coconut milk, cocoa powder, almond butter, maple syrup, vanilla, and salt. Whisk well until smooth. Add the cinnamon stick and heat over medium heat, stirring frequently, until almost boiling, 7 to 10 minutes.

2. Remove from the heat and scoop out the cinnamon stick. Pour the hot chocolate into mugs or festive glasses. Top with Chantilly and a sprinkle of shaved chocolate, if desired.

Serves 1

Wally's Chocolate Coffee Freakshake

Vegan ✳ Gluten-free ✳ Soy-free ✳ Refined Sugar-free Option ✳ Raw/No-bake

This chocolate coffee smoothie is a tribute to an ultra-cool café in Lille called Wally's Coffee, started by my talented friend Wally. This Euro-contemporary café is renowned in Lille for its Freakshakes—ultra-decadent milkshakes topped with a brownie or doughnut and whipped cream, with a tall straw to help devour it all. Although this particular recipe is a much healthier spin, and wholesome enough to enjoy for breakfast, it is just as decadent and luxurious. Get freaky by topping it with Chantilly (page 298) or your favourite store-bought vegan whipped cream and a good drizzle of chocolate sauce.

1. Make the Super-Quick Oat Milk, if using.

2. In a high-speed blender, combine the oat milk, oats, frozen banana, date, espresso, almond butter, cocoa powder, cinnamon, salt, and 3 ice cubes. Blend until smooth. If you prefer a colder and thicker shake, add more ice cubes, then blend again.

3. Pour the shake into a large glass. If desired, top with Chantilly and drizzle with chocolate sauce. Serve with a wide reusable straw for sipping.

1 cup Super-Quick Oat Milk (page 82)
    or unsweetened store-bought

¼ cup gluten-free old-fashioned
    rolled oats

1 large frozen banana, chopped

1 Medjool date, pitted

1 shot of espresso

2 tablespoons natural almond butter

2 tablespoons cocoa powder

½ teaspoon cinnamon

Pinch of fine sea salt

3 to 5 ice cubes

FREAKY TOPPINGS (OPTIONAL)

Chantilly (page 298) or vegan
    whipped cream

Vegan chocolate sauce, to drizzle

TIPS

1. This recipe is refined sugar–free without the toppings. I enjoy the smoothie without the toppings, but my husband, Mitch, loves it styled up with whipped cream and chocolate sauce.

2. The oat milk can be replaced with unsweetened almond milk.

REFINED SUGAR-FREE

Omit the Freaky Toppings (Chantilly and vegan chocolate sauce).

Serves 2

Supreme Blueberry Smoothie

Vegan ✳ Gluten-free ✳ Grain-free ✳ Oil-free ✳ Soy-free ✳ Refined Sugar-free ✳ Raw/No-bake

1 cup frozen blueberries

1 frozen banana

1 small red beet, peeled and chopped
    (see Tip)

3 tablespoons hemp hearts

1 tablespoon natural almond butter

½ teaspoon cinnamon

1½ cups unsweetened almond milk

3 ice cubes

2 to 3 teaspoons pure maple syrup
    (optional)

This blueberry smoothie is easy to make, bold in colour, and packed with antioxidants. It's invigorating, luscious, and comforting. I love to start my day with this smoothie, especially in the late summer and early fall with its cinnamon-spiced flavour.

1. In a high-speed blender, combine the blueberries, banana, beet, hemp hearts, almond butter, cinnamon, almond milk, and ice. Blend until smooth and creamy, 45 seconds to 1 minute. (If using a standard blender, blend for 2 minutes or until smooth.) Taste, and add the maple syrup to sweeten, if desired; blend on low speed just to combine.

DO AHEAD

This smoothie can be prepared the night before. Store in a glass bottle or jar in the refrigerator. Shake or stir well before drinking.

TIPS

1. If using a high-speed blender, you can use a raw beet in this recipe. However, if you are using a standard blender, then I recommend using a cooked beet.

2. I like to cook a batch of beets to have them handy. To cook the beets, place them in a large pot and add water to cover by 1 to 2 inches. Bring to a boil over high heat. Reduce the heat to medium-low, cover with a lid, and simmer until the beets are fork-tender, about 45 minutes. Using a cooked beet no longer makes this recipe raw/no-bake.

Serves 2

Green Detox Smoothie

Vegan * Gluten-free * Grain-free * Oil-free * Soy-free * Refined Sugar-free * Raw/No-bake

This green detox smoothie is sweet, thirst-quenching, and easy to sip. My secret ingredient in green smoothies is parsley—surprising, I know! Parsley is delicious in smoothies, offering bright and fresh flavour, and it is known for being high in antioxidants and for freshening breath. My friends are now converts to parsley in smoothies. I am certain that this healthful smoothie will become a morning favourite for you as well.

1. In a high-speed blender, combine the spinach, parsley, orange, hemp hearts, date, ginger, almond butter, almond milk, and ice. Blend until smooth and creamy, about 1 minute. (If using a standard blender, blend for 2 minutes or until smooth.)

2 cups tightly packed baby spinach

¼ cup tightly packed fresh flat-leaf parsley leaves

1 large orange, peeled and roughly chopped (navel, Valencia, or blood orange)

3 tablespoons hemp hearts

1 Medjool date, pitted

1 (1-inch) piece fresh ginger, peeled and chopped

1 tablespoon natural almond butter

1¼ cups unsweetened almond milk

3 ice cubes

TIP
During the summer months, try a ripe peach in place of the orange.

DO AHEAD
This smoothie can be prepared the night before. Store in the refrigerator in a glass bottle or jar. Shake or stir well before drinking.

Immunity Boost Juice

Vegan   ✳   Gluten-free   ✳   Grain-free   ✳   Nut-free   ✳   Oil-free   ✳   Soy-free   ✳   Refined Sugar-free   ✳   Raw/No-bake

4 navel oranges, peeled

1 lemon, peeled

2 large carrots, peeled and roughly
    chopped

1 (3-inch) piece fresh ginger, peeled
    and chopped

1 (2-inch) piece fresh turmeric, peeled
    and chopped

1 tablespoon agave, more if desired

2 tablespoons hot water if using a juicer
    (or ¾ to 1 cup room-temperature
    water if using a high-speed blender)

STORAGE

Store the juice in a glass bottle or jar
in the refrigerator for up to 4 days.
Shake well before drinking.

This glowing juice is sweet but mighty. Spiced with fresh turmeric and ginger, and packed with vitamin C and antioxidants from orange and lemon, it's an immunity-fighting and metabolism-boosting drink that I love to sip on pre- or post-morning workout. It is especially loved around our home during the winter months to help ward off colds and flu.

Fresh-pressed juice can be expensive, but making your own is a cost-effective way to juice up your day. I like to make this recipe using the juicer attachment of my 3-in-1 food processor, but it's just as good made in a high-speed blender and squeezed through a nut-milk bag.

USING A JUICER

1. One at a time, push the oranges, lemon, carrots, ginger, and turmeric through the juicer.
2. In a small cup, whisk together the agave and hot water. Pour the sweet water into the juice and stir to combine. Taste, and add more agave if you prefer it sweeter. Transfer the juice to a glass bottle or jar and place the lid on tightly.

USING A HIGH-SPEED BLENDER

1. Slice the oranges and lemon in half crosswise and scoop out any seeds. In the high-speed blender, combine the oranges, lemon, carrots, ginger, and turmeric. Add ¾ to 1 cup of water (as much as needed) and blend on medium-high speed until pulverized. Use a tamper if needed if things get stuck while blending. If you do not have a tamper, occasionally stop the blender and stir with a wooden spoon to help the blending process.
2. Place an open nut milk bag over a medium bowl. Pour the blended juice into the bag and squeeze to strain all the juice into the bowl. (Alternatively, you can use a thin kitchen towel or a couple of layers of cheesecloth to strain the juice.)
3. Return the strained juice to the blender. Add the agave and blend for a few seconds to combine. Taste, and add more agave if you prefer it sweeter. Transfer the juice to a glass bottle or jar and place the lid on tightly.

Makes 2½ cups

Energizing Green Tonic

Vegan * Gluten-free * Grain-free * Nut-free * Oil-free * Soy-free * No Added Sugar * Refined Sugar-free * Raw/No-bake

This energizing green juice is refreshing, perfectly tart, and full of detoxifying spinach, parsley, green apples, and cucumber. I love to make this juice after returning from vacation, or in January after the holidays. It helps me to refuel, recharge, and restart those healthy habits. This tonic can be made in a juicer or a high-speed blender.

USING A JUICER

1. One at a time, push the spinach, parsley, green apples, cucumber, lemon, and ginger through the juicer. Pour the juice into a glass bottle or jar and place the lid on tightly.

USING A HIGH-SPEED BLENDER

1. In the high-speed blender, combine the spinach, parsley, green apples, cucumber, lemon, and ginger. Add ¾ to 1 cup of water (as much as needed) and blend on medium-high speed until pulverized. Use a tamper if needed if things get stuck while blending. If you do not have a tamper, occasionally stop the blender and stir with a wooden spoon to help the blending process.

2. Place an open nut milk bag over a medium bowl. Pour the blended juice into the bag and squeeze to strain all the juice into the bowl. (Alternatively, you can use a thin kitchen towel or a couple of layers of cheesecloth to strain the juice.)

3. Return the strained juice to the blender (so it's easier to pour), then pour the juice into a glass bottle or jar and place the lid on tightly.

4 cups tightly packed baby spinach

1 cup tightly packed fresh flat-leaf parsley leaves

2 green apples, roughly chopped

1 English cucumber, roughly chopped

1 lemon, peeled and roughly chopped

1 (1-inch) piece fresh ginger, peeled and chopped

¾ to 1 cup water (if using a high-speed blender)

STORAGE

Store the juice in a glass bottle or jar in the refrigerator for up to 4 days. Shake well before drinking.

Sweet Treats, Cakes, and Bites

Family and friends know that I have a major sweet tooth. I love noshing on little treats like muffins, cookies, and loaves mid-afternoon as a pick-me-up snack.

If you are like-minded, this chapter is dedicated to you. I have shared all sorts of sweet snacks, from healthy squares like Pumpkin Chickpea Blondies (page 139) to Raspberry Jam Thumbprint Cookies (page 121), and moist fluffy cakes like Chocolate Almond Torte (page 140) for entertaining loved ones.

I found vegan baking intimidating when I was first adopting a plant-based diet. Over time, I have learned how to make vegan versions of my favourite baked goods that do not compromise on taste or texture. I know you, too, will soon become a confident vegan baker through this chapter. As you progress in your baking, try some of the more ambitious recipes that I have included, which bring the wow factor, like my Chocolate Macarons (page 113) or mouth-watering Cannelés (page 125). I am certain this chapter will grow with you, just as it has with me.

Sweet Assortment Menus

I love to throw an afternoon tea party on special occasions like an engagement party or baby shower. Whip out Grandma's teacups and saucers, and get all the floral patterns flowing! Who doesn't love tucking into sweet hand-held treats with a hot cup of tea? That is how the best conversations commence, if you ask me.

Teatime was a fun ritual when we were kids. My mum is a master baker, and her occasional afternoon teas always featured fancy fare. Try it with your family for a fun weekend activity. If you are entertaining beyond your household, ask your guests to bring containers so they can take home any leftovers. They will be thanking you for the sweet snack later in the workweek!

Teatime with Besties

Raspberry Jam Thumbprint
Cookies (page 121)
Madeleines (page 117)
Sneaky Zucchini and Walnut Bread
(page 144)

Teatime for Two

Chocolate Hazelnut Swirl Muffins
(page 149) or Feel-Good Raspberry
Muffins (page 146)
Cannelés (page 125)

Family Fun

Baked Beignets (page 127)
Raspberry Jam Thumbprint Cookies
(page 121) or My Darling Flourless
Chocolate Chip Cookies (page 118)
Chocolate Chip Banana Bread (page 143)

Teatime for Entertaining

Sweet Sablés (page 107)
Pretty Petites Meringues (page 110)
or Chocolate Macarons (page 113)
Brookies (page 135)
Pain d'Épices (page 129) or
Chocolate Almond Torte (page 140)

Quick and Easy

My Darling Flourless Chocolate Chip
Cookies (page 118) or Ginger Snap
or Chewy Cookies (page 122)
Pumpkin Chickpea Blondies (page 139)
Healthier Millionaire Bars (page 133)

Sweet Sablés

Vegan ✳ Soy-free

In France, vegan shortbread cookies are better known as sablés, which means "sand." But I assure you these cookies taste nothing like sand! They are perfectly sweet, lightly spiced, soft, and buttery. They are everything we could want in a classic shortbread cookie and will certainly please a crowd.

Make these a feast for the eyes by dipping in a sugar glaze and decorating with edible rose petals or candied sprinkles. If you want to keep things simple, though, just sprinkle the baked shortbreads with icing sugar.

1. Make the Sablés: Sift the flour and icing sugar into a large bowl. Add the almond flour, cardamom, and salt and stir to combine.
2. Cut the vegan butter into small cubes and add to the flour mixture. Using your hands, massage the butter into the flour mixture to form a shaggy and loosely combined dough. Add the agave and vanilla and mix together. If the dough is too dry, add 2 or 3 teaspoons of almond milk, a teaspoon at a time, and knead to form a shaggy dough.
3. Turn the dough out onto a work surface. Using your hands, bring the dough together and knead to form a smooth ball. It is okay if there are a few dry spots. (Do not over-knead the dough or the sablés will be dense.) Wrap the dough in reusable wrap and chill in the refrigerator for 30 minutes.
4. Place the oven racks in the upper and lower thirds of the oven. Preheat the oven to 350°F (180°C). Line 2 baking sheets with parchment paper.
5. Lightly dust the work surface with all-purpose flour. Using a rolling pin, roll out the dough into a rectangle or oval about ¼ inch thick. (Try to handle the dough as little as possible for a light and flaky texture when baked.) Using a 2½-inch round cookie cutter, cut out rounds and transfer to the prepared baking sheets, leaving a small space between each cookie. Reroll the scraps and cut out more rounds. You should have at least 18 cookies.

SABLÉS

1¼ cups (162 g) all-purpose flour, more for dusting

¼ cup (25 g) organic icing sugar

¼ cup (25 g) almond flour

¼ teaspoon ground cardamom

⅛ teaspoon fine sea salt

½ cup (4 ounces/115 g) vegan butter, cold

2 tablespoons agave

½ teaspoon pure vanilla extract

2 to 3 teaspoons unsweetened almond milk, if needed

SUGAR GLAZE

½ cup (50 g) organic icing sugar

2 to 3 teaspoons unsweetened almond milk

GARNISHES (OPTIONAL)

2 to 3 tablespoons dried edible rose petals

2 to 3 tablespoons candied sprinkles

Recipe continues

Store the cookies in an airtight container in the refrigerator for up to 1 week or in the freezer for up to 1 month.

TIP

You can easily double this recipe to make a large batch of cookies for gifting or entertaining.

DO AHEAD

The cookie dough can be made up to 2 days in advance. Keep wrapped in a ball and stored in the refrigerator. If the dough is too hard for rolling, let it sit at room temperature for 10 to 20 minutes to soften slightly.

6. Bake the cookies until lightly golden on top, 8 to 10 minutes. For even baking, rotate the baking sheets front to back and top to bottom halfway through. Let the cookies cool in the pan for 5 minutes, then transfer to a wire rack to cool completely.

7. Make the Sugar Glaze: Sift the icing sugar into a small flat-bottomed bowl. Add 2 teaspoons of the almond milk and whisk together until smooth. If needed, add the remaining 1 teaspoon almond milk to thin the glaze.

8. Turn the cookies upside down on a baking sheet. One at a time, dip the top of each cookie in the glaze to cover the surface. Place the cookies, iced side up, back on the baking sheet. While the icing is wet, garnish the cookies with the dried rose petals and/or candied sprinkles, if desired. Chill the cookies in the refrigerator until the icing has hardened, about 2 hours.

Pretty Petites Meringues

Vegan   ✱   Gluten-free   ✱   Grain-free   ✱   Oil-free   ✱   Soy-free   ✱   Refined Sugar-free

¾ cup aquafaba (liquid from
    canned chickpeas)

½ teaspoon pure vanilla extract

¼ teaspoon cream of tartar

Pinch of fine sea salt

¾ cup (160 g) granulated sugar (see Tip)

STORAGE

Store the meringues in an airtight container lined with parchment paper, separating each layer of meringues with parchment. Store at room temperature for up to 2 weeks or in the freezer for up to 2 months. If frozen, bring to room temperature, tightly sealed, before serving.

TIPS

1. Granulated sugar is not always vegan. To make your own granulated sugar, add ¾ cup organic cane sugar to a high-speed blender and pulse a few times. Measure out ¾ cup of the fine sugar for this recipe and keep the rest for another use. (You should only have a little extra.)

2. The meringues will soften over time if exposed to the air. It is best to store them in an airtight container. If your meringues have gone a little sticky to the touch, heat them in the oven at 200°F (100°C) for 10 to 20 minutes, or until they are firm. Let cool with the oven door slightly ajar.

These mini meringues are like sweet little clouds. They are light, airy, and sugary. Pop one in your mouth and let it melt away into sweet nothings. These vegan meringues are made using aquafaba, the liquid from canned chickpeas, whipped into stiff peaks, piped into swirls, and baked at a low temperature until firm and crispy. At chic French cafés, you will often find little meringues served with a hot drink. I have fond memories admiring them served with my tea at the famous Aux Merveilleux de Fred in Lille. They are also lovely to share during the holidays, and are adored by adults and kids alike.

1. Place the oven racks in the upper and lower thirds of the oven. Preheat the oven to 200°F (100°C). Line 2 baking sheets with parchment paper. The parchment paper must lie flat inside the baking sheet, so trim if necessary.

2. In the bowl of a stand mixer fitted with the whisk attachment, combine the aquafaba, vanilla, cream of tartar, and salt. (Alternatively, you can use a hand mixer and a large bowl.) Whip on medium-high speed until bubbles begin to form, then increase the speed to high and slowly add the granulated sugar, a tablespoon at a time, whipping until the aquafaba forms stiff and glossy peaks, 7 to 10 minutes (or about 15 minutes if using a hand mixer). Test that the whipped meringue is stiff enough by gently tilting the bowl at a 90-degree angle. If the meringue stays in place without sliding, it is ready.

3. Fit a large piping bag with a large star piping tip (No. 32) and fill the bag with the meringue. Pipe 2-inch-wide swirls, ½ inch apart, onto the baking sheet. (You should be able to fit 5 meringues across, and 7 down the pan.)

4. Bake for 90 minutes, rotating the baking sheets from top to bottom halfway through the bake. The meringues should be firm and dry to the touch when ready. Turn the oven off and let the meringues cool in the oven for 1 hour with the door slightly open. (This will stop them from cracking from the sudden temperature change.)

Makes 16 macarons * Requires: cooling time + drying time

Chocolate Macarons

Vegan * Gluten-free * Grain-free * Oil-free * Soy-free

These chocolate macarons bring the Parisian patisserie into your home. The patisserie-perfect macarons have a light and crispy chocolate shell, a soft meringue interior, and a sweet chocolate hazelnut filling. This recipe certainly proves that even the most challenging sweets can be made vegan without compromising on taste or texture.

I will admit that my first few attempts did not yield window-shop macarons. So do not worry if your macarons are not a perfect uniform shape. It is all about the taste, which is delightful! Like everything in life, practice makes perfect.

Measure out the ingredients before starting, so you have everything ready. For this recipe, it is beneficial to weigh the ingredients if you have a scale, to ensure exact measurement.

½ cup Chocolate Hazelnut Spread (page 69)

1 cup aquafaba (liquid from canned chickpeas)

1 cup (100 g) almond flour

1 cup (100 g) organic icing sugar

2 tablespoons (13 g) cocoa powder

¼ teaspoon cream of tartar

¼ cup + 1 tablespoon (70 g) granulated sugar (see Tip)

1. Make the Chocolate Hazelnut Spread. Cover and set aside until ready to use.

2. Make the Batter: Line 2 baking sheets with parchment paper. The parchment paper must lie flat inside the baking sheet, so trim if necessary. Using a pencil and a 1½-inch round cookie cutter or same size flat round object, trace sixteen 1½-inch circles, 1 inch apart, onto each sheet of parchment paper. Flip the paper over to prevent the marks from transferring to the macarons. Fit a large piping bag with a plain round piping tip (No. 12).

3. Pour the aquafaba into a small saucepan and bring to a low simmer over medium-low heat. Reduce the aquafaba to ⅓ cup. Transfer to a large bowl and let cool to room temperature.

4. Sift the almond flour, icing sugar, and cocoa powder into a small bowl. (If the sieve holes are too small to sift the almond flour, add the almond flour to the bowl first and whisk well to aerate and break up any clumps. Then sift the remaining ingredients into the bowl.)

5. Add the cream of tartar to the cooled aquafaba. Using a hand mixer, beat on high speed until soft peaks begin to form, about 6 minutes.

Recipe continues

The macarons will keep in an airtight container in the refrigerator for up to 3 days or in the freezer for up to 2 months. Bring to room temperature before eating.

TIPS

1. Save the parchment paper with the traced circles to make more macarons another time.

2. Granulated sugar is not always vegan. To make your own vegan granulated sugar, add ¼ cup + 1 tablespoon organic cane sugar to a high-speed blender and pulse a few times. Measure out ¼ cup + 1 tablespoon of the fine sugar for this recipe and keep the rest for another use. (You should only have a little extra.)

3. Store any leftover Chocolate Hazelnut Spread in a jar at room temperature for up to 10 days.

Sprinkle in the granulated sugar, a spoonful at a time, while beating until the meringue is glossy and holds stiff peaks, 6 to 10 minutes. To test that the meringue is stiff enough, gently tilt the bowl at a 90-degree angle. If the meringue stays in place without sliding, it is ready.

6. Add the sifted dry ingredients to the meringue and gently fold into the batter until smooth and combined and the batter falls gently in a slow stream from the lifted spatula. (If it is still stiff when lifted, fold a few more times and test again. It should take only a few more folds to achieve the right consistency.)

7. Pipe the Batter: Fill the piping bag with the batter and twist the top of the bag to enclose. Lift up the four corners of the parchment paper, pipe a small dot of batter on the baking sheet, and smooth out the paper again to lay flat. (This will glue the corners of the parchment paper and stop the paper from shifting.) Hold the piping tip upright over the centre of a pencilled circle and squeeze until the batter is a 1½-inch circle. It is okay if the piping does not fit exactly in the circles. Use them as a guideline for size, and it will get easier with practice. Gently tap the baking sheet against the counter to release any air bubbles. (This should also help the small peak left by the piping tip to fall, for a smooth, rounded shell. If there is still a peak at the top, you can lightly moisten your fingertip and gently push down for a smoother top.) Let the piped shells sit at room temperature until the surface does not stick to your fingers when gently touched, 30 minutes to 1 hour.

8. Bake the Macaron Shells: Place the oven rack in the middle of the oven. Preheat the oven to 250°F (120°C).

9. Bake one baking sheet at a time, rotating the baking sheet at the 5-minute mark to ensure even baking, for 20 to 25 minutes, or until the macaron shells are puffed, look dry, and form "feet"—the bubbly-looking bottom. When you touch the top of a shell, it should not move, and the macaron can be lifted easily off the parchment paper. Let cool completely on the baking sheet, about 20 minutes.

10. Pipe the Macaron Shells and Assemble: Fit a piping bag with a No. 12 small round tip and fill it with the Chocolate Hazelnut Spread.

11. Arrange the macaron shells in rows, pairing shells of similar size. Pipe a dollop of the Chocolate Hazelnut Spread onto the flat side of one cookie from each pair. When all of the bottom shells are piped, gently place its pair, right side up, on top to create a sandwich. Serve the macarons at room temperature.

Make the Batter

Pipe the Batter onto the Template

Fill the Shells and Top to Create a Sandwich

Madeleines

Vegan * Soy-free * Refined Sugar-free

Light and airy, sweet and spongy is how I describe my vegan madeleines. It is a taste profile so typical in French baking. Madeleines are in fact delicate little cakes, although many people call them cookies. Do as the Parisians do and serve them with afternoon tea or coffee.

You will need a 16-mould non-stick madeleine pan for creating these pretty shell-shaped cookies. You can find madeleine pans in most kitchenware stores or online.

1. In a small bowl, combine the coconut sugar, melted vegan butter, almond milk, lemon zest and juice, and vanilla. Whisk to combine.
2. Sift the all-purpose flour into a large bowl. Add the almond flour, arrowroot powder, baking powder, and salt. Mix together.
3. Pour the wet ingredients into the dry ingredients and stir to combine. Cover the bowl with a kitchen towel and chill in the refrigerator for at least 1 hour.
4. Preheat the oven to 350°F (180°C). Lightly brush the shell-shaped moulds of a madeleine pan with the avocado oil.
5. Spoon about 2 teaspoons of batter into each mould; the moulds should be almost full. Lightly tap the pan on the counter a few times to release any air bubbles.
6. Bake until the madeleines are golden around the edges and a small hump forms in the middle, 12 to 14 minutes. Remove from the oven and let the madeleines cool in the pan for 5 minutes. Turn the madeleines out onto a wire rack or kitchen towel to cool completely.
7. If desired, dust the shell side of the cooled madeleines with icing sugar. The madeleines are best enjoyed on the day they are made.

¼ cup (35 g) coconut sugar

3 tablespoons (40 g) vegan butter, melted

½ cup unsweetened almond milk

Zest of 1 lemon

2 tablespoons lemon juice

1 teaspoon pure vanilla extract

⅓ cup (43 g) all-purpose flour

⅔ cup (70 g) almond flour

¼ cup (30 g) arrowroot powder

1½ teaspoons baking powder

¼ teaspoon fine sea salt

Avocado oil, for brushing the pan

1 tablespoon organic icing sugar, for dusting (optional)

TIP

This recipe requires a madeleine pan to achieve the beautiful traditional madeleine shape. I used a 16-mould non-stick metallic baking pan. If you have a 12-mould madeleine pan, you will need to bake the madeleines in two batches.

DO AHEAD

The batter can be prepared 1 day in advance. Store, covered, in the refrigerator.

Makes 18 cookies ✳ Requires: chill time

My Darling Flourless Chocolate Chip Cookies

Vegan ✳ Gluten-free ✳ Grain-free ✳ Soy-free ✳ One-bowl

3 cups (300 g) almond flour

1 cup (72 g) unsweetened
   shredded coconut

2 tablespoons ground chia seeds
   or ground flaxseed

1 teaspoon baking powder

½ teaspoon fine sea salt

½ teaspoon cinnamon

¾ cup pure maple syrup

⅓ cup (65 g) coconut oil, melted

2 teaspoons pure vanilla extract

1 bar (8 ounces/225 g) dairy-free semi-
   sweet chocolate, cut into chunks
   (or 1 cup semi-sweet chocolate chips)

STORAGE

Store the cookies in an airtight container
at room temperature for up to 1 week or
in the freezer for up to 2 months.

TIPS

1. It's normal for this cookie dough to
feel a bit more wet in texture. Chilling
the dough makes it easier to roll. It also
helps to clean your hands from time to
time if things start to get too sticky.

2. For a less expensive version or as an
alternative, replace 1 cup of almond flour
with 1 cup gluten-free old-fashioned
rolled oats. However, this recipe will no
longer be grain-free.

These flourless chocolate chip cookies are such a favourite on
my blog and in real life. They are sweet and moist, with a lightly
crispy exterior and ultra-soft interior, and are bejewelled with
big chocolate chips. Not bad for a simple one-bowl recipe with
wholesome ingredients! My friends and family go absolutely
bonkers over these cookies, and kids love them too. Not a single
party ends without a handful of people asking for the recipe. Let
this cookie recipe become your go-to for a sweet and simple treat.

1. Place the oven racks in the upper and lower thirds of the oven.
Preheat the oven to 350°F (180°C). Line 2 baking sheets with
parchment paper.

2. In a large bowl, combine the almond flour, shredded coconut,
ground chia seeds, baking powder, salt, and cinnamon. Stir to combine.

3. Pour the maple syrup, melted coconut oil, and vanilla into the flour
mixture. Stir until combined and a dough-like texture. (The batter will
be a bit wetter than regular cookie dough.) Add the chocolate chunks
and mix in evenly. Cover and refrigerate for 20 minutes.

4. Using your hands, gently roll the cookie dough into eighteen
2-inch balls. Arrange the balls on the prepared baking sheets,
about 2 inches apart. Press down on the balls with the heel of your
hand to slightly flatten. If any chocolate chunks fall out while forming
the balls, press them into the tops of the cookies after flattening them
on the baking sheet.

5. Bake the cookies until lightly golden on top and lightly brown
around the edges, 12 to 15 minutes. Let the cookies cool on the pan
for 5 minutes, then transfer to a wire rack to cool completely.

Raspberry Jam Thumbprint Cookies

Vegan * Gluten-free * Soy-free * Refined Sugar-free

It is such a treat sinking your teeth into these thumbprint cookies. With their sweet, jammy interior, they are a comforting childhood classic that pleases all ages. Enjoy these cookies any time of year— in the summer when raspberries are plentiful, or during the holidays as a festive cookie.

1. Make the Raspberry Chia Jam, if using.
2. Preheat the oven to 350°F (180°C). Line a baking sheet with parchment paper.
3. In a food processor or high-speed blender, pulse the oats until they reach a flour-like consistency. Transfer the oat flour to a large bowl and add the almond flour, cinnamon, and salt. Stir to combine.
4. In a small bowl, whisk together the maple syrup, melted coconut oil, almond butter, and vanilla. Pour the wet ingredients into the dry ingredients and stir well to combine.
5. Using your hands, roll the dough into fifteen 1½-inch balls. Place the balls on the prepared baking sheet, leaving ample space between them. (They may slightly flatten during baking.) Using your thumb, gently push into the middle of each cookie to make an indent. Fill each indent to the brim with the Raspberry Chia Jam.
6. Bake the cookies until the edges are crispy and golden, 10 to 12 minutes. Let the cookies cool on the pan for 5 minutes, then transfer to a wire rack to cool completely.

½ cup Raspberry Chia Jam (page 66) or jam of choice

1½ cups (200 g) gluten-free old-fashioned rolled oats

1 cup (100 g) almond flour

1 teaspoon cinnamon

¼ teaspoon fine sea salt

½ cup pure maple syrup

⅓ cup (65 g) coconut oil, melted

2 tablespoons natural almond butter

1 teaspoon pure vanilla extract

STORAGE

Store the cookies in an airtight container at room temperature for up to 2 days, in the refrigerator for up to 5 days, or in the freezer for up to 1 month.

TIP

To make these cookies holiday festive, drizzle cooled cookies with sugar glaze. Mix ½ cup icing sugar with 2 to 3 teaspoons unsweetened almond milk until desired drizzle texture is reached. This recipe will no longer be refined sugar-free with the sugar glaze.

DO AHEAD

The Raspberry Chia Jam can be made in advance. Store in a jar in the refrigerator for up to 1 week.

Ginger Snap or Chewy Cookies

Vegan * Nut-free * Soy-free

1½ cups (195 g) all-purpose flour

2 teaspoons baking soda

2 teaspoons ground ginger

1 teaspoon cinnamon

½ teaspoon ground allspice

Pinch of freshly ground black pepper

½ cup (4 ounces/115 g) vegan butter

¼ cup (32 g) lightly packed dark
   brown sugar

¼ cup (55 g) + 2 tablespoons demerara
   sugar, divided

¼ cup fancy molasses

STORAGE

Store the cookies in an airtight container
at room temperature for up to 5 days
or in the freezer for up to 1 month.

We are big fans of ginger cookies in my household. They need to be well spiced (but not overpowering), buttery (but not greasy), and sweet (but not *too* sweet!). This recipe ticks all the boxes. They are a perfect balance. Different bake times allow you to make cookies that are chewy or crunchy. I will leave it to you to pick your favourite type. These cookies are great to bake up for the holidays, and they make a lovely gift for neighbours and friends. They are especially delicious when enjoyed with a hot cup of tea or coffee.

1. Place the oven racks in the upper and lower thirds of the oven. Preheat the oven to 350°F (180°C). Line 2 baking sheets with parchment paper.

2. Into a small bowl, sift the flour, baking soda, ginger, cinnamon, allspice, and pepper.

3. In a large bowl, combine the vegan butter, brown sugar, and ¼ cup of the demerara sugar. Using a hand mixer on medium-high speed, cream together until fluffy and light, about 2 minutes. Add the molasses and beat to combine.

4. Gradually add the dry ingredients to the butter mixture, stirring with a spatula to combine into a thick dough.

5. Sprinkle the remaining 2 tablespoons demerara sugar onto a small plate. Scoop 1 heaping tablespoon of the dough and roll into a ball using your hands. Roll each ball in the sugar to coat and place on the prepared baking sheet, 1½ to 2 inches apart. Lightly press down on the top of each ball with the heel of your hand to flatten them slightly. Repeat to make 24 cookies.

6. Bake the cookies until lightly browned around the edges and bottom, about 10 minutes (for a softer, chewy cookie) or until a deeper golden brown around the edges and bottom, about 12 minutes (for a crunchier "snap" cookie). Let the cookies cool on the pan for 5 minutes, then transfer to a wire rack to cool completely.

Cannelés

Vegan * Soy-free

Cannelés are a sweet delicacy originating from the Bordeaux region of France. Expect a crunchy and caramelized exterior shell with a spongy and custardy interior. I loved ogling them in pastry-shop windows, but unfortunately they were never made vegan—so I took to making them myself. This is a show-stopping recipe, both in taste and in the fact that you would never believe cannelés could be vegan! This recipe is a bit more involved than some of my other treats and it requires a special cannelé pan to achieve the timeless shape. However, it is well worth the effort. Hands-down, this is one of my favourite recipes in the book, and my husband, Mitch's, too.

1. In a small bowl, whisk together the aquafaba and ground flaxseed to make the flax egg. Set aside for at least 10 minutes.

2. Into a medium bowl, sift the flour, cane sugar, arrowroot powder, and tapioca powder.

3. In a separate medium bowl, combine the flax egg, almond milk, melted vegan butter, rum, and vanilla. Whisk well to combine. Gradually whisk in the flour mixture, a little at a time, to make a smooth batter. Cover and refrigerate the batter for at least 24 hours, preferably up to 48 hours. (The flavour and texture improve significantly with time.)

4. When ready to bake, preheat the oven to 450°F (230°C). Bring the batter back to room temperature and whisk to reincorporate.

5. Lightly brush a 6-cavity non-stick cannelé pan with melted vegan butter. Alternatively, you can use 6 (2-inch) copper cannelé moulds. Using a spoon, divide the batter evenly among the moulds, filling three-quarters full.

6. Bake for 10 minutes, then reduce the oven temperature to 375°F (190°C). Continue baking for 50 minutes, until the tops are a uniform deep caramel colour. Let the cannelés cool slightly in the mould for 5 minutes, then invert them onto a wire rack to cool completely and set, 1½ to 2 hours. These are best enjoyed the same day.

3 tablespoons aquafaba
(liquid from canned chickpeas)

1 tablespoon ground flaxseed

½ cup (65 g) all-purpose flour

½ cup (108 g) organic cane sugar

2 tablespoons arrowroot powder

2 tablespoons tapioca powder

¾ cup + 2 tablespoons unsweetened
almond milk

1 tablespoon vegan butter, melted,
more for the pan

2 tablespoons dark rum

2 teaspoons pure vanilla extract

TIPS

1. I recommend using a 6- or 12-cavity non-stick cannelé pan. It achieves the perfect crunchy exterior desired in a cannelé, and it is less expensive than the traditional individual copper cannelé moulds. Cannelé pans can be found at kitchen stores or online. Silicon cannelé pans can be used, but I do not recommend them because they do not achieve the same crunchy exterior as a metal pan.

2. If using a 12-cavity non-stick cannelé pan, this recipe can easily be doubled to fill the pan. Or simply fill 6 cavities and bake as directed.

Baked Beignets

Vegan ✳ Soy-free

Beignets are a treat found in abundance during the yearly Braderie de Lille, a famous antiques market where people from all over Europe participate. During the Braderie, it's as much about the food as it is about the antiques! Visitors will buy a bagful of beignets from boulangeries as they walk and shop for trinkets.

These mini baked beignets are lightly sweet and airy. Served warm out of the oven and sprinkled with icing sugar, they are a true treat for entertaining larger groups, and they please all ages. Since they are baked instead of fried, they are a healthier option for indulging. We love to dip them into my Chocolate Hazelnut Spread.

1. Prepare the Chocolate Hazelnut Spread, if using.

2. Make the Dough: In a small bowl, whisk together ¼ cup of the almond milk and the apple cider vinegar. This is your buttermilk.

3. In the bowl of a stand mixer, whisk together the water, sugar, and yeast and let sit until tiny bubbles have formed on the surface, about 10 minutes. Add the buttermilk, aquafaba, vanilla, salt, and 1 tablespoon of the melted vegan butter. Fit the bowl into the stand mixer, fit it with the whisk attachment, and mix on medium-low speed until well combined, about 3 minutes.

4. Replace the whisk attachment with the dough hook. With the mixer on low speed, gradually add the flour, mixing until the dough is well combined, soft and plush, 7 to 8 minutes. The dough will be sticky to the touch.

5. Proof the Dough: Lightly coat a large bowl with avocado oil and transfer the dough to the bowl. Cover the bowl with reusable wrap and proof at room temperature for 2 hours, or until almost doubled in size.

6. Bake the Beignets: Place the oven rack in the middle of the oven. Preheat the oven to 350°F (180°C). Line 2 baking sheets with parchment paper.

Chocolate Hazelnut Spread (page 69), for dipping (optional)

¼ cup + 1 tablespoon unsweetened almond milk, divided

¾ teaspoon apple cider vinegar

6 tablespoons warm water

2 tablespoons (30 g) organic cane sugar

Heaping ½ teaspoon active dry yeast

1 tablespoon aquafaba (liquid from canned chickpeas)

1 teaspoon pure vanilla extract

½ teaspoon fine sea salt

2 tablespoons vegan butter, melted and divided

1¾ cups (227 g) all-purpose flour, more for dusting

½ teaspoon avocado oil, for coating

2 to 3 tablespoons organic icing sugar, for sprinkling

DO AHEAD

Steps 1 to 4 of the dough can be prepared 1 day in advance. Cover with plastic wrap and refrigerate overnight (8 to 9 hours). When ready to use, proof the dough following step 5 onwards.

Recipe continues

7. Dust a work surface with flour. Turn out the dough, and using a rolling pin, roll out the dough into a rectangle about ¼ inch thick. Lightly sprinkle the dough with flour as needed to stop it from sticking to the rolling pin. Cut the dough lengthwise into 1½-inch strips, then cut each strip crosswise into 1½-inch squares. Place the squares on the prepared baking sheets, about 1 inch apart. Slide each baking sheet into a large plastic bag to enclose, and place 2 juice cups upside down on either side of each baking sheet so the bag doesn't touch the dough. Let proof at room temperature until the beignets are slightly puffed and nearly doubled in size, about 30 minutes.

8. Remove one of the baking sheets from the bags and lightly brush the tops of the beignets with some of the remaining almond milk. Bake until the beignets are puffed and lightly golden, 12 to 15 minutes. Remove from the oven and immediately lightly brush the tops of the beignets with some of the remaining melted butter. Dust with the icing sugar and serve warm with Chocolate Hazelnut Spread for dipping, if using. Repeat with the second baking sheet to make all the beignets. Best enjoyed fresh from the oven, while warm.

Makes 16 slices

Pain d'Épices

Vegan ✳ Soy-free

Pain d'Épices is a French spice cake that is popularly served around the holidays, and it has become a tradition in our home. It is loaded with warming winter flavours: ginger, nutmeg, cloves, and peppercorns. Quatre-Épices, literally "four spices," is a popular blend in France. It can be bought premixed and is called "quatre-épices," but it's a lot easier and cheaper to mix the spices yourself for this glorious recipe.

     More than just flavour makes this cake so desirable. The texture is spot on: fluffy, light, and moist. Spread thick with a vanilla icing for the perfect marriage of sweet and spiced. The cake goes down all too easy with a hot cup of tea.

1. Preheat the oven to 350°F (180°C). Grease a 12-cup Bundt pan with melted vegan butter, making sure to get into all the nooks and crannies of the pan.

2. Make the Quatre-Épices: In a small bowl, stir together the pepper, ginger, nutmeg, and cloves. Set aside.

3. Make the Cake: In a small bowl, whisk together the ground flaxseed and water until combined. Let sit for 10 minutes. This is your flax egg.

4. In a separate small bowl, cover the dates with the hot water. Let soak for 10 minutes to soften the dates.

5. Transfer the soaked dates and soaking water to a high-speed blender. Add the almond milk and blend on high speed until smooth.

6. Pour the sweet milk mixture into a large bowl. Add the flax egg, cane sugar, salt, and melted vegan butter. Whisk well to combine.

7. Into a medium bowl, sift the all-purpose flour, whole wheat flour, baking powder, baking soda, and 6 teaspoons of the Quatre-Épices. Gently fold the dry ingredients into the wet ingredients, a little at a time, until the batter is well combined and smooth.

QUATRE-ÉPICES

1 tablespoon freshly ground black pepper

1½ teaspoons ground ginger

1½ teaspoons ground nutmeg

1½ teaspoons ground cloves

CAKE

3 tablespoons ground flaxseed

6 tablespoons water

½ cup (90 g) Medjool dates, pitted

½ cup hot water

1½ cups unsweetened almond milk

1½ cups (325 g) organic cane sugar

1½ teaspoons fine sea salt

½ cup (4 ounces/115 g) vegan butter, melted, more for the pan

1½ cups (195 g) all-purpose flour

1½ cups (185 g) whole wheat flour

2 teaspoons baking powder

1 teaspoon baking soda

VANILLA ICING

2 cups (200 g) organic icing sugar, sifted

2 tablespoons vegan butter, softened

1 teaspoon pure vanilla extract

2 to 4 tablespoons unsweetened almond milk

Candied sprinkles, for garnish (optional)

Recipe continues

The cake can be stored in an airtight container at room temperature for up to 5 days or in the refrigerator for up to 9 days. This cake can also be frozen for up to 3 months. Wrap well in resealable plastic wrap and freeze in an airtight container. I like to cut the cake into slices before freezing, so that I can just defrost the number of desired slices for eating.

8. Pour the batter into the prepared pan and bake until the cake is browned and springy, the cake just starts to pull away from the sides of the pan, and a toothpick inserted in the centre comes out clean, 40 to 50 minutes. Let the cake cool in the pan for 5 minutes, then invert the cake onto a wire rack to cool completely.

9. Make the Vanilla Icing: In a medium bowl, combine the sifted icing sugar, vegan butter, and vanilla. Using a hand mixer, mix on low speed to combine. Pour in 2 tablespoons of the almond milk and beat on medium until smooth. Thin with more almond milk, a tablespoon at a time, for desired consistency.

10. Spread the icing on top of the cooled cake. Garnish with candied sprinkles, if desired.

TIPS

1. You will have 1½ teaspoons of the Quatre-Épices left over. Store it in a small airtight container at room temperature for up to 6 months.

2. A well-greased Bundt pan will help the cake release smoothly from the pan. If you are having trouble releasing your cake from the pan, cover the inverted pan with a kitchen towel and tap around the pan to help release the grip. You can also leave the pan inverted on the cooling rack for a few minutes and allow gravity to do the trick.

3. If you do not have a Bundt pan, this recipe can also be made in two 8½ x 4½-inch loaf pans.

Makes 9 squares * Requires: soak time + chill time

Healthier Millionaire Bars

Vegan * Gluten-free * Soy-free

These millionaire bars are my healthier rendition of the traditional, yet just as indulgent with their almond oat crust, date caramel filling, and a covering of chocolate. With their three distinct layers, they are as beautiful as they are delicious. This is a bar to please a variety of eaters, from young to old, healthy to not so healthy, and vegan food lovers to skeptics. What more could you ask for in a sweet treat? I often enjoyed sweet bites like millonaire bars at more trendy cafes in France.

1. In a small bowl, cover the dates with boiling water. Let sit for at least 20 minutes to soften.

2. Make the Crust Layer: Preheat the oven to 350°F (180°C). Line an 8-inch square baking pan with parchment paper, leaving a 1-inch overhang of parchment on the sides.

3. In a food processor or high-speed blender, pulse the oats until they reach a flour-like consistency. Transfer the oat flour to a small bowl and add the almond flour, melted coconut oil, maple syrup, and sea salt. Stir together to create a crumbly dough.

4. Tip the dough into the prepared baking pan and press down firmly into an even layer. Bake until the top is lightly golden brown, 12 to 15 minutes. Let cool for at least 10 minutes.

5. Meanwhile, Make the Date Caramel Layer: Drain the dates and peel away and discard the outer skin. (The skins should peel away easily after soaking. It's okay if a few pieces remain.) In a food processor, combine the dates, almond butter, coconut milk, maple syrup, vanilla, and sea salt. Process until smooth.

6. Pour the date caramel layer over the slightly cooled crust and smooth with a spatula to make an even layer. Freeze for 30 minutes.

¾ cup Medjool dates, pitted

CRUST LAYER

¼ cup (33 g) gluten-free old-fashioned rolled oats

1½ cups (150 g) almond flour

3 tablespoons coconut oil, melted

2 tablespoons pure maple syrup

¼ teaspoon fine sea salt

DATE CARAMEL LAYER

½ cup natural almond butter

¼ cup canned full-fat coconut milk

2 tablespoons pure maple syrup

1 teaspoon pure vanilla extract

½ teaspoon fine sea salt

CHOCOLATE LAYER

¾ cup dairy-free semi-sweet chocolate chips

1 tablespoon coconut oil

Flaky sea salt, for sprinkling (optional)

Recipe continues

Store the bars in an airtight container in the refrigerator for up to 2 weeks or in the freezer for up to 3 months.

TIPS

It's helpful to use a very sharp knife to score the chocolate before cutting these squares. Otherwise, the chocolate may crack when cutting. Chill the Millionaire Bars until the chocolate is almost set, about 30 minutes, and then run the tip of the knife a few times over the chocolate where you plan to cut. Chill completely and then cut completely into 9 squares.

DO AHEAD

The Date Caramel Layer can be made up to 3 days in advance. Store in an airtight container in the refrigerator.

7. Make the Chocolate Layer: In a small saucepan, bring 2 inches of water to a low simmer over low heat. Place a small heatproof bowl on top of the pot, making sure the bottom of the bowl is not touching the water. Add the chocolate chips and the coconut oil and melt the chocolate, stirring often until completely smooth. (Alternatively, you can melt the chocolate in the microwave in 30-second intervals.)

8. Drizzle the melted chocolate over the caramel layer and gently tilt the pan to spread the chocolate in an even layer. Refrigerate until the chocolate has hardened, at least 1 hour.

9. When ready to eat, remove from the refrigerator. Lift the bars out of the pan using the parchment overhang. Using a serrated knife, cut into 9 squares. Sprinkle with flaky sea salt, if desired.

Brookies

Vegan ✳ Soy-free

What is a brookie, you ask? Well, it is a marriage of half brownie and half cookie, for those times when you want both but just cannot choose between the two!

I discovered these fun squares at hip cafés and bakeries around the city in Lille. Although they do not really *seem* traditionally French, they were often displayed in Euro-contemporary cafés, among mouth-watering arrays of luxurious cakes, cookies, and brownies, often with signs reading "It is forbidden to drool on the cakes!" I suppose they spoke from experience. I agree, it is near impossible not to drool over this decadent cookie and brownie combination. This is the ultimate sweet treat to indulge in.

1. Preheat the oven to 350°F (180°C). Line an 8-inch non-stick square baking pan with parchment paper, leaving a 1-inch overhang of parchment on the sides.
2. Make the Brownie Batter: In a small bowl, whisk together the ground flaxseed and water until combined. Let sit for 10 minutes. This is your flax egg.
3. In a medium bowl, combine the melted vegan butter, cane sugar, and vanilla. Add the flax egg and whisk well to combine. Sift in the flour, cocoa powder, and salt and stir until smooth. Pour the batter into the prepared pan. Smooth with a spatula to level, if needed.
4. Make the Cookie Batter: In a small bowl, whisk together the ground flaxseed and water until combined. Let sit for 10 minutes. This is your flax egg.
5. In a medium bowl, combine the vegan butter, cane sugar, and brown sugar. Using a hand mixer on medium speed, cream together until light and fluffy, 2 minutes. Pour in the flax egg and vanilla and beat on medium until combined, 2 minutes.

BROWNIE BATTER

2 tablespoons ground flaxseed

¼ cup water

½ cup (4 ounces/115 g) vegan butter, melted

1 cup (215 g) organic cane sugar

1 teaspoon pure vanilla extract

½ cup (65 g) all-purpose flour

⅓ cup (30 g) cocoa powder

¼ teaspoon fine sea salt

COOKIE BATTER

2 teaspoons ground flaxseed

4 teaspoons water

¼ cup (2 ounces/57 g) vegan butter, room temperature

2 tablespoons organic cane sugar

¼ cup (32 g) dark brown sugar

½ teaspoon pure vanilla extract

¾ cup (97 g) all-purpose flour

¼ teaspoon fine sea salt

¼ teaspoon baking soda

⅛ teaspoon baking powder

¼ cup dairy-free semi-sweet chocolate chips

Recipe continues

STORAGE

Store the brookies in an airtight container at room temperature for up to 3 days or in the refrigerator for up to 1 week. The brookies can also be frozen for up to 2 months. Bring to room temperature before serving.

6. Sift in the flour, salt, baking soda, and baking powder and mix together using a spatula until combined. Sprinkle in the chocolate chips and fold into the batter.

7. Drop spoonfuls of the cookie batter evenly onto the brownie batter layer. (It is okay if there are gaps of exposed brownie; the cookie batter will spread as it cooks.) Cover with foil and bake for 20 minutes. Uncover and continue baking until the brownie edges are shiny and the cookie top is golden brown, 15 to 20 minutes. Let the brookies cool in the pan for 10 minutes, then lift from the pan and transfer to a wire rack to cool completely before cutting into squares.

Makes 12 squares

Pumpkin Chickpea Blondies

Vegan * Gluten-free * Oil-free * Soy-free

These delicious blondies are made with chickpeas. You will not believe how the humble chickpea can transform into this stellar sweet treat! I absolutely love to make these pumpkin blondies when I want a healthy snack that hits the sweet spot but is also fibre-fuelled and sticks with me. They are especially popular in our home during the fall season with their pumpkin, cinnamon, and maple flavours.

1. Preheat the oven to 350°F (180°C). Line an 8-inch square baking pan with parchment paper, leaving a 1-inch overhang of parchment on the sides.

2. In a food processor, pulse the oats until they reach a flour-like consistency. Add the chickpeas, almond butter, pumpkin purée, maple syrup, vanilla, pumpkin spice, cinnamon, baking powder, baking soda, and salt. Process until well combined and a smoothish batter-like consistency. (The batter will not be completely smooth because of the chickpeas.)

3. Remove the blade from the food processor and sprinkle in 6 tablespoons of the chocolate chips. Fold into the batter with a spatula. Pour the batter into the prepared pan and spread evenly with a spatula. Sprinkle the remaining 2 tablespoons chocolate chips evenly over the batter.

4. Bake until the blondies look firm and a toothpick inserted into the centre comes out clean, 25 to 30 minutes. Let cool in the pan for 10 minutes, then lift from the pan and transfer to a wire rack to cool completely before cutting into squares.

½ cup (66 g) gluten-free old-fashioned rolled oats

1⅓ cups cooked chickpeas, drained and rinsed (see Tip)

½ cup natural almond butter

⅓ cup canned pure pumpkin purée

¼ cup pure maple syrup

2 teaspoons pure vanilla extract

1 teaspoon pumpkin spice

½ teaspoon cinnamon

½ teaspoon baking powder

½ teaspoon baking soda

½ teaspoon fine sea salt

½ cup dairy-free semi-sweet chocolate chips, divided

STORAGE

Store the blondies in an airtight container in the refrigerator for up to 5 days or in the freezer for up to 2 months. If frozen, thaw before serving.

TIP

One (14-ounce/400 mL) can of chickpeas is equivalent to 1½ cups cooked chickpeas. If using canned chickpeas, you will need 1 can for this recipe.

Serves 8

Chocolate Almond Torte

Vegan * Gluten-free * Soy-free

1 tablespoon ground flaxseed

2 tablespoons water

1 cup (140 g) gluten-free baking flour

⅓ cup (30 g) almond flour

6 tablespoons (45 g) cocoa powder,
     more for the pan

1 teaspoon baking powder

1 teaspoon baking soda

¼ teaspoon fine sea salt

¼ cup (54 g) organic cane sugar

1 cup unsweetened almond milk

⅓ cup pure maple syrup

¼ cup olive oil, more for the pan

2 tablespoons espresso

1 teaspoon pure vanilla extract

¼ teaspoon pure almond extract

FOR SERVING

1 batch Chantilly (page 298; optional)

1 to 2 tablespoons organic icing sugar,
     for sprinkling

½ cup fresh raspberries

STORAGE

Store the torte, without toppings, in an
airtight container at room temperature for
up to 5 days or in the refrigerator for up to
1 week. To freeze, wrap the cake, without
toppings, in plastic wrap and store in an
airtight container in the freezer for up to
3 months. I like to cut the cake into slices
before freezing, so that I can just defrost
the number of desired slices for eating.

If you are looking for a simple, spongy, moist, and rich chocolate
cake, well, this is it. I absolutely love this gluten-free chocolate cake
for any occasion—be it a birthday celebration, holiday, or just because
I have a craving for cake. (We do not always need a reason to have our
cake and eat it too!) As they often do in France, sprinkle the cake with
icing sugar and serve alongside raspberries and Chantilly (page 298).
You can also frost it with my Mousse au Chocolat (page 281) as a
whipped icing.

1. Preheat the oven to 350°F (180°C). Grease a 9-inch non-stick round
cake pan with olive oil. Lightly sprinkle the base and sides of the pan
with cocoa powder and tap out the excess over the sink.

2. In a small bowl, whisk together the ground flaxseed and water until
combined. Let sit for at least 10 minutes. This is your flax egg.

3. Into a medium bowl, sift the gluten-free baking flour, almond flour,
cocoa powder, baking powder, baking soda, and salt. Add the cane sugar
and stir to combine.

4. In a large bowl, combine the almond milk, maple syrup, olive oil,
espresso, vanilla, and almond extract. Add the flax egg and whisk until
well combined. Add the dry ingredients, a little at a time, and whisk
until the batter is smooth and well combined.

5. Pour the batter into the prepared pan and gently wiggle the pan to
smooth out the top. Bake until the cake is puffed and springy, it just
starts to pull away from the sides of the pan, and a toothpick inserted
in the centre comes out clean, 25 minutes. Let cool in the pan for
5 minutes, then invert the cake onto a wire rack to cool completely.

6. Prepare the Chantilly (if using) just before serving.

7. Sprinkle the top of the cake with icing sugar, slice, and serve with
Chantilly (if using) and fresh raspberries.

TIPS

1. This torte is also delicious frosted with my Mousse au Chocolat (page 281). To thin the mousse into a spreadable frosting, add about ¼ cup more almond milk, a tablespoon at a time, while blending the mousse.

2. You can easily double the recipe to make a 2-layer cake (serves 12). Follow the directions and divide the batter between two 9-inch non-stick round cake pans. Fill the middle with a layer of my Mousse au Chocolate and some fresh raspberries.

TIPS

1. Bananas that are overripe (mostly brown) can result in a denser bread. It's best to use bananas that are spotty but not too brown.

2. Overworking the batter can also lead to a dense banana bread. To ensure light and fluffy banana bread, gently fold the batter to combine, but do not over-mix.

Serves 8

Chocolate Chip Banana Bread

Vegan ＊ Gluten-free ＊ Soy-free

This banana bread is moist, chocolatey, and wholesome—a loaf to suit all ages and all eaters. It is hard to perfect a gluten-free, mostly refined sugar–free, and vegan banana bread, but I did it! It took a few tries and a little troubleshooting to get this banana bread recipe right. It is fluffy, perfectly sweet, cinnamony, and flecked with gorgeous chocolate chips. I love to reserve a handful of the chocolate chips to sprinkle on top of the loaf just before baking for a picture-perfect loaf that will have your family begging for a slice.

1. Preheat the oven to 350°F (180°C). Lightly grease an 8½ x 4½-inch loaf pan with the vegan butter or coconut oil. Line the greased pan with enough parchment paper to hang over the two long sides.

2. In a small bowl, whisk together the ground flaxseed and water until combined. Let sit for 10 minutes. This is your flax egg.

3. In a large bowl, combine the vegan butter and coconut sugar. Using a hand mixer on medium speed, cream together until fluffy and combined. Add the flax egg, mashed banana, maple syrup, and vanilla and beat together on medium until well combined.

4. In a food processor or high-speed blender, pulse the oats until they reach a flour-like consistency. Transfer the oat flour to a medium bowl and add the gluten-free baking flour, buckwheat flour, baking soda, baking powder, cinnamon, and salt. Stir to combine.

5. Gradually fold the dry ingredients into the wet ingredients, folding gently to combine. (Be sure not to over-mix the ingredients or the loaf will be too dense.) Toss in ⅓ cup of the chocolate chips and gently fold again.

6. Scrape the batter into the prepared loaf pan and sprinkle evenly with the remaining 2 tablespoons chocolate chips. Bake until the top is golden and puffed and a toothpick inserted into the centre comes out clean, 45 to 50 minutes. Let the banana bread cool slightly in the pan, then turn out onto a wire rack to cool completely.

½ teaspoon vegan butter or coconut oil, for greasing the pan

WET INGREDIENTS

2 tablespoons ground flaxseed

¼ cup water

½ cup (4 ounces/115 g) vegan butter, softened

½ cup (70 g) coconut sugar

1½ cups mashed banana (about 3 large bananas)

¼ cup + 1 tablespoon pure maple syrup

1 teaspoon pure vanilla extract

DRY INGREDIENTS

½ cup (66 g) gluten-free old-fashioned rolled oats

1 cup (140 g) gluten-free baking flour

½ cup (75 g) buckwheat flour

1 teaspoon baking soda

1 teaspoon baking powder

1 teaspoon cinnamon

¾ teaspoon fine sea salt

⅓ cup (60 g) + 2 tablespoons dairy-free semi-sweet chocolate chips, divided

STORAGE

Store the loaf, covered with a kitchen towel or reusable wrap, at room temperature for up to 4 days or in the refrigerator for up to 1 week. To freeze, wrap the loaf in plastic wrap and store in an airtight container in the freezer for up to 3 months.

Serves 8

Sneaky Zucchini and Walnut Bread

Vegan ✳ Soy-free

½ teaspoon vegan butter or coconut oil,
  for greasing the pan

WET INGREDIENTS

⅓ cup (5⅓ ounces/75 g) vegan butter,
  melted
½ cup pure maple syrup
½ cup mashed banana
  (about 1 large banana)
¼ cup unsweetened almond milk
1 teaspoon pure vanilla extract

DRY INGREDIENTS

1½ cups (195 g) all-purpose flour
1 tablespoon ground flaxseed
1 teaspoon baking soda
½ teaspoon baking powder
½ teaspoon fine sea salt
1 teaspoon cinnamon
¼ teaspoon ground nutmeg
¼ teaspoon ground cardamom
1 cup (115 g) grated zucchini
½ cup (60 g) chopped raw walnuts

STORAGE

Store the loaf, covered with a kitchen
towel or reusable wrap, at room
temperature or in the refrigerator for
up to 1 week. To freeze, wrap the loaf
in plastic wrap and store in an airtight
container in the freezer for up to
3 months.

This zucchini loaf is so soft, spongy, and beautifully spiced, with
crunchy walnut chunks. Despite the name, you would never know
there is zucchini in it—which is why I have called it "sneaky"! I love
when you can sneak some extra greens into your day. Enjoy this
bread for a snack or breakfast to go.

1. Preheat the oven to 350°F (180°C). Lightly grease an 8½ x 4½-inch
loaf pan with the vegan butter or coconut oil. Line the greased pan
with enough parchment paper to hang over the two long sides.
2. In a large bowl, whisk together the melted vegan butter, maple
syrup, mashed banana, almond milk, and vanilla.
3. In a medium bowl, combine the flour, ground flaxseed, baking soda,
baking powder, salt, cinnamon, nutmeg, and cardamom. Stir gently
to combine.
4. Gradually and gently fold the dry ingredients into the wet
ingredients until just combined. Do not over-mix or the bread will
be too dense. Toss in the grated zucchini and walnuts and gently
fold again.
5. Scrape the batter into the prepared loaf pan and bake until the top
is golden and puffed and a toothpick inserted into the centre comes
out clean, 45 to 55 minutes. Let the zucchini bread cool slightly in the
pan, then turn out onto a wire rack to cool completely.

Feel-Good Raspberry Muffins

Vegan ✳ Soy-free ✳ Refined Sugar-free Option

DRY INGREDIENTS

¾ cup (100 g) gluten-free old-fashioned
    rolled oats

¾ cup (90 g) whole wheat flour

¼ cup (25 g) almond flour

2 tablespoons ground chia seeds
    or ground flaxseed

1 teaspoon baking powder

½ teaspoon baking soda

½ teaspoon fine sea salt

WET INGREDIENTS

¾ cup (123 g) plain coconut yogurt

½ cup pure maple syrup

6 tablespoons unsweetened almond milk

⅓ cup olive oil, more for the pan

1 teaspoon pure vanilla extract

2 cups fresh or frozen raspberries, divided

TOPPINGS (OPTIONAL)

2 tablespoons slivered almonds

1 teaspoon organic icing sugar, for dusting

TIP

Leaving the muffins in the pan to cool
slightly before transferring to a wire rack
will allow them to firm up. If the muffins
are too hot, the tops will separate from the
bottoms as you lift them out of the pan.

REFINED SUGAR-FREE

Omit the icing sugar for dusting.

These muffins taste as heavenly as they look. They are wholesome,
and the perfect combination of sweet and tart. With their blend
of oat, almond, and whole wheat flour, you can feel good about
indulging in these muffins.

1. Preheat the oven to 350°F (180°C). Lightly grease a 12-cup muffin
pan with olive oil.

2. In a food processor or high-speed blender, pulse the oats until they
reach a flour-like consistency. Transfer the oat flour to a large bowl and
add the whole wheat flour, almond flour, ground chia seeds, baking
powder, baking soda, and salt. Stir to combine.

3. In a medium bowl, whisk together the coconut yogurt, maple syrup,
almond milk, olive oil, and vanilla. Pour the wet ingredients into the
dry ingredients and stir to combine. Cover the bowl with a kitchen
towel and let thicken, 10 to 15 minutes.

4. Gently fold 1 cup of the raspberries into the batter.

5. Divide the batter evenly among the muffin cups until just full.
Divide the remaining 1 cup raspberries over the muffins, then sprinkle
with the almond slivers, if using.

6. Bake until golden and a toothpick inserted in the centre comes
out clean, 25 to 30 minutes. Let the muffins cool in the pan for 10 to
12 minutes, then lift them out onto a wire rack to cool completely.
Dust with the icing sugar, if desired.

STORAGE

Store the muffins, covered with a kitchen towel or reusable wrap,
at room temperature for up to 2 days or in the refrigerator for up to
5 days. To freeze, store the muffins in an airtight container in the
freezer for up to 2 months.

Makes 12 muffins

Chocolate Hazelnut Swirl Muffins

Vegan ⁕ Soy-free

These chocolate hazelnut muffins are sweet, fluffy, and delightful. My husband, Mitch, says they are the best muffins he has ever had. They are a delicious snack with a cup of tea or coffee, and gorgeous looking with their swirly muffin top. Enjoy serving these at an afternoon get-together with your loved ones.

1. Make the Chocolate Hazelnut Spread.

2. Preheat the oven to 350°F (180°C). Line a 12-cup muffin pan with paper muffin liners.

3. In a small bowl, whisk together the ground flaxseed and water until combined. Let sit for at least 10 minutes. This is your flax egg.

4. Into a small bowl, sift the all-purpose flour, whole wheat flour, baking powder, salt, and cinnamon.

5. In a large bowl, combine the vegan butter and sugar. Cream together with a hand mixer on medium-low speed until whipped and combined, 2 minutes. Add the flax egg, vanilla, coconut yogurt, and almond milk and beat on medium until combined, 2 minutes.

6. Sprinkle the dry ingredients over the wet ingredients, a little at a time, and fold into the batter until smooth. Be sure not to over-mix to ensure light and fluffy muffins.

7. Divide the batter evenly among the muffin cups until almost full. Scoop a heaping ½ teaspoon of the Chocolate Hazelnut Spread into the middle of each muffin and swirl it around with a skewer.

8. Bake the muffins until golden and a toothpick inserted in the centre comes out clean, about 20 minutes. Let the muffins cool in the pan for about 5 minutes, then turn out onto a wire rack to cool completely.

6 to 8 teaspoons Chocolate Hazelnut Spread (page 69)

2 tablespoons ground flaxseed

¼ cup water

1½ cups (195 g) all-purpose flour

½ cup (60 g) whole wheat flour

1 teaspoon baking powder

½ teaspoon fine sea salt

½ teaspoon cinnamon

½ cup (4 ounces/115 g) vegan butter, room temperature

⅔ cup (143 g) organic cane sugar

1 teaspoon pure vanilla extract

½ cup (82 g) plain coconut yogurt

⅓ cup unsweetened almond milk

STORAGE

Store the muffins in an airtight container at room temperature for up to 3 days, in the refrigerator for up to 5 days, or in the freezer for up to 2 months.

Store any leftover Chocolate Hazelnut Spread in a jar at room temperature for up to 10 days.

TIP

Make this recipe without using paper liners by lightly greasing a 12-cup non-stick muffin pan with avocado oil, ensuring you get into the edges and up the sides.

L'Apéritif

Appetizers and Nibbles

This chapter will help you create unforgettable plant-based charcuterie boards, with colourful dips, spreads, finger foods, and fauxmages that all eaters will adore.

The recipes take classic favourites to the next level with fun and creative twists. Why have beige hummus when it can be pink or orange? Take a pass on bagged potato chips and try my Cheesy Kale Chips (page 180) instead.

For you savoury-snack lovers, this chapter is chock full of delicious snack recipes. Crunchy Curried Roasted Chickpeas (page 179) are a great protein-rich snack to grab and go, and come midday, I love to slather my Herb and Garlic Cheese (page 159) over Super-Seedy Crackers (page 183).

Having some of these recipes ready-made to snack on through the week makes it so easy to throw a charcuterie board together in the evenings. Take joy in putting together gorgeous platters from these recipes, and try out some of my Platter Menus for your entertaining.

Platter Menus

In France, l'apéritif is a gathering of friends in the evening for light food and drinks. It is so common that it is more often referred to as l'apéro. Essentially, it is a cocktail hour featuring drinks and nibbles that often ends up lasting through the night and even into the early hours of the morning.

Putting together a colourful and well-intentioned charcuterie board is an art. It has to be colourful and enticing, and have something for everyone—fauxmage, spreads, finger foods, and crunchy things. I love to snap a photo just before everyone arrives to document my masterpiece. The pleasure is all mine when the boards are wiped clean by the end of the night.

Nibbles with Besties

Dreamy Cashew Cream Cheese (page 155)

Pink Beet Hummus (page 168) with
Super-Seedy Crackers (page 183)

Cheesy Kale Chips (page 180)

Crackers, figs, grapes, and nuts

Nibbles for Two

Luxurious Baked Brie (page 160)

Roasted Eggplant Baba Ganoush
(page 172)

Crispy Baked Frites (page 184)

Sourdough or baguette

Family Fun Nibbles

Dreamy Cashew Cream Cheese (page 155)

Golden Roasted Carrot Hummus (page 171)

Broccoli and Potato Croquettes (page 187)

Crunchy Curried Roasted Chickpeas
(page 179)

Crackers

Nibbles for Entertaining

Ooey Gooey Cheesy Fondue (page 163)

Blue Cheese (page 156)

Faux Gras (page 176)

Pink Beet Hummus (page 168) with
Super-Seedy Crackers (page 183)

Baguette, olives, and nuts

Quick and Easy Nibbles

Herb and Garlic Cheese (page 159)

Creamy Avocado Mousse (page 175)

Cheesy Kale Chips (page 180)

Crackers, baguette, olives, and nuts

Dreamy Cashew Cream Cheese

Vegan ✳ Gluten-free ✳ Grain-free ✳ Oil-free ✳ Soy-free ✳ No Added Sugar ✳ Refined Sugar-free ✳ Raw/No-bake

This light, spreadable cashew cheese is creamy and silky smooth. In my opinion, it beats any store-bought brand. Whenever I make this simple cashew cream cheese for friends and family, they always ask for the recipe. The requests continue when they serve it at their gatherings too. Slather this cream cheese over baguette, sourdough bread, or Super-Seedy Crackers (page 183), or scoop it inside savoury Buckwheat Crepes (page 55).

1. Place the cashews in a small bowl and add boiling water to cover. Soak for 1 hour, then drain. (Alternatively, soak the cashews in room-temperature water to cover for at least 6 hours or overnight, then drain.)

2. In a high-speed blender, combine the cashews, coconut yogurt, apple cider vinegar, and salt. Blend on medium speed until smooth and creamy, about 3 minutes. Stop to scrape down the sides of the bowl as needed to ensure a consistent smooth texture.

3. Transfer the cream cheese to a small bowl and sprinkle with the chives. Stir to combine.

1½ cups raw cashews

½ cup plain coconut yogurt

2 tablespoons + 1 teaspoon apple cider vinegar

¾ teaspoon fine sea salt

¼ cup finely chopped chives

STORAGE

Store the cheese in an airtight container in the refrigerator for up to 5 days or in the freezer for up to 3 months. If frozen, let thaw for at least 30 minutes before serving.

TIP

Using a high-speed blender is best for ultra-smooth consistency. However, you can use a food processor; the cream cheese just won't be as smooth.

Blue Cheese

Vegan * Gluten-free * Grain-free * Oil-free * No Added Sugar * Refined Sugar-free * Raw/No-bake

2 cups raw cashews

¼ cup water

2 cloves garlic, finely chopped

2 tablespoons apple cider vinegar

2 tablespoons nutritional yeast

2 teaspoons white miso

½ teaspoon fine sea salt

¼ to ½ teaspoon blue spirulina powder

STORAGE

Store the cheese in the ramekins, covered with plastic wrap, in the refrigerator for up to 5 days or in an airtight container in the freezer for up to 1 month. If frozen, let thaw for at least 30 minutes before serving.

TIPS

1. Using a high-speed blender is best for ultra-smooth consistency. However, you can also use a food processor; the cheese just won't be as smooth.

2. Blue spirulina is not necessary for making this cheese. The cheese will still have the same delicious taste without it. The spirulina provides beautiful blue veins similar to Roquefort; you can also substitute with green spirulina. You can find blue spirulina at most health food and supplement stores or online. See Pantry Staples (page 17) for my favourite brand.

This soft blue cheese is packed with umami flavour for a rich, tangy, and creamy cheese. The blue veins are made by weaving spirulina into the filling to give the illusion of a real blue cheese. Serve with sliced baguette, grapes, or Super-Seedy Crackers (page 183), and use it to top my Balsamic Roasted Beets with Toasted Pine Nuts and Blue Cheese (page 227).

1. Place the cashews in a small bowl and add boiling water to cover. Soak for 1 hour, then drain. (Alternatively, soak the cashews in room-temperature water to cover for at least 6 hours or overnight, then drain.)

2. In a high-speed blender, combine the cashews, water, garlic, apple cider vinegar, nutritional yeast, miso, and salt. Blend on medium speed until smooth and creamy, about 3 minutes. Stop to scrape down the sides of the bowl as needed to ensure a consistent smooth texture.

3. Snugly line three 4-ounce ramekins with plastic wrap, leaving some overhang on all sides. Scoop the cheese mixture into the lined ramekins, filling half full. Using a small spoon, sprinkle a bit of the blue spirulina on top. Spoon the remaining cheese mixture on top and sprinkle with more spirulina.

4. Using a toothpick, swirl the cheese in a lazy zigzag pattern, going back and forth and up and down a few times. This will create blue veins in the cheese. Be careful not to over-mix, or the cheese will become a solid blue colour.

5. Fold the plastic wrap over the cheese, making sure there is no air exposure. Refrigerate for at least 6 to 8 hours or overnight. When ready to serve, fold back the plastic wrap and invert the cheese onto a plate or cheese board. Peel away the wrap and serve.

Serves 6 * Requires: soak time + chill time

Herb and Garlic Cheese

Vegan * Gluten-free * Grain-free * No Added Sugar * Refined Sugar-free * Raw/No-bake

This herb and garlic cheese is creamy and spreadable. It is a flavourful cheese, made with fragrant herbes de Provence and fresh garlic. Enjoy it sliced or spread onto Super-Seedy Crackers (page 183) or baguette, and served with figs and grapes.

1. Place the cashews in a small bowl and add boiling water to cover. Soak for 1 hour, then drain. (Alternatively, soak the cashews in room-temperature water to cover for at least 6 hours or overnight, then drain.)

2. In a high-speed blender, combine the cashews, water, garlic, nutritional yeast, lemon juice, mustard, herbes de Provence, salt, and miso. Blend on medium speed until smooth and creamy, about 3 minutes. Stop to scrape down the sides of the bowl as needed to ensure a consistent smooth texture.

3. Snugly line a small bowl with plastic wrap, leaving some overhang on all sides. Scoop the cheese mixture into the lined bowl. Fold the plastic wrap over the cheese, making sure there is no air exposure. Refrigerate for at least 6 hours or overnight. When ready to serve, fold back the plastic wrap and invert the cheese onto a plate or cheese board. Peel away the wrap. If desired, sprinkle the top with more herbes de Provence.

1½ cups raw cashews

⅓ cup water

3 cloves garlic, finely chopped

¼ cup nutritional yeast

2 tablespoons lemon juice

1 tablespoon Dijon mustard

2 teaspoons herbes de Provence, more for sprinkling (optional)

1 teaspoon fine sea salt

1 teaspoon white miso

STORAGE

Store the cheese in the bowl, wrapped with the plastic wrap, in the refrigerator for up to 5 days or wrapped and stored in an airtight container in the freezer for up to 1 month. If frozen, let thaw for at least 40 minutes before serving.

TIP

This recipe works best in a high-speed blender for ultra-smooth consistency. However, you can also use a food processor; the cheese just won't be as smooth.

Serves 4 * Requires: soak time

Luxurious Baked Brie

Vegan * Gluten-free * Grain-free * Oil-free * No Added Sugar * Refined Sugar-free

1 cup raw cashews

6 cloves garlic, divided

1½ cups water

¼ cup tapioca powder

2 tablespoons tahini

2 tablespoons nutritional yeast

1 tablespoon + 1 teaspoon apple cider
    vinegar

1½ teaspoons fine sea salt

1 teaspoon white miso

1 tablespoon fresh thyme leaves

STORAGE

Store the cheese, covered with reusable
wrap, in the refrigerator for up to 5 days.
Reheat in the oven at 350°F (180°C)
for 10 to 15 minutes before serving.

TIP

If you prefer a less garlicky brie, you
can skip the sliced garlic topping.

This baked brie is rich, creamy, and garlicky. I love serving this
luxurious cheese when entertaining in the cold winter months to
soothe the soul. Tuck into this warming dish with fresh baguette
or crackers and a glass of red wine.

1. Place the cashews in a small bowl and add boiling water to cover.
Soak for 1 hour, then drain. (Alternatively, soak the cashews in
room-temperature water to cover for at least 6 hours or overnight,
then drain.)

2. Preheat the oven to 350°F (180°C).

3. Chop 3 cloves of the garlic and add to a high-speed blender along
with the cashews, water, tapioca powder, tahini, nutritional yeast,
apple cider vinegar, salt, and miso. Blend on medium-high speed
until smooth, about 1 minute.

4. Pour the cheese mixture into a 7½ x 2-inch round brie baking dish.
Thinly slice the remaining 3 garlic cloves and arrange them on top of
the cheese. Sprinkle with the thyme. Bake, uncovered, until the cheese
has formed a skin on the top and is lightly brown around the edges,
25 minutes.

Serves 4 to 6 * Requires: soak time

Ooey Gooey Cheesy Fondue

Vegan * Gluten-free Option * Grain-free Option * No Added Sugar * Refined Sugar-free

My Ooey Gooey Cheesy Fondue reminds me of ski trips abroad, where steaming pots of fondue would pass by our table as we defrosted in a snuggly restaurant for lunch. The rich cheese and white wine notes filled our noses as we sat down on faux fur benches, preferably near a blazing fire. This vegan fondue delivers on all these expectations. It is warm, rich, cheesy, and winey. Serve it piping hot with chopped baguette pieces, steamed broccoli, and roasted potatoes for dipping. This is a great dish to nourish yourself on a cold winter day, and even better for entertaining friends.

1. Place the cashews in a small bowl and add boiling water to cover. Soak for 1 hour, then drain. (Alternatively, soak the cashews in room-temperature water to cover for at least 6 hours or overnight, then drain.)

2. In a medium cast-iron skillet, heat the olive oil over medium heat. Add the onion and garlic and cook, stirring often, until the onion has softened, about 10 minutes.

3. Transfer the onion mixture to a high-speed blender. Add the cashews, 1 cup of the vegetable broth, miso, lemon juice, mustard, arrowroot powder, salt, and pepper. Blend on medium-high speed until smooth.

4. Pour the cheesy mixture back into the cast-iron skillet. Whisk over medium heat, adding the white wine, a little at a time, until the cheese has thickened and is gooey in texture. If the mixture is too thick, add a splash more vegetable broth to thin.

5. Serve the fondue immediately, alongside chopped baguette (if not gluten-free), steamed broccoli, and roasted baby potatoes for dipping.

TIPS

1. Serving this fondue in a cast-iron skillet helps to retain the heat as time passes. However, it can also be prepared in a medium stainless steel pot.

2. If the fondue starts to thicken as it sits, reheat for a few minutes over medium heat. Thin with a splash more vegetable broth or water, if needed.

3. You can substitute vegetable broth for the white wine.

1½ cups raw cashews

1 tablespoon olive oil

1 small yellow onion, finely chopped

2 cloves garlic, finely chopped

1 cup vegetable broth, more as needed

3 tablespoons white miso

2 tablespoons lemon juice

1 tablespoon Dijon mustard

4 teaspoons arrowroot powder

1 teaspoon fine sea salt

¼ teaspoon freshly ground black pepper

¾ cup dry white wine

FOR SERVING

½ baguette, cut into bite-size pieces (optional)

Roasted baby potatoes (1½ pounds/675 g)

Steamed broccoli florets (from 2 bunches; 1½ pounds/675 g total)

GLUTEN-FREE AND GRAIN-FREE

Omit the baguette for serving.

DO AHEAD

The cheese can be made 1 day in advance. Let cool completely, then cover tightly with resealable plastic and store in the refrigerator overnight. When ready to serve, heat, whisking frequently, over medium heat until warmed through, about 8 minutes. Thin with a splash more vegetable broth or water, if needed.

Refreshing Ricotta Cheese

Vegan ✳ Gluten-free ✳ Grain-free ✳ Oil-free Option ✳ No Added Sugar ✳ Refined Sugar-free ✳ Raw/No-bake

1 cup raw cashews

1 block (12 ounces/350 g) firm tofu

3 cloves garlic, finely chopped

Zest of 1 lemon

⅓ cup nutritional yeast

2 tablespoons olive oil

1 tablespoon lemon juice

2 teaspoons Italian seasoning

1½ teaspoons fine sea salt

Pinch of freshly ground black pepper

2 to 4 tablespoons unsweetened
   almond milk

STORAGE

Store the ricotta in an airtight container in the refrigerator for up to 5 days.

OIL-FREE

Omit the olive oil.

This plant-based ricotta cheese is light, bright, and tangy. Made with tofu and cashews, it is mild in flavour and protein-packed. Slather this ricotta on Chickpea Omelettes (page 62), stuff into pasta shells (page 257), or add a big dollop to a bowl of ratatouille (page 253) to elevate each dish.

1. Place the cashews in a small bowl and add boiling water to cover. Soak for 1 hour, then drain. (Alternatively, soak the cashews in room-temperature water to cover for at least 6 hours or overnight, then drain.)

2. Drain and rinse the tofu and wrap in a clean kitchen towel. Place on the countertop. Place a large cutting board securely on top, followed by a heavy cast-iron skillet or heavy pot. Let the weight of the pot "press" the excess water out of the tofu for 15 to 20 minutes. Unwrap the tofu and tear it into 1-inch chunks.

3. In a food processor, combine the cashews, tofu, garlic, lemon zest, nutritional yeast, olive oil, lemon juice, Italian seasoning, salt, and pepper. Pulse to combine. Add 2 tablespoons of the almond milk and blend to form a smooth ricotta-like consistency. Add an additional 1 to 2 tablespoons of the remaining almond milk for a smoother texture, if needed. Transfer the ricotta to a small bowl, cover with reusable wrap, and refrigerate until ready to serve.

Makes about 1 cup

Sprinkle-on-Everything Parmesan

Vegan * Gluten-free * Grain-free * Oil-free * Soy-free * No Added Sugar * Refined Sugar-free * Raw/No-bake

This vegan parmesan cheese is salty, savoury, cheesy, and nutty. I can eat it by the spoonful! We love it sprinkled on pretty much everything, from pasta dishes to roasted veggies, for some extra umami flavour.

Enjoy this cheese on Cheesy Kale Chips (page 180), Shaved Brussels Sprouts Salad with Coconut Bacon, Pomegranate, and Parmesan (page 215), Creamy Crunchy Kale Caesar Salad (page 216), Grilled Asparagus with Cherry Tomatoes and Parmesan (page 224), Moroccan Stuffed Eggplant with French Lentils and Parmesan (page 241), Spinach and Ricotta Stuffed Shells (page 257), and Cauliflower au Gratin (page 258).

1 cup raw cashews

⅓ cup nutritional yeast

¼ teaspoon garlic powder

¼ teaspoon fine sea salt

STORAGE

Store the cheese in an airtight container in the refrigerator for up to 1 month.

1. In a food processor, combine the cashews, nutritional yeast, garlic powder, and salt. Pulse to a fine meal, 30 seconds to 1 minute.

Makes 4 cups

Pink Beet Hummus

Vegan ✻ Gluten-free ✻ Grain-free ✻ Nut-free ✻ Oil-free Option ✻ Soy-free ✻ No Added Sugar ✻ Refined Sugar-free

2 small red beets, stems removed
    and scrubbed clean
2 cups cooked chickpeas, drained and
    rinsed (reserve chickpea liquid for
    oil-free option; see Tip)
3 cloves garlic, chopped
⅓ cup tahini
¼ cup olive oil, more for drizzling
¼ cup lemon juice
½ teaspoon fine sea salt

GARNISHES

2 tablespoons chopped fresh basil leaves
Sesame seeds, for sprinkling (optional)
Pinch of freshly ground black pepper

STORAGE

Store the hummus in an airtight container in the refrigerator for up to 5 days or in the freezer for up to 3 months. If frozen, thaw in the refrigerator the day before using.

OIL-FREE

Use the reserved chickpea liquid in place of the olive oil in step 3. Omit the oil drizzle.

Why have beige hummus when you can make it pink? This beet hummus is as delicious as it is pretty. The beets also adds a slight sweetness to the chickpea purée. Enjoy this Middle Eastern-inspired hummus on toast or as a dip with crunchy veggies and pita bread.

1. Place the beets in a medium pot and add water to cover by 1 to 2 inches. Bring to a boil over high heat. Reduce the heat to medium-low, cover with a lid, and simmer until the beets are fork-tender, about 45 minutes.
2. Drain the beets and rinse under cold running water until they are cool to the touch. Peel off the skins and chop into rough chunks.
3. In a food processor, pulse the beets a few times until finely chopped. Add the chickpeas, garlic, tahini, olive oil, lemon juice, and salt. Blend until smooth and creamy, 5 to 7 minutes. Stop to scrape down the sides of the bowl as needed to ensure a consistent texture.
4. Transfer the pink beet hummus to a small bowl. Garnish with a sprinkle of fresh basil and pepper. Drizzle with more olive oil and sprinkle with sesame seeds, if desired.

TIPS

1. One (14-ounce/400 mL) can of chickpeas is equivalent to 1½ cups cooked chickpeas. If using canned chickpeas, you will need 2 cans to have enough chickpeas for this recipe. (You will have chickpeas left over.)
2. You can purchase precooked beets to speed up prep time. Skip steps 1 and 2. Be sure the skins have been removed from the cooked beets before using.

Makes 4½ cups

Golden Roasted Carrot Hummus

Vegan ⁕ Gluten-free ⁕ Grain-free ⁕ Nut-free ⁕ Soy-free ⁕ No Added Sugar ⁕ Refined Sugar-free

This golden hummus is smooth and creamy, with sweetness and smoky umami flavours—not to mention a beautiful colour—from the oven-roasted carrots. Inspired by Middle Eastern flavours, it's the perfect companion for my Super-Seedy Crackers (page 183) or sourdough toast.

1. Preheat the oven to 400°F (200°C). Line a baking sheet with parchment paper.
2. In a medium bowl, mix together the carrots, 2 tablespoons of the olive oil, 1 teaspoon of the salt, and ginger. Pour the carrot mixture onto the prepared baking sheet and spread out in an even layer. Roast until the carrots are fork-tender, about 30 minutes.
3. Transfer the carrots to a food processor and pulse into fine chunks. (Optional to reserve a handful of the roasted carrots for garnish.) Add the remaining ½ cup olive oil, the remaining ½ teaspoon salt, the chickpeas, ¼ cup of the reserved chickpea liquid, garlic, tahini, and lemon juice. Blend until smooth, 5 to 7 minutes. Stop to scrape down the sides of the bowl as needed to ensure a consistent texture. Add more chickpea liquid, a tablespoon at a time, to thin, if desired.
4. Transfer the carrot hummus to a medium bowl. Garnish with reserved roasted carrots (if using), a sprinkle of fresh basil, sesame seeds (if using), and pepper. Drizzle with more olive oil, if desired.

1½ pounds (675 g) orange carrots, peeled and chopped (4 cups)
½ cup + 2 tablespoons olive oil, divided, more for drizzling
1½ teaspoons fine sea salt, divided
½ teaspoon ground ginger
2 cups cooked chickpeas (reserve chickpea liquid), drained and rinsed (see Tip)
3 cloves garlic
⅓ cup tahini
¼ cup lemon juice

GARNISHES
2 tablespoons chopped fresh basil leaves
Sesame seeds, for sprinkling (optional)
Pinch of freshly ground black pepper

STORAGE
Store the hummus in an airtight container in the refrigerator for up to 5 days or in the freezer for up to 3 months. If frozen, thaw in the refrigerator the day before using.

TIPS
1. One (14-ounce/400 mL) can of chickpeas is equivalent to 1½ cups cooked chickpeas. If using canned chickpeas, you will need 2 cans for this recipe. (You will have chickpeas left over.)
2. When roasting the carrots, be sure that they are fork-tender. This will ensure a smoother and creamier hummus when blended.

Makes 3½ cups

Roasted Eggplant Baba Ganoush

Vegan * Gluten-free * Grain-free * Soy-free * No Added Sugar * Refined Sugar-free

2 medium Italian eggplants
    (about 1 pound/450 g each)
1 tablespoon avocado oil or olive oil
½ teaspoon + pinch of fine sea salt,
    divided
1 clove garlic
⅓ cup plain coconut yogurt
¼ cup tahini, more for drizzling
3 tablespoons lemon juice
2 tablespoons olive oil
¼ teaspoon ground cumin
¼ teaspoon sweet paprika

GARNISHES (OPTIONAL)
1 to 2 tablespoons finely chopped
    fresh flat-leaf parsley
1 to 2 tablespoons pomegranate seeds

STORAGE
Store the baba ganoush in an airtight
container in the refrigerator for up to
5 days.

TIP
If your tahini is too thick for drizzling at
the end, add a heaping tablespoon to a
small bowl and mix with water, a teaspoon
at a time, until drizzly.

This classic Lebanese-inspired dip is made with roasted eggplant, garlic, and tahini. It's smooth, smoky, and savoury. I love the addition of tart coconut yogurt to add lightness and creamy flavour, and a sprinkle of pomegranate seeds for a sweet crunch! I like to serve it as a dip with bread or crackers or with fresh veggies like endive and carrots.

1. Preheat the oven to 400°F (200°C). Line a baking sheet with parchment paper.

2. Slice the eggplants in half lengthwise and brush the fleshy side with the avocado oil. Sprinkle with a pinch of salt.

3. Place the eggplants flesh side down on the prepared baking sheet and roast until tender and the skin is wrinkly and collapsed, about 35 minutes. Let cool slightly. Scoop out the fleshy interior, discarding the skins.

4. In a food processor, combine the eggplant, garlic, coconut yogurt, tahini, lemon juice, olive oil, cumin, paprika, and ½ teaspoon salt. Blend until smooth and creamy. Transfer the baba ganoush to a medium bowl. Drizzle with more tahini, and sprinkle with parsley and pomegranate seeds, if desired.

Serves 4 to 6

Creamy Avocado Mousse

Vegan * Gluten-free * Grain-free * Nut-free * Oil-free * Soy-free * No Added Sugar * Refined Sugar-free * Raw/No-bake

I like to think of this creamy avocado mousse as my French spin on guacamole! Instead of the traditional chunky texture and bold flavour, I blend the avocados until smooth, and the taste and texture are more subtle and refined—light, airy, creamy, and citrusy. This is a lovely mousse to slather on baguette, sourdough, or my Super-Seedy Crackers (page 183). This mousse is also delicious as a topping for Super-Stuffed Sweet Potatoes with Chickpea Chili (page 237).

1. In a high-speed blender, combine the avocados, coconut yogurt, lime juice, garlic, and salt. Blend until ultra-smooth. Taste, and adjust flavours if desired, adding more salt to enhance flavour, more garlic if you like it garlicky, or more lime juice for more brightness. Transfer to a small bowl.

3 ripe avocados, pitted and peeled
¼ cup plain coconut yogurt
3 tablespoons lime juice
1 clove garlic, finely chopped
Pinch of fine sea salt

TIPS

1. If you are having trouble with blending, use the tamper accessory to mix together the mousse for perfect consistency. If you do not have a tamper, occasionally stop the blender and stir with a wooden spoon to help the blending process.
2. This recipe can also be made in a small blender or bullet blender.

DO AHEAD

The mousse is best served immediately, as the avocados can brown over time. If you want to prepare it a few hours in advance, I suggest covering the serving bowl well with plastic wrap, gently pressing it against the mousse so there is no air exposure. Store in the refrigerator until ready to serve.

Faux Gras

Vegan • Gluten-free Option • Grain-free Option • Oil-free Option • Refined Sugar-free

FAUX GRAS

Heaping ½ cup dried French green lentils
(du Puy lentils)

2 tablespoons coconut oil

2 cloves garlic, finely chopped

1 shallot, finely chopped

8 ounces (225 g) white button
mushrooms, chopped

2 teaspoons chopped fresh rosemary

2 teaspoons fresh thyme leaves

½ cup raw walnuts

2 tablespoons nutritional yeast

2 tablespoons lemon juice

1 tablespoon gluten-free tamari

1 teaspoon pure maple syrup

1 teaspoon tomato paste

¾ teaspoon dried cilantro

¼ teaspoon cinnamon

⅛ teaspoon ground cloves

½ teaspoon fine sea salt

Pinch of freshly ground black pepper

GARLICKY BREAD

1 baguette, cut into 1-inch-thick slices

2 cloves garlic, halved lengthwise

2 to 3 tablespoons vegan butter

1 cup arugula, for topping (optional)

This faux gras is made from mushrooms and lentils and well-seasoned for an umami-rich spread that is very similar in taste to pâté. Foie gras is really popular in France, and when living there I discovered a tasty plant-based version at a small vegan shop called Végétal & Vous. Back home in Canada, my homemade version has become the perfect replacement for the little tin of faux gras that I used to buy in Lille. The best way to enjoy it, in my opinion, is generously spread on toasted garlic bread.

1. Make the Faux Gras: In a medium saucepan, combine the lentils and 4 cups of water. Bring to a boil over high heat, then reduce heat to medium-low and simmer until the lentils are soft, about 20 minutes. Drain and set aside.

2. Heat the coconut oil in a large skillet over medium heat. Add the garlic and shallot and cook, stirring frequently, until softened, about 7 minutes. Increase the heat to medium-high. Add the mushrooms and cook, stirring occasionally, until softened and the juices from the mushrooms have mostly evaporated, about 10 minutes. Add the rosemary and thyme and cook until fragrant, another 3 to 4 minutes.

3. Scrape the mushroom medley into a food processor. Add the lentils, walnuts, nutritional yeast, lemon juice, tamari, maple syrup, tomato paste, cilantro, cinnamon, cloves, salt, and pepper. Pulse until well combined and smooth. Transfer to 2 small jars. Serve or chill for later. Serve topped with a few arugula greens, if desired.

4. When Ready to Serve, Make the Garlicky Bread: Set the oven to broil. Line a baking sheet with parchment paper. Rub one side of each slice of baguette with cut side of garlic, then butter each slice. Lay the bread on the prepared baking sheet and toast under the broiler for 2 to 3 minutes, until golden brown and crisp. Serve baguette slices alongside the faux gras for slathering.

STORAGE

Store the faux gras in an airtight container in the refrigerator for up to 5 days or in the freezer for up to 3 months. If frozen, thaw in the refrigerator the day before using.

GLUTEN-FREE AND GRAIN-FREE
Omit the baguette and instead
serve with my Super-Seedy Crackers
(page 183).

OIL-FREE
Omit the coconut oil and instead cook
the garlic and shallots with a splash of
water. Watch closely as they are more
prone to burning.

DO AHEAD
The faux gras can be made up to
5 days in advance (see Storage).

Makes about 1 cup

Crunchy Curried Roasted Chickpeas

Vegan ＊ Gluten-free ＊ Grain-free ＊ Nut-free ＊ Soy-free ＊ No Added Sugar ＊ Refined Sugar-free ＊ One-bowl

Transform chickpeas into this crunchy, spicy, and protein-packed snack. These curried roasted chickpeas are seasoned with paprika, cumin, and turmeric, making them so easy to pop into your mouth. They also make a delicious topper on my Creamy Crunchy Kale Caesar Salad (page 216) or Butternut Squash, Apple, and Sage Soup (page 197).

1. Preheat the oven to 400°F (200°C). Line a baking sheet with parchment paper.
2. Spread the chickpeas onto a kitchen towel and pat until very dry. Discard any loose skins. Transfer to another dry kitchen towel and let sit for at least 15 minutes to dry out further. The chickpeas should not feel wet to the touch.
3. Transfer the chickpeas to a medium bowl. Add the avocado oil, paprika, cumin, turmeric, sea salt, and pepper. Toss to coat well.
4. Pour the chickpeas onto the prepared baking sheet and spread them out in an even layer. Sprinkle with flaky sea salt, if desired. Bake until golden, crispy, and dry on the outside, 35 to 40 minutes. Let the chickpeas cool on the baking sheet before serving.

1 can (14 ounces/400 mL) chickpeas, drained and rinsed (see Tip)
4 teaspoons avocado oil
½ teaspoon sweet paprika
¼ teaspoon ground cumin
¼ teaspoon ground turmeric
¼ teaspoon fine sea salt
Pinch of freshly ground black pepper
Pinch of flaky sea salt (optional)

STORAGE
Store the roasted chickpeas in an airtight container at room temperature for up to 5 days.

TIPS
1. It is important to pat the chickpeas very dry with the kitchen towel before seasoning. This will ensure optimal crunchiness after roasting.
2. If you prefer to cook chickpeas from scratch, you will need to soak and cook ½ cup dried chickpeas to get 1½ cups cooked (the equivalent of 1 can).

Serves 4

Cheesy Kale Chips

Vegan ✳ Gluten-free ✳ Grain-free ✳ Soy-free ✳ No Added Sugar ✳ Refined Sugar-free ✳ One-bowl

½ cup Sprinkle-on-Everything Parmesan
   (page 167)
1 bunch of kale (11 ounces/300 g),
   stems removed, leaves torn into
   2- to 3-inch pieces
3 tablespoons avocado oil
Pinch of fine sea salt

STORAGE
Store the kale chips in an airtight
container at room temperature for
up to 1 day.

DO AHEAD
The Sprinkle-on-Everything Parmesan
can be made well in advance. Store in
an airtight container in the refrigerator
for up to 1 month.

These kale chips are crispy, cheesy, salty, nutty—and so simple to
make. You will not believe that healthy chips can be this addictive!
I love to serve these as part of a vegan platter, as they are always
sure to wow our guests.

1. Make the Sprinkle-on-Everything Parmesan.
2. Place the oven racks in the upper and lower thirds of the oven.
Preheat the oven to 300°F (150°C). Line 2 baking sheets with
parchment paper.
3. Place the torn kale in a large bowl and drizzle with the avocado
oil. Toss and massage the kale with your hands to ensure the kale is
evenly coated with oil. Sprinkle with the parmesan and a pinch of salt,
and toss again to combine.
4. Scatter the kale onto the prepared baking sheets in an even layer.
Be sure not to overcrowd the pan or the kale will not crisp. Bake
until the kale looks crisp and some of the edges are lightly browned,
20 to 25 minutes. Rotate the baking sheets from top to bottom after
10 minutes for even baking. Watch closely as they can brown quickly.
Let the kale cool on the pan for a few minutes, then transfer to a bowl
and serve.

Serves 8

Super-Seedy Crackers

Vegan ☀ Gluten-free ☀ Grain-free ☀ No Added Sugar Option ☀ Refined Sugar-free ☀ Soy-free

These Super-Seedy Crackers are exactly what their name says; seedy and super! Made with oats, flax, chia, sesame, and pumpkin seeds, this is a wholesome, thin, and crispy cracker. Enjoy these crackers with any of my spreads, cheeses, or soups.

1. Place the oven racks in the upper and lower thirds of the oven. Preheat the oven to 375°F (190°C).

2. In a large bowl, combine the oats, pumpkin seeds, flax seeds, sesame seeds, chia seeds, rosemary, salt, and garlic powder. Stir to combine.

3. In a small bowl, whisk together the olive oil, maple syrup, and warm water.

4. Pour the wet ingredients over the dry ingredients and stir to combine well. Cover with a kitchen towel and let sit for 10 minutes, stirring occasionally, to ensure everything is absorbed and well combined.

5. Cut 4 pieces of parchment paper to fit a standard baking sheet. Divide the dough between 2 pieces of parchment. Using your hands, form each portion of dough into a disc 1 inch thick. Place a piece of parchment paper on top of each disc. (This will stop the rolling pin from sticking to the dough.) Using a rolling pin, roll out the dough until ⅛ inch thick. Slide the parchment-encased dough onto 2 baking sheets and gently peel away the top sheet of parchment. (If you have only 2 standard baking sheets, bake just one sheet of dough at a time on the middle rack. You will need the second baking sheet to invert the crackers.)

6. Bake until golden brown around the edges, about 20 minutes. Rotate the baking sheets from top to bottom after 10 minutes for even baking. Remove from the oven and place another baking sheet, bottom side up, on top of the hot baking sheet. Using oven mitts, hold the 2 baking sheets together tightly and gently invert. Remove the top (hot) baking sheet and peel off the parchment. Repeat with the second baking sheet of crackers. Return both sheets to the oven and bake until the crackers are golden and crispy on top, 10 to 15 minutes. Let the crackers cool completely on the baking sheets, then break into pieces with your hands.

DRY INGREDIENTS

1 cup gluten-free old-fashioned rolled oats

½ cup raw pumpkin seeds

⅓ cup flax seeds

⅓ cup sesame seeds

3 tablespoons chia seeds

2 tablespoons fresh rosemary leaves, coarsely chopped

¾ teaspoon fine sea salt

¼ teaspoon garlic powder

WET INGREDIENTS

1 tablespoon + 1 teaspoon olive oil

1 tablespoon pure maple syrup (optional)

1 cup warm water

STORAGE

Store the crackers in an airtight container at room temperature for up to 1 week.

TIP

The water should be warm enough to easily whisk the liquid ingredients together, but not boiling.

NO ADDED SUGAR

Omit the maple syrup.

Serves 2 or 3 ✳ Requires: soak time

Crispy Baked Frites

Vegan ✳ Gluten-free ✳ Grain-free ✳ Nut-free ✳ Soy-free ✳ Refined Sugar-free

HOMEMADE KETCHUP

¼ cup tomato sauce

2 tablespoons tomato paste

1 tablespoon lemon juice

1½ teaspoons pure maple syrup

¼ to ½ teaspoon fine sea salt

CRISPY BAKED FRITES

1½ pounds (675 g) russet potatoes
    (about 4 medium potatoes), scrubbed

3 tablespoons avocado oil

1 tablespoon chopped fresh rosemary

½ teaspoon lemon dill seasoning or
    dried dill

½ teaspoon fine sea salt

½ teaspoon garlic powder

¼ teaspoon onion powder

¼ teaspoon freshly ground black pepper

Flaky sea salt and coarse black pepper,
    for sprinkling

TIP

Soaking the potatoes in cold water helps to remove excess starch. This allows the potatoes to get gorgeously crispy when baked.

DO AHEAD

The ketchup can be made up to 2 days in advance. Store in an airtight container in the refrigerator.

These addictive baked frites are beautifully crispy, seasoned, and salty. I have fond memories of afternoons spent sitting in La Grand Place in Lille, sipping cold Belgian beer and stuffing our bellies with pommes frites.

These are what I like to call "accidentally vegan," because even the vegan skeptics devour these frites. Though they're typically served with mayonnaise, I prefer my frites with my tangy homemade ketchup.

1. Make the Homemade Ketchup: In a small bowl, whisk together the tomato sauce, tomato paste, lemon juice, maple syrup, and ¼ teaspoon salt. Taste, and add more salt if desired.

2. Make the Crispy Baked Frites: Fill a large bowl with cold water. Cut the potatoes into quarters and then slice into matchsticks. Drop into the bowl of water and let soak for 30 minutes.

3. Preheat the oven to 375°F (190°C). Line a baking sheet with parchment paper.

4. Drain and rinse the potato matchsticks, then pat very dry with a kitchen towel. Dry the bowl. Return the matchsticks to the bowl and drizzle with the avocado oil. Sprinkle with rosemary, lemon dill seasoning, salt, garlic powder, onion powder, and pepper. Mix gently with a spatula to coat thoroughly.

5. Spread the potato matchsticks onto the prepared baking sheet in an even layer. Bake for 20 minutes. Toss and flip the matchsticks, increase the oven temperature to 425°F (220°C), and roast for another 20 to 25 minutes, or until golden brown and very crispy. Sprinkle with flaky sea salt and coarse pepper. Serve immediately with the Homemade Ketchup.

Broccoli and Potato Croquettes

Vegan * Gluten-free Option * No Added Sugar * Refined Sugar-free * Soy-free

These warm croquettes are scrumptious. A pillowy soft potato filling rolled in bread crumbs, pan-fried until crispy, and served with a creamy yogurt and green onion sauce for dipping—does finger food get better than this?

1. Make the Yogurt Dip: In a small bowl, stir together the coconut yogurt, lime juice, salt, and green onions. Chill in the refrigerator until ready to use.

2. Make the Croquette Filling: Bring a large pot of water to a boil. Add a generous pinch of salt and drop in the potatoes. Cook for 15 minutes, or until the potatoes are fork-tender. Drain the potatoes and transfer to a medium bowl. Add the coconut milk, vegan butter, and ¾ teaspoon of the salt. Using a potato masher or large fork, mash the potatoes until fluffy. Cover with a kitchen towel and set aside.

3. Chop the broccoli florets into fine pieces, discard any large green stems. To a large skillet, add the coconut oil, onion, garlic, and remaining ¼ teaspoon salt and cook over medium heat, stirring often, until the onion is softened, about 10 minutes. Add the broccoli and continue cooking, stirring often, until the broccoli is very soft and bright green, about 12 minutes.

4. Transfer the broccoli mixture to the mashed potatoes, sprinkle with nutritional yeast, and mix together well. Cover with a kitchen towel and refrigerate until the mixture is cool enough to handle, about 20 minutes.

5. Line a baking sheet with parchment paper. Using your hands, roll the potato mixture into 18 small logs, each 1½ inches thick and 2 inches long. Arrange on the prepared baking sheet and freeze until the potatoes are very cold, about 25 minutes.

6. For the Breading: Have ready 2 small bowls and 1 shallow medium dish. Place the flour in one bowl. In the second bowl, whisk together the almond milk, tapioca starch, and salt. In the shallow dish, stir together the bread crumbs and pepper.

YOGURT DIP

¾ cup plain coconut yogurt

2 tablespoons lime juice

Pinch of fine sea salt

2 green onions, white and light green parts only, finely chopped

CROQUETTE FILLING

1½ pounds (675 g) white potatoes, cut into 1-inch chunks (4 medium potatoes)

3 tablespoons full-fat coconut milk or unsweetened almond milk

1 tablespoon vegan butter

¾ teaspoon + ¼ teaspoon fine sea salt, divided

1 bunch broccoli, cut into florets

3 tablespoons coconut oil

1 yellow onion, finely chopped

3 cloves garlic, finely chopped

3 tablespoons nutritional yeast

BREADING

½ cup all-purpose flour

1 cup unsweetened almond milk

2 tablespoons tapioca starch

¼ teaspoon fine sea salt

1½ cups dry bread crumbs

¼ teaspoon freshly ground black pepper

⅓ to ⅔ cup coconut oil, for frying

Recipe continues

Clean hands allow for easier breading. If you find that your hands are getting too sticky while breading the potato logs, rinse and dry your hands and then continue.

GLUTEN-FREE

Replace the all-purpose flour and bread crumbs with gluten-free versions.

7. Dip and roll each potato log in the flour, followed by the milk mixture, then the bread crumbs, and place back on the baking sheet.

8. Heat about ⅓ cup of coconut oil in a small non-stick skillet over medium heat. (The oil should come about ½ inch up the sides.) When the oil is hot, working in batches, add a few croquettes to the skillet—they should sizzle when added to the hot oil—and cook, turning frequently, until the outside is golden brown, 4 to 6 minutes. Using a slotted spoon, transfer the croquettes to a plate lined with paper towel to absorb the excess oil. Fry the remaining croquettes, adding more coconut oil, a tablespoon at a time, as needed. Serve the croquettes hot with the Yogurt Dip.

Soups and Salads

The soup recipes in this chapter are as cozy as they come. I've shared a little something for everyone, from go-to puréed soups like butternut squash or carrot, to chunky vegetable soups that kids will love, to spiced stews. Soups are always welcomed when feeding a crowd, and they are just as perfect for a light lunch served with crusty bread. Better yet, they can be frozen and reheated in a flash.

As for salads, gone are the days of boring basic salads. In this chapter I share some of my favourite recipes for colourful, flavourful salads that are so nourishing and tasty they will take up at least three-quarters of your plate at dinnertime.

Serves 6

Chunky Vegetable Soup

Vegan * Gluten-free * Grain-free * Nut-free * Soy-free * No Added Sugar * Refined Sugar-free * One-pot

This chunky vegetable soup is so comforting and wholesome. It's my version of a simple dish called pot-au-feu de légumes that I often ordered for lunch at the local restaurants in Lille. The rainy winter months could chill you to the bone, and this soup always warmed me back to good spirits from tummy to toes. Just like in Lille, I like to serve it with fresh bread.

1. In a large pot, heat the olive oil over medium heat. Add the onion and salt and cook, stirring often, until softened, 10 minutes. Add the celery, carrots, and potatoes. Cook, stirring often, until the vegetables start to soften, 7 to 10 minutes.

2. Pour in the vegetable broth and season with the bay leaves, herbes de Provence, and pepper. Add the diced tomatoes. Reduce the heat to medium-low and simmer, with the lid slightly ajar, until the vegetables are very soft, 10 to 15 minutes.

3. Add the peas and kale and stir until the kale is wilted and the peas are bright green, about 1 minute. Add the lemon juice and a pinch of chili flakes to taste. Serve the soup in bowls with a dollop of coconut yogurt, if desired.

3 tablespoons olive oil

1 yellow onion, finely chopped

1 teaspoon fine sea salt

2 ribs celery, chopped

3 large carrots, peeled and chopped

2 medium white potatoes, peeled and chopped

4 cups vegetable broth

2 bay leaves

2 teaspoons herbes de Provence

¼ teaspoon freshly ground black pepper

1 can (14 ounces/400 mL) diced tomatoes, with their juices

1 cup frozen peas

2 cups tightly packed stemmed and chopped Tuscan kale or curly kale

1 teaspoon lemon juice

Pinch of red chili flakes

Coconut yogurt, for serving (optional)

STORAGE

Store the soup in an airtight container in the refrigerator for up to 5 days or in the freezer, in small or big batches, for up to 2 months. If frozen, thaw before reheating.

Creamy Carrot and Ginger Soup

Vegan * Gluten-free * Grain-free * Nut-free Option * Soy-free * No Added Sugar * Refined Sugar-free * One-pot

1 tablespoon coconut oil

1 yellow onion, finely chopped

3 cloves garlic, chopped

1½ pounds (675 g) carrots, peeled
    and chopped (4 cups)

1 medium sweet potato, peeled
    and chopped

¾ teaspoon fine sea salt

2 bay leaves

1 tablespoon dried cilantro

2 teaspoons peeled and grated
    fresh ginger

4 cups vegetable broth, more as needed

1 can (14 ounces/400 mL) full-fat
    coconut milk

1 tablespoon lemon juice

FOR SERVING

¼ cup pine nuts (optional)

Pinch of freshly ground black pepper

STORAGE

Store the soup in an airtight container
in the refrigerator for up to 5 days or
in the freezer, in small or large batches,
for up to 2 months. If frozen, thaw
before reheating.

NUT-FREE

Omit the pine nuts.

This carrot soup is so dreamy and creamy. It is smooth and velvety,
with coconut and ginger spice flavours. Enjoy it as a light lunch or
as a warm starter when you are entertaining family or friends. This
carrot soup has quickly become one of my favourites.

1. In a large pot, heat the coconut oil over medium heat. Add the onion
and garlic and cook, stirring occasionally, until softened and fragrant,
about 10 minutes. Add the carrots, sweet potato, and salt. Cover with a
lid, reduce the heat to medium-low, and simmer, stirring occasionally,
until the vegetables are slightly softened, about 15 minutes.

2. Add the bay leaves, cilantro, and ginger. Pour in the vegetable broth
and bring to a low simmer. Cook with the lid slightly ajar, stirring
occasionally, until the vegetables are very soft, another 20 minutes.

3. Discard the bay leaves. Using an immersion blender, purée the
soup until smooth and creamy. (Alternatively, blend the soup in a
high-speed blender, starting on low speed and increasing as needed.
Return the soup to the pot.) Pour in the coconut milk and lemon
juice and stir to combine. Thin with a splash more vegetable broth,
if needed. (Optional to reserve 2 to 3 tablespoons of the coconut milk
for garnish.)

4. If using the pine nuts, in a small skillet over medium-high heat,
toast the nuts, stirring often, until golden, about 7 minutes. Transfer
to a small bowl.

5. Pour the soup into bowls and spoon a few drops of reserved
coconut milk and swirl with a toothpick, if desired. Sprinkle with
the toasted pine nuts (if using) and a pinch of pepper.

TIP

Puréeing vegetables in a high-speed blender results in a smoother
and creamier blend. You might need to do this in batches. To avoid a
mess, start by blending on low speed and slowly increase to medium-
high. Otherwise, the blender lid might pop off, causing a soup explosion!

Serves 6

Butternut Squash, Apple, and Sage Soup

Vegan * Gluten-free * Grain-free * Nut-free * Soy-free * No Added Sugar * Refined Sugar-free

I would be remiss if I didn't include a rich and reliable butternut squash soup in my cookbook. I love to make this recipe for my in-laws at Christmas and Thanksgiving. Each year we divide the menu, and this soup is always requested. The butternut squash and apple make for a sweet blend, seasoned with sage, thyme, bay leaf, and cardamom. Garnish with fried sage leaves and Crunchy Curried Roasted Chickpeas for a little crunch.

1. Make the Crunchy Curried Roasted Chickpeas, if using.

2. In a large pot, heat the olive oil over medium heat. Add the garlic, celery, onion, salt, and pepper and cook, stirring often, until the onions are softened and fragrant, about 10 minutes.

3. Make the Soup: Sprinkle in the sage and thyme and stir together until the sage is wilted and fragrant, about 1 minute. Add the butternut squash and apple and stir together. Cover the pot with the lid, reduce the heat to medium-low, and simmer, stirring occasionally, until the squash and apple are softened, about 15 minutes.

4. Pour in the vegetable broth and add the bay leaves and cardamom pods. Bring the soup to a simmer and cook with the lid slightly ajar, stirring occasionally, until the squash and apple are very soft, 20 to 30 minutes.

5. Discard the bay leaves and cardamom pods. Using an immersion blender, purée the soup until smooth and creamy. (Alternatively, blend the soup in a high-speed blender, starting on low speed and increasing as needed. Return the soup to the pot.) Pour in the coconut milk and lemon juice and stir to combine.

Crunchy Curried Roasted Chickpeas
    (page 179), for topping (optional)

SOUP

3 tablespoons olive oil

4 cloves garlic, finely chopped

2 ribs celery, chopped

1 yellow onion, finely chopped

½ teaspoon fine sea salt

Pinch of freshly ground black pepper

1 sprig fresh sage, leaves only, chopped

1 teaspoon fresh thyme leaves

1 small butternut squash (2 pounds/900 g),
    peeled, seeded, and cubed (5 cups)

1 Honeycrisp apple, peeled, cored,
    and chopped

4 cups vegetable broth

2 bay leaves

2 cardamom pods

¼ cup full-fat coconut milk

2 teaspoons lemon juice

FRIED SAGE

2 tablespoons olive oil

2 sprigs fresh sage, leaves only

Pinch of fine sea salt

Recipe continues

STORAGE

Store the soup in an airtight container in the refrigerator for up to 5 days or in the freezer, in small or big batches, for up to 2 months. If frozen, thaw before reheating.

TIP

Puréeing vegetables in a high-speed blender results in a smoother and creamier blend. You might need to do this in batches. To avoid a mess, start by blending on low speed and slowly increase to medium-high. Otherwise, the blender lid might pop off, causing a soup explosion!

DO AHEAD

The Crunchy Curried Roasted Chickpeas can be prepared up to 5 days in advance. Store in an airtight container at room temperature.

6. Make the Fried Sage: In a small skillet, heat the olive oil over high heat. When the oil is hot, add the sage leaves and sizzle for 4 to 8 seconds per side, turning with a spoon, until the leaves are crispy and a deep green colour. Transfer the fried sage to a small plate lined with paper towel to absorb excess oil. Sprinkle with salt.

7. Ladle the soup into bowls and top each with a few fried sage leaves. Sprinkle with the Crunchy Curried Roasted Chickpeas (if using) and more freshly ground black pepper.

Serves 4

Gourmet French Onion Soup

Vegan　❋　Gluten-free Option　❋　Soy-free　❋　Refined Sugar-free

This vegan French onion soup is gourmet through and through. It begins with cooking onions until they are caramelized, sweet, and fragrant, then flavouring them with thyme, tamari, and white wine. It's rich, hearty, and bursting with umami flavour.

To top it off, literally, I use toasted baguette with Ooey Gooey Cheesy Fondue. Are you drooling yet? Certainly, this French onion soup is so lush you could serve it as a stand-alone dish.

1. Make the Ooey Gooey Cheesy Fondue. Cover with a lid and let cool until ready to use. (Alternatively, you can use your favourite store-bought vegan mozzarella cheese. Set aside to use in step 7.)
2. Make the Soup: In a large pot, melt the vegan butter and coconut oil over medium heat. Add the onions and cook, stirring occasionally, until softened, about 10 minutes.
3. Add the coconut sugar, salt, and pepper and cook until the onions are golden and caramelized and the liquid has mostly evaporated, about 30 minutes.
4. Add the flour and stir to combine. Pour in the vegetable broth, white wine, and tamari. Stir to combine.
5. Add the thyme and bay leaves to the pot. Simmer the soup over medium-low heat, with the lid slightly ajar, until the broth is thickened and flavourful, about 20 minutes. Remove the thyme and bay leaves and discard. Add splashes more vegetable broth to thin, if needed.
6. Reheat the Ooey Gooey Cheesy Fondue, adding splashes of vegetable broth or water if needed for smooth consistency.

½ cup Ooey Gooey Cheesy Fondue
　　(page 163) or store-bought shredded
　　vegan mozzarella cheese (see Tip)

SOUP

3 tablespoons vegan butter,
　　more for spreading
1 tablespoon coconut oil
3½ pounds (1.6 kg) white onions
　　(about 5 large onions), halved
　　lengthwise and thinly sliced
2 teaspoons coconut sugar
1 teaspoon fine sea salt
½ teaspoon freshly ground black pepper
1 tablespoon all-purpose flour
4 cups vegetable broth, more as needed
½ cup dry white wine (see Tip)
1 tablespoon gluten-free tamari
8 sprigs fresh thyme, tied with twine
2 bay leaves
1 baguette, cut into twelve 1-inch-thick
　　slices
1 clove garlic, peeled and halved
　　lengthwise
2 to 3 teaspoons fresh thyme leaves,
　　for garnish (optional)

Recipe continues

GLUTEN-FREE

Replace the all-purpose flour with gluten-free baking flour. Replace the baguette with gluten-free bread of choice, topped with the cheesy fondue, or omit the baguette and cheese altogether.

7. Toast the baguette: Set the oven to broil. Line a baking sheet with parchment paper. Rub one side of each bread slice with the cut side of the garlic, then butter each slice. Lay the bread on the prepared baking sheet and toast under the broiler until golden brown and crisp, 2 to 3 minutes. Remove from the oven and spoon a dollop of the cheesy fondue on top of each slice. (If using store-bought cheese, sprinkle over the toasted slices and pop back in the oven under the broiler until melted, about 30 seconds to 1 minute.)

8. Ladle the soup into bowls and top each with 3 slices of cheesy baguette. Sprinkle with thyme, if desired.

TIPS

1. If you are using store-bought vegan mozzarella cheese in place of the Ooey Gooey Cheesy Fondue, I recommend looking for a brand that melts when heated. It should say on the packaging whether it's a "melty" cheese. I find the Daiya brand to be very good. Store-bought vegan cheese may alter this recipe from being soy-free.

2. More vegetable broth can be used instead of the white wine. Add a squeeze of lemon juice to brighten the dish, if desired.

TIP
If you prefer to cook chickpeas from scratch, you will need to soak and cook ½ cup dried chickpeas to get 1½ cups cooked (the equivalent of 1 can).

GLUTEN-FREE AND GRAIN-FREE
Serve without pita or sourdough bread.

Serves 8 to 10

Hearty Moroccan Lentil Soup

Vegan * Gluten-free Option * Grain-free Option * Nut-free * No Added Sugar * Refined Sugar-free * Soy-free * One-pot

This North African–inspired soup is so hearty and warming. The lentils and veggies are cooked in bold spices like cinnamon, sweet paprika, ginger, and chili flakes. This is an easy, budget-friendly soup that can last you through the week for lunch or dinner.

I love to serve this bowl topped with a dollop of coconut yogurt to offset the heat and some comforting whole wheat pita bread or sourdough.

1. In a large pot, heat the olive oil over medium heat. Add the onion, garlic, and salt and cook, stirring occasionally, until the onion is softened, about 10 minutes. Add the bell pepper, carrots, and sweet potatoes, cover with a lid, and cook, stirring occasionally, until the vegetables have softened, about 15 minutes.

2. Add the ginger, cinnamon, cilantro, cumin, paprika, chili flakes, and black pepper. Pour in the lentils and stir gently to combine. Pour in the vegetable broth and diced tomatoes and stir again. Cover the soup with the lid slightly ajar and bring to a boil over medium-high heat. Reduce the heat to medium-low and simmer until the lentils are tender, about 20 minutes. Stir in the chickpeas and add the baby spinach, cover with the lid, and simmer until the spinach has wilted, 2 to 3 minutes. Stir to combine.

3. Squeeze in the lime juice, then pour in the water to thin the soup. Add more water or vegetable broth if needed for desired consistency.

4. Ladle the soup into bowls. If desired, top with a dollop of coconut yogurt and sprinkle with chili flakes for more heat. Serve with pita bread or a thick slice of sourdough, if desired.

STORAGE

Store the soup in an airtight container in the refrigerator for up to 5 days or in the freezer, in small or large batches, for up to 2 months. If frozen, thaw before reheating.

1 tablespoon olive oil

1 small sweet onion, finely chopped

4 cloves garlic, finely chopped

½ teaspoon fine sea salt

1 red bell pepper, finely chopped

2 large carrots, peeled and sliced into coins

2 small sweet potatoes, peeled and cut into bite-size pieces

2 teaspoons peeled and grated fresh ginger

1½ teaspoons cinnamon

1 teaspoon dried cilantro

1 teaspoon ground cumin

1 teaspoon sweet paprika

½ teaspoon red chili flakes, more for serving

¼ teaspoon freshly ground black pepper

1½ cups dried French green lentils (du Puy lentils)

5 cups vegetable broth, more as needed

1 can (14 ounces/400 mL) diced tomatoes, with their juices

1 can (14 ounces/400 mL) chickpeas, drained and rinsed (see Tip)

2 cups tightly packed baby spinach

2 tablespoons lime juice

½ cup water, more as needed

FOR SERVING (OPTIONAL)

Plain coconut yogurt

Pita bread or sourdough bread

Chilled Tomato Gazpacho

Vegan ✳ Gluten-free ✳ Grain-free ✳ Nut-free ✳ Soy-free ✳ No Added Sugar ✳ Refined Sugar-free ✳ Raw/No-bake

2 pounds (900 g) vine-ripe tomatoes
  (6 tomatoes)
2 cloves garlic, finely chopped
1 red bell pepper, chopped
1 shallot, finely chopped
½ large English cucumber, chopped
¼ cup olive oil
2 tablespoons lemon juice
1 teaspoon fine sea salt
¼ teaspoon freshly ground black pepper

GARNISHES

½ cup chopped cherry tomatoes (optional)
¼ cup tightly packed fresh basil leaves,
  chopped

STORAGE

Store the soup in an airtight container
in the refrigerator for up to 5 days or in
the freezer, in small or large batches, for
up to 2 months. Stir well before serving.

This refreshing Chilled Tomato Gazpacho is one of my favourite recipes to make in the summertime, when local tomatoes are abundant, juicy, and sweet. My father-in-law grows tomatoes in his garden every summer, and it's a treat to receive a big bag full. I won't allow any of those premium tomatoes to go to waste, so this recipe is a godsend. Enjoy it as a light lunch with bread, or as an appetizer on a hot summer's day.

1. Peel the Skins From the Tomatoes: Fill a large bowl with ice water. Bring a large pot of water to a boil. Slice a small "X" into the bottom of each tomato and drop them into the boiling water for 30 seconds. Using a slotted spoon, remove the tomatoes from the boiling water and submerge them in the ice water for 1 to 2 minutes. The skins should now easily peel away. Discard the skins. Chop the tomatoes into chunks.

2. Make the Gazpacho: In a large bowl, combine the chopped tomatoes, garlic, bell pepper, shallot, cucumber, olive oil, lemon juice, salt, and black pepper. Stir together. Cover with a kitchen towel and leave to marinate at room temperature for at least 20 minutes or up to 1 hour.

3. Transfer the marinated medley to a high-speed blender and blend on high speed until smooth. Chill the soup in the refrigerator for at least 2 hours.

4. When ready to serve, give the soup a quick stir with a wooden spoon to recombine if separated. Pour the gazpacho into bowls and top with the cherry tomatoes, if desired. Sprinkle with the fresh basil.

TIP

If you prefer to cook chickpeas from scratch, you will need to soak and cook ½ cup dried chickpeas to get 1½ cups cooked (the equivalent of 1 can).

DO AHEAD

The Lemon Dijon Dressing can be prepared up to 3 days in advance. Store in a jar in the refrigerator. Bring to room temperature and shake before using.

Serves 4

Chickpea Salad Niçoise

Vegan * Gluten-free * Grain-free * Nut-free * Soy-free * No Added Sugar * Refined Sugar-free

This niçoise is fully loaded with hearty potatoes, seasoned chickpeas, colourful vegetables, and crispy lettuce. It is summery, crunchy, and full of flavours you would typically find in a salad niçoise from the South of France—one of my favourite places in France to visit. The freshness of this salad takes me back to the morning markets in the Old Town of Nice, where I used to buy the ingredients to prepare this vibrant salad. We loved to pack it in containers and picnic on the stony beach. Enjoy this salad as a delicious healthy lunch, dinner, or side salad.

1. Make the Lemon Dijon Dressing: In a small bowl, combine the olive oil, lemon juice, mustard, shallots, garlic, agave, miso, salt, pepper, and oregano. Whisk to combine. Set aside to allow the flavours to meld together.

2. Prepare the Chickpeas: In a medium bowl, combine the chickpeas, lemon juice, mustard, oregano, and salt. Stir to combine. Set aside.

3. Make the Salad: Fill a medium bowl with ice water. Bring a large pot of water to a boil over high heat. When the water is boiling, reduce the heat to medium-high, add the green beans, and cook until the beans are vivid green and just tender, 3 to 4 minutes. Using a slotted spoon, scoop out the green beans and submerge them in the ice water. Add the potatoes to the boiling water and cook until fork-tender, 10 to 12 minutes. Drain the potatoes and rinse under cool running water. Drain the green beans. Pat dry the potatoes and green beans.

4. Spread the romaine lettuce on a large serving platter. Evenly arrange the green beans, potatoes, tomatoes, cucumber, olives, and red onion over the romaine. Sprinkle with the seasoned chickpeas, chives, capers, and a pinch each of salt and pepper. Serve the Lemon Dijon Dressing on the side for drizzling. (Alternatively, you can toss all the ingredients together in a large salad bowl and toss with the dressing to taste just before serving.)

LEMON DIJON DRESSING

⅓ cup olive oil

¼ cup lemon juice

2 tablespoons Dijon mustard

2 tablespoons finely diced shallots

1 clove garlic, finely diced

1½ teaspoons agave

½ teaspoon white miso

½ teaspoon fine sea salt

¼ teaspoon freshly ground black pepper

¼ teaspoon dried oregano

CHICKPEAS

1 can (14 ounces/400 mL) chickpeas, drained and rinsed (see Tip)

2 teaspoons lemon juice

1 teaspoon Dijon mustard

1 teaspoon dried oregano

Pinch of fine sea salt

SALAD

7 ounces (200 g) green beans, trimmed

7 ounces (200 g) baby potatoes, colour of choice, cut into bite-size pieces

2 cups chopped romaine lettuce

1 cup grape tomatoes, halved

1 cup thinly sliced English cucumber

¼ cup pitted mixed Greek olives

½ small red onion, thinly sliced

2 tablespoons chopped fresh chives

¼ cup drained capers

Pinch of fine sea salt

Pinch of freshly ground black pepper

Serves 6

Herby Quinoa Tabbouleh Salad

Vegan ✳ Gluten-free ✳ Nut-free ✳ Soy-free ✳ No Added Sugar ✳ Refined Sugar-free

SALAD

1 cup uncooked white quinoa (see Tip)

½ red onion, finely chopped

½ English cucumber, finely chopped

1 red bell pepper, finely chopped

1½ cups cherry tomatoes, finely chopped

1½ cups tightly packed fresh flat-leaf
    parsley leaves, very finely chopped

1 cup tightly packed fresh mint leaves,
    very finely chopped

2 green onions, white and light green
    parts only, finely chopped

Pinch of fine sea salt, more as needed

Pinch of freshly ground black pepper,
    more as needed

DRESSING

⅓ cup olive oil

¼ cup lemon juice

2 cloves garlic, finely chopped

½ teaspoon fine sea salt

½ teaspoon dried oregano

¼ teaspoon freshly ground black pepper

DO AHEAD

The salad dressing can be prepared up
to 2 days in advance. Store in a jar in the
refrigerator. Bring to room temperature
and shake before using.

This Lebanese-inspired quinoa tabbouleh salad is delightfully fresh, herby, crunchy, and bright. Lebanese cuisine was often our first choice when we were tired of going to French restaurants in Lille. Authentic Lebanese food is hugely popular in France, and you can find a premixed tabbouleh salad in almost every grocery store.

I love using quinoa as opposed to bulgur to keep this salad gluten-free and add protein to the dish. Enjoy this tabbouleh as a light lunch or served with dinner.

1. Prepare the Salad: In a medium saucepan, stir together the quinoa and 2 cups of water. Bring to a boil over medium-high heat. Reduce the heat to medium-low, cover with the lid slightly ajar, and simmer the quinoa until cooked and pleasantly chewy, 12 to 15 minutes. Transfer the cooked quinoa to a shallow bowl for quicker cooling and cover with a kitchen towel.

2. In a large bowl, combine the cooled quinoa, red onion, cucumber, bell pepper, cherry tomatoes, parsley, mint, green onion, and a pinch each of salt and black pepper. Toss to combine.

3. Make the Dressing: In a small bowl, whisk together the olive oil, lemon juice, garlic, salt, oregano, and black pepper.

4. Pour the dressing over the salad and toss to combine. Season with more salt and black pepper to taste.

TIPS

1. Quinoa cooking time can vary depending on the brand. It is always helpful to read the package instructions for perfect consistency.

2. The finer you chop the herbs and veggies in this salad, the more enjoyable the texture will be. Take joy in the slicing and dicing. It can be a peaceful pursuit.

Serves 8

French Lentil and Walnut Salad

Vegan ✳ Gluten-free ✳ Grain-free ✳ Soy-free ✳ Refined Sugar-free

While living in France, our favourite healthy fast-food restaurants often served a lentil and walnut salad like this one inspired by our time abroad. Often we would bring it along as sustenance on long train rides for weekend getaways. It's fresh yet wholesome, and protein-packed from the lentils and walnuts. Enjoy this salad when you need a nourishing meal away from home.

1. Make the Dressing: In a small bowl, combine the olive oil, garlic, shallots, mustard, balsamic vinegar, lemon juice, maple syrup, herbes de Provence, salt, and pepper. Whisk to combine. Set aside.

2. Prepare the Salad: In medium saucepan, combine the lentils and 6 cups of water. Add the bay leaf, thyme, and a generous pinch of salt. Bring to a simmer over medium-high heat and cook, with the lid on, until the lentils are al dente, 10 to 15 minutes. Add the carrots and celery to the pot and simmer for 5 more minutes.

3. Discard the bay leaf and thyme sprigs. Drain the lentil mixture and transfer to a large bowl. Add the parsley, walnuts, pomegranate seeds, and shallot. Pour in the dressing and toss to combine. Season with more salt and pepper. Serve warm or chilled.

STORAGE

Store the salad in an airtight container in the refrigerator for up to 5 days.

TIP

Lentil cooking time can vary depending on the brand. It is always helpful to read the package instructions for perfect consistency.

DRESSING

¼ cup olive oil

2 cloves garlic, finely chopped

2 tablespoons chopped shallot

2 tablespoons Dijon mustard

2 tablespoons balsamic vinegar

2 tablespoons lemon juice

1 teaspoon pure maple syrup

¼ teaspoon herbes de Provence

¼ teaspoon fine sea salt, more as needed

Pinch of freshly ground black pepper,
    more as needed

SALAD

1 cup dried French green lentils
    (du Puy lentils)

1 bay leaf

5 sprigs fresh thyme, tied with twine

Pinch of fine sea salt

2 carrots, peeled and finely chopped

2 ribs celery, finely chopped

1 cup tightly packed flat-leaf parsley leaves,
    finely chopped

1 cup raw walnuts, chopped

¾ cup pomegranate seeds

1 shallot, finely chopped

DO AHEAD

The salad dressing can be prepared up to 3 days in advance. Store in a jar in the refrigerator. Bring to room temperature and shake before using.

Autumn Wild Rice Salad

Vegan * Gluten-free * Soy-free * Refined Sugar-free

WILD RICE SALAD

1 cup wild rice blend

3 tablespoons avocado oil, divided

1 small butternut squash (2 pounds/900 g),
    cubed (about 4 cups)

½ teaspoon fine sea salt

¼ teaspoon freshly ground black pepper

½ cup raw pecans, chopped

2 ribs celery, chopped

2 cups tightly packed stemmed and
    chopped curly kale leaves

½ cup tightly packed curly or flat-leaf
    parsley leaves, finely chopped

½ cup unsweetened dried cranberries

BALSAMIC VINAIGRETTE
DRESSING

1 clove garlic, finely chopped

¼ cup balsamic vinegar

3 tablespoons olive oil

1 tablespoon pure maple syrup

2 teaspoons Dijon mustard

¼ teaspoon cinnamon

¼ teaspoon fine sea salt

¼ teaspoon freshly ground black pepper

STORAGE

Store the salad in an airtight container
in the refrigerator for up to 5 days.

This warm autumn-inspired salad is a gorgeous mix of sweet, savoury, and satiating that I love to serve around Thanksgiving. A delicious wild rice blend is tossed with roasted squash, hearty kale, cranberries, and toasted pecans and then drizzled with a cinnamon-infused balsamic dressing. It makes an excellent side salad that just happens to be vegan and gluten-free.

1. Preheat the oven to 400°F (200°C). Line a baking sheet with parchment paper.

2. Make the Wild Rice Salad: In a large saucepan, combine the wild rice, 1¾ cups of water, and 1 tablespoon of the avocado oil. Bring to a boil over high heat, then reduce the heat to medium-low, cover with the lid, and simmer until cooked and pleasantly chewy, 35 to 45 minutes. Remove from the heat and fluff the rice with a fork. Cover the pot with a clean kitchen towel to catch the steam and place the lid on top. Let sit for at least 10 minutes.

3. Meanwhile, toss the cubed squash into a medium bowl. Drizzle with the remaining 2 tablespoons avocado oil, sprinkle with salt and pepper, and toss to combine. Evenly spread the squash on the prepared baking sheet and roast until lightly golden and fork-tender, about 30 minutes.

4. Meanwhile, in a small skillet over medium-high heat, toast the pecans, stirring often, until fragrant and lightly browned, about 7 minutes.

5. Make the Balsamic Vinaigrette Dressing: In a small bowl, combine the garlic, balsamic vinegar, olive oil, maple syrup, mustard, cinnamon, salt, and pepper. Whisk to combine.

6. In a large bowl, combine the cooked rice, roasted squash, toasted pecans, celery, kale, parsley, and cranberries. Drizzle with the Balsamic Vinaigrette Dressing and toss gently to combine. Serve warm or at room temperature.

DO AHEAD

This salad can be prepared up to 2 days in advance, but add the toasted pecans and the cranberries just before serving. Store in an airtight container in the refrigerator. Serve chilled or at room temperature.

Serves 6

Shaved Brussels Sprouts Salad with Coconut Bacon, Pomegranate, and Parmesan

Vegan ✳ Gluten-free ✳ Grain-free ✳ Refined Sugar-free

I like to serve this salad around the holidays, when Brussels sprouts and pomegranate are fresh and abundant. This hearty salad is rich with umami flavours from the coconut bacon and parmesan. Dressed to impress and great for entertaining.

1. Make the Sprinkle-on-Everything Parmesan.

2. Make the Dressing: In a small bowl, stir together the tahini, apple cider vinegar, maple syrup, water, and salt. Set aside.

3. Make the Salad: Preheat the oven to 350°F (180°C). Line a baking sheet with parchment paper.

4. In a food processor fitted with the shredding disc, shred the Brussels sprouts. (Alternatively, thinly slice the sprouts with a sharp knife.)

5. Transfer the shredded Brussels sprouts to a large bowl. Pour the dressing over top and toss to combine. Cover with a kitchen towel and refrigerate, to let the Brussels sprouts marinate in the dressing.

6. Meanwhile, Make the Coconut Bacon: In a small bowl, stir together the avocado oil, tamari, maple syrup, paprika, and a pinch each of salt and pepper. Add the coconut flakes and toss to coat. Evenly spread the coconut on the prepared baking sheet, breaking up any clumps. Bake until golden brown and crispy, 5 to 10 minutes. Let cool.

7. Add the pomegranate seeds and Coconut Bacon to the Brussels sprouts. Sprinkle with the Sprinkle-on-Everything Parmesan and toss to combine.

DO AHEAD

1. The Coconut Bacon can be prepared up to 1 week ahead. Store in an airtight container at room temperature.

2. This salad gets better over time as the dressing tenderizes the tough green leaves. Feel free to make the salad a few hours in advance. Sprinkle with the Coconut Bacon just before serving.

2 tablespoons Sprinkle-on-Everything Parmesan (page 167), for serving

DRESSING

⅓ cup tahini

4 teaspoons apple cider vinegar

2 teaspoons pure maple syrup

½ cup water

Pinch of fine sea salt

SALAD

⅔ pound (300 g) Brussels sprouts, trimmed and halved lengthwise

⅔ cup pomegranate seeds

COCONUT BACON

1 teaspoon avocado oil

2 teaspoons gluten-free tamari

1 teaspoon pure maple syrup

1 teaspoon smoked paprika

Fine sea salt

Freshly ground black pepper

⅔ cup unsweetened coconut flakes

Serves 6

Creamy Crunchy Kale Caesar Salad

Vegan * Gluten-free * Grain-free * Soy-free * Refined Sugar-free

2 tablespoons Sprinkle-on-Everything
    Parmesan (page 167)
1 cup Crunchy Curried Roasted Chickpeas
    (page 179)

DRESSING
4 tablespoons warm water, divided
1 teaspoon white miso
¼ cup tahini
¼ cup lemon juice
1 teaspoon Dijon mustard
1 teaspoon pure maple syrup
1 clove garlic, finely chopped
¼ teaspoon fine sea salt
Pinch of freshly ground black pepper

SALAD
1 bunch curly kale, stems removed,
    leaves torn into bite-size pieces
    (12 cups tightly packed/155 g)
Pinch of fine sea salt
Pinch of freshly ground black pepper

This delicious Caesar salad is creamy, hearty, and full of flavour. Made with sturdy kale and served with crunchy chickpeas in place of croutons and savoury vegan parmesan cheese, this signature salad is always appreciated for its creamy taste and crunchy texture. It can be dressed well in advance of serving, and it keeps well for delicious next-day leftovers. I like to enjoy this salad year-round, be it at barbecues with friends or holiday gatherings.

1. Make the Sprinkle-on-Everything Parmesan and Crunchy Curried Roasted Chickpeas.
2. Make the Dressing: In a small bowl, stir 1 tablespoon of the warm water with the miso, ensuring there are no clumps. Add the remaining 3 tablespoons water, the tahini, lemon juice, mustard, maple syrup, garlic, salt, and pepper. Whisk well to combine.
3. Make the Salad: In a large bowl, sprinkle the torn kale with a pinch of salt and then massage the leaves by lightly scrunching them with your hands a few times. (This will help to soften the leaves for better absorption of the dressing.)
4. Drizzle the kale with the dressing and toss to combine. Add the Sprinkle-on-Everything Parmesan and toss again. Transfer the salad to a large serving bowl and sprinkle with the Crunchy Curried Roasted Chickpeas. Sprinkle with pepper and serve.

DO AHEAD
1. Feel free to make the salad a few hours in advance, but add the Crunchy Curried Roasted Chickpeas right before serving to ensure crunchiness.
2. The Sprinkle-on-Everything Parmesan can be made well in advance. Store in an airtight container in the refrigerator for up to 1 month.
3. The Crunchy Curried Roasted Chickpeas can be prepared up to 5 days in advance. Store in an airtight container at room temperature.

Delicious Mains, Sharing Plates, and Wholesome Bowls

Making a plant-based dinner wholesome and flavourful can sometimes be a challenge, especially when you're new to plant-based cooking. How do you work in protein? How do you transform humble chickpeas into a gourmet feast? Over the years, I've found many tips and tricks for enhancing flavour to elevate bland tofu or a can of chickpeas into restaurant-worthy dishes. Now, I am sharing all my knowledge in this chapter.

The best compliment I receive from friends and family after they try one of my dishes is, "I didn't even miss the meat!" These recipes certainly prove that there is no compromise on taste when it comes to plant-based meals. Pretty soon your family will be jumping on the bandwagon with you! In this chapter you'll find gourmet dishes like Mushroom Bourguignon with Buttery Mashed Potatoes (page 247), bubbling Summer Rainbow Ratatouille (page 253), gorgeous curries and flavourful tofu bowls, and lots of nourishing side dishes that can be paired together for a colourful feast. Be sure to check out my Dinner Menus for my favourite pairings.

Dinner Menus

Deciding what to make for a special dinner can sometimes be an onerous task. I have taken all the guesswork out of it for you with my favourite menu pairings. Whether you are looking to entertain a crowd or you're cooking for a romantic night in for two, the menus below offer a wonderful selection that ties together taste, texture, colour, and sensation for a well-balanced meal.

Of course, what is a meal without dessert? These menus include some of my favourite desserts that are a perfect marriage with the main meal, whether you want something quick and easy or a showstopper to impress a crowd.

Dinner with Besties

Creamy Carrot and Ginger Soup (page 194)

Shaved Brussels Sprouts Salad with Coconut Bacon, Pomegranate, and Parmesan (page 215)

Oven-Baked Falafels (page 231)

Roasted Cauliflower with Pesto and Tahini Drizzle (page 238)

Lemon Tart (page 265) or Blueberry Ginger Galette (page 291)

Family Fun

Chunky Vegetable Soup (page 193)

Creamy Crunchy Kale Caesar Salad (page 216)

Spinach and Ricotta Stuffed Shells (page 257) or Balsamic Mushroom Risotto (page 251)

Level-Up Chocolate Mousse Tart (page 277) or Just Peachy Crumble (page 286)

Dinner for Two

Chickpea Salad Niçoise (page 207)

Mushroom Bourguignon with Buttery Mashed Potatoes (page 247)

Kryptonite Chocolate Lava Cakes (page 278) or Classic Crème Brûlée (page 293)

Dinner for Entertaining

French Lentil and Walnut Salad (page 211)

Balsamic Roasted Beets with Toasted Pine Nuts and Blue Cheese (page 227)

Maple Spiced Roasted Carrots (page 228)

Cauliflower au Gratin (page 258)

Summer Rainbow Ratatouille (page 253)

Sweet Cherry Frangipane Tart (page 271) or French Apple Tart (page 273)

Chocolate Peanut Butter Truffles (page 282—good for after-dinner nibbles!)

Quick and Easy

Butternut Squash, Apple, and Sage Soup (page 197)

Green Beans Amandine (page 223) or Grilled Asparagus with Cherry Tomatoes and Parmesan (page 224)

Moroccan Stuffed Eggplant with French Lentils and Parmesan (page 241)

Mousse au Chocolat (page 281) or Raspberry Clafoutis (page 285)

Serves 4

Green Beans Amandine

Vegan * Gluten-free * Grain-free * Soy-free * No Sugar Added * Refined Sugar-free

Green beans amandine is a simple dish of sautéed green beans and garlic, toasted almonds, and a squeeze of lemon. It is bright, citrusy, and nutty for a healthy side dish worth sharing. My family loves this classic recipe. If you ask me, it's far too delicious for how quickly it comes together.

½ cup slivered almonds

3 tablespoons olive oil

4 cloves garlic, finely chopped

2 shallots, finely chopped

1 pound (450 g) green beans, trimmed

½ teaspoon fine sea salt

Pinch of freshly ground black pepper

1 tablespoon lemon juice

Zest of 1 lemon

1. In a small skillet over medium heat, toast the almonds, stirring often, until fragrant and golden brown, 5 to 7 minutes. (Keep a close watch on the almonds, as they can quickly go from lightly brown to burnt.) Set aside.

2. Heat the olive oil in a large skillet (preferably cast-iron) over medium heat. Add the garlic and shallots and cook, stirring frequently, until the shallots are softened, 2 to 4 minutes.

3. Increase the heat to high and add the green beans, salt, and pepper. Sauté the green beans until al dente, 5 to 7 minutes. Pour in the lemon juice, and sprinkle with the toasted almonds and lemon zest. Toss to combine. Serve hot.

Serves 3 or 4

Grilled Asparagus with Cherry Tomatoes and Parmesan

Vegan * Gluten-free * Grain-free * Soy-free * No Sugar Added * Refined Sugar-free

2 tablespoons Sprinkle-on-Everything
    Parmesan (page 167)

2 tablespoons olive oil

1 pound (450 g) asparagus, trimmed

4 cloves garlic, finely chopped

¼ teaspoon fine sea salt

Pinch of freshly ground black pepper

2 teaspoons lemon juice

4 ounces (115 g) cherry tomatoes,
    chopped

TIP

This recipe is the stuffing for my Chickpea
Omelette with Ricotta, Grilled Asparagus,
and Tomato (page 62).

DO AHEAD

The Sprinkle-on-Everything Parmesan
can be made well in advance. Store in an
airtight container in the refrigerator for
up to 1 month.

Fresh asparagus is one of the first indications that local vegetables are back in season. Asparagus is clean and earthy, and not too much effort is needed to enjoy the fullness of its flavour. In this recipe, I sauté asparagus in a cast-iron skillet until lightly charred, then top it with cherry tomatoes and nutty vegan parmesan—it's that simple. People will fork-fight for a second serving!

1. Make the Sprinkle-on-Everything Parmesan.
2. Heat the olive oil in a large cast-iron skillet over medium-high heat. Add the asparagus, garlic, salt, and pepper. Give everything a shake, then sprinkle with the lemon juice. Cook the asparagus, stirring often, until lightly charred and just softened, about 7 minutes. Remove from the heat, top with the tomatoes and Sprinkle-on-Everything Parmesan and serve.

Serves 3

Balsamic Roasted Beets with Toasted Pine Nuts and Blue Cheese

Vegan * Gluten-free * Grain-free * Soy-free * Refined Sugar-free

I was never a huge fan of roasted beets until I made this recipe. The list of ingredients—balsamic vinegar, Dijon, rosemary, and toasted pine nuts—truly elevates these beets into a luxurious side dish. If you are looking for ways to incorporate this nutritious root vegetable into your diet, this recipe has you covered. I have used a combination of red and golden beets for a colourful platter, but feel free to use classic red beets if that's what is available at your local grocers or farmers' market. Try these roasted beets in my Winter Bliss Bowl (page 233).

1. Make the Blue Cheese.

2. Preheat the oven to 400°F (200°C). Line a baking sheet with parchment paper.

3. Separate the golden and red beets into 2 small bowls and divide the rosemary and olive oil between the two. Sprinkle each with a pinch of pepper and toss to coat the beets in the oil. Spread the golden beets on one side of the prepared baking sheet and the red beets on the other side. (This will prevent the deep red colour from bleeding into the golden.) Roast until lightly golden and a fork meets with slight resistance, about 20 minutes.

4. Meanwhile, in a small skillet over medium heat, toast the pine nuts, stirring often, until golden and fragrant, 5 to 7 minutes.

5. In a small bowl, whisk together the balsamic vinegar, mustard, agave, salt, and garlic.

6. Drizzle the balsamic sauce over the semi-cooked beets. (Use a pastry brush if needed to evenly distribute the sauce.) Return the beets to the oven to roast until the edges are golden brown and sizzling and the beets are fork-tender, another 10 to 15 minutes.

7. Transfer the roasted beets to a serving plate and sprinkle with the toasted pine nuts and fresh rosemary, if desired. Top with small dollops of the blue cheese.

1 to 2 tablespoons Blue Cheese (page 156)

1½ pounds (675 g) beets (red and golden mix), peeled and cut into wedges

4 teaspoons fresh rosemary leaves, more for garnish

1 tablespoon olive oil

Pinch of freshly ground black pepper

2 tablespoons pine nuts

1 tablespoon balsamic vinegar

2 teaspoons Dijon mustard

2 teaspoons agave

¼ teaspoon fine sea salt

2 cloves garlic, finely chopped

TIP

Feel free to use only one colour of beets for this recipe. You will not need to divide the beets into separate bowls. Simply toss them all into a medium bowl and follow the instructions for seasoning.

DO AHEAD

Be sure to make the Blue Cheese ahead of time, because it needs at least 6 to 8 hours to chill. It can be made up to 5 days in advance. Store in an airtight container in the refrigerator. Alternatively, you can use your favourite store-bought cashew-based cheese to top the roasted beets.

Serves 4

Maple Spiced Roasted Carrots

Vegan ✳ Gluten-free ✳ Grain-free ✳ Nut-free ✳ Soy-free ✳ Refined Sugar-free

2 heaping tablespoons Roasted Eggplant Baba Ganoush (page 172), for serving (optional)

1½ pounds (675 g) carrots, trimmed

2 tablespoons avocado oil

½ teaspoon cinnamon

½ teaspoon ground cumin

½ teaspoon ground ginger

Fine sea salt

Freshly ground black pepper

2 tablespoons pure maple syrup

2 tablespoons lime juice

FOR SERVING

1 tablespoon chopped fresh flat-leaf parsley

1 teaspoon toasted sesame seeds

DO AHEAD

The Roasted Eggplant Baba Ganoush can be made up to 5 days in advance. Store in an airtight container in the refrigerator.

These roasted carrots are infused with warm winter spices and glazed with a sweet maple and lime sauce. I especially love to serve them plated over my Roasted Eggplant Baba Ganoush. I like to use rainbow carrots for a visual wow factor, but traditional orange carrots come out just as tasty.

1. Make the Roasted Eggplant Baba Ganoush, if using. Cover and refrigerate until ready to use.

2. Preheat the oven to 400°F (200°C). Line a baking sheet with parchment paper.

3. If you have very thick carrots, cut them in half lengthwise for consistent sizing. If the carrots are very large, cut into quarters lengthwise. Spread the carrots on the prepared baking sheet.

4. In a small bowl, whisk together the avocado oil, cinnamon, cumin, ginger, and a generous pinch each of salt and pepper. Pour the mixture over the carrots and massage with your hands to coat. Evenly spread the carrots in a single layer and roast until golden and sizzling, about 20 minutes.

5. In the same small bowl, whisk together the maple syrup and lime juice. Pour the mixture over the carrots and continue roasting for another 5 minutes, until fork-tender. Serve the roasted carrots as is, or smear baba ganoush onto a serving plate and layer the carrots on top. Sprinkle with parsley and sesame seeds.

Serves 4 to 6

Oven-Baked Falafels

Vegan * Gluten-free Option * Nut-free * Soy-free * No Added Sugar * Refined Sugar-free

These falafels are baked instead of the traditional fried, making them deliciously healthy to devour for lunch or dinner. Count on these Lebanese-inspired falafels to be the best baked falafels you'll ever make. This is one of the first recipes that truly won over my vegan-skeptic friends. They are full of flavour from cardamom, cilantro, cumin, red chili flakes, and fresh parsley. Also, chickpeas and oat flour mean they're packed with protein. Serve with my Awesome Green Sauce to drizzle. It adds beautiful brightness. You can also enjoy these baked falafels on top of my Winter Bliss Bowl (page 233) and on salads.

1. Make the Falafels: Preheat the oven to 375°F (190°C). Line a baking sheet with parchment paper.
2. In a food processor, pulse the oats until they reach a flour-like consistency. Transfer the oat flour to a small bowl.
3. In the food processor, combine the onion, garlic, and parsley and pulse until finely chopped. Add the oat flour, chickpeas, tahini, nutritional yeast, lemon juice, 1 tablespoon of the olive oil, salt, cumin, cilantro, cardamom, chili flakes, and pepper. Pulse until the mixture has a crumbly dough-like texture.
4. Scoop a heaping tablespoon of the dough and gently form a 2-inch ball with your hands. Repeat with the remaining dough, evenly spacing the balls on the prepared baking sheet. You should have 18 falafel balls. Brush with the remaining 1 tablespoon olive oil. Bake until golden and crispy, 15 to 20 minutes.
5. Make the Awesome Green Sauce: In the cleaned food processor or a high-speed blender, combine the avocado, garlic, cilantro, hemp hearts, lemon juice, water, and ¼ teaspoon of salt. Blend until smooth and creamy. Taste, and add more salt if desired to enhance flavour.
6. Build your falafel wraps in a pita or whole-grain tortilla, using the red cabbage, cucumber, and 3 or 4 falafel balls. Drizzle with the Awesome Green Sauce.

FALAFELS

⅓ cup gluten-free old-fashioned rolled oats

1 small yellow onion, roughly chopped

3 cloves garlic, roughly chopped

½ cup tightly packed fresh flat-leaf parsley leaves

1 can (14 ounces/400 mL) chickpeas, drained and rinsed (see Tip)

3 tablespoons tahini

2 tablespoons nutritional yeast

2 tablespoons lemon juice

2 tablespoons olive oil, divided

½ teaspoon fine sea salt

½ teaspoon ground cumin

½ teaspoon dried cilantro

¼ teaspoon ground cardamom

¼ teaspoon red chili flakes

¼ teaspoon freshly ground black pepper

AWESOME GREEN SAUCE

1 small avocado, pitted and peeled

1 clove garlic

1 cup tightly packed fresh cilantro or flat-leaf parsley leaves

½ cup hemp hearts

½ cup lemon juice

½ cup water

¼ to ½ teaspoon fine sea salt

FOR SERVING

6 pita breads or whole-grain tortillas

1 cup shredded red cabbage

2 mini cucumbers, sliced into thin rounds

Recipe continues

GLUTEN-FREE

Replace the pitas or whole wheat wraps with gluten-free versions, or serve the falafels with rice or quinoa.

DO AHEAD

The falafel mixture can be made a day in advance. Store the dough in an airtight container, or cover the food processor bowl with reusable wrap, and store in the refrigerator until ready to roll into balls for baking.

STORAGE

1. Store leftover falafel balls in an airtight container in the refrigerator for up to 4 days.

2. Store the Awesome Green Sauce in a jar in the refrigerator for up to 4 days. Shake before serving.

TIPS

1. If you prefer to cook chickpeas from scratch, you will need to soak and cook ½ cup dried chickpeas to get 1½ cups cooked (the equivalent of 1 can).

2. If your hands get too sticky when rolling the falafels, rinse them clean and continue rolling. Clean or even slightly damp hands allow for easier rolling.

3. In my opinion, the Awesome Green Sauce is a titch more delicious made with cilantro.

Serves 4

Winter Bliss Bowl

Vegan * Gluten-free * Soy-free * Refined Sugar-free

This Winter Bliss Bowl is warm, hearty, and full of protein. It is a delicious way to serve roasted veggies for a nourishing bowl that you can enjoy for lunch or dinner. This bowl is a feast for the eyes and taste buds! It features roasted beets and broccoli, along with my Oven-Baked Falafels (page 231) and a simple creamy tahini drizzle. This winter bowl is a great way to repurpose leftovers and transform them into a loveable dish. See my swap-up ideas on the next page.

1. Make the Tahini Dressing: In a small bowl, whisk together the tahini, water, lemon juice, and salt. Thin with a splash more water if needed. Set aside.

2. Place the oven racks in the upper and lower thirds of the oven. Preheat the oven to 375°F (190°C). Make the Oven-Baked Falafels.

3. Increase the oven temperature to 400°F (200°C). Prepare the Balsamic Roasted Beets with Toasted Pine Nuts and Blue Cheese. (You can omit the blue cheese to save time. Set aside the toasted pine nuts and sprinkle over the bliss bowl once assembled.) Roast the beets on the upper rack for 15 minutes.

4. Meanwhile, in a medium bowl, toss the broccoli florets with 3 to 4 tablespoons of olive oil to lightly coat. Sprinkle with salt and pepper and toss again. Spread the broccoli evenly on a second baking sheet lined with parchment paper.

5. Once the beets have roasted for 15 minutes, slide the baking sheet with the broccoli into the oven on the lower rack. Bake until the broccoli is vivid green and lightly charred and the beets are fork-tender with lightly browned edges, about another 20 minutes.

TAHINI DRESSING

¼ cup tahini

¼ cup water

¼ cup lemon juice

Pinch of fine sea salt

BLISS BOWL

1 batch Oven-Baked Falafels (page 231)

1 batch Balsamic Roasted Beets with Toasted Pine Nuts and Blue Cheese (page 227)

1 medium bunch broccoli (1½ pounds/ 675 g), cut into florets (4 cups)

3 to 4 tablespoons olive oil

Pinch of fine sea salt

Pinch of ground black pepper

1½ cups uncooked white quinoa (see Tip)

2 avocados, pitted and peeled

Recipe continues

TIP

Cooking time can vary depending on the brand of quinoa. It's always helpful to read the package instructions for perfect consistency.

DO AHEAD

The Tahini Dressing can be prepared up to 5 days in advance. Store in an airtight container in the refrigerator. Bring to room temperature before using for drizzle consistency. Add a splash of water to thin, if desired.

6. While the beets and broccoli are roasting, prepare the quinoa. In a large saucepan, combine the quinoa and 3 cups of water. Bring to a boil over medium-high heat. Reduce the heat to medium-low, cover with the lid slightly ajar, and simmer the quinoa until cooked and pleasantly chewy, 12 to 15 minutes. Remove from the heat and fluff with a fork. Cover the pot with a clean kitchen towel to catch the steam and place the lid on top. Let sit for at least 10 minutes or until ready to serve.

7. Assemble the Bliss Bowls: Divide the quinoa among bowls, followed by 3 or 4 falafel balls per bowl and a heaping spoonful of roasted beets and broccoli. Scoop half an avocado into each bowl and top with the Tahini Dressing. Sprinkle with the toasted pine nuts to finish.

SWAP-UP IDEAS

1. To save time, swap the falafels for 1 can (14 ounces/400 mL) chickpeas (1½ cups cooked chickpeas), drained and rinsed, or my Crunchy Curried Roasted Chickpeas (page 179).

2. Swap the Tahini Dressing for my Awesome Green Sauce from the Oven-Baked Falafels recipe (page 231). Both dressings are delicious.

3. Swap the roasted broccoli for my Roasted Cauliflower with Pesto and Tahini Drizzle (page 238). Use the Tahini Dressing amounts given in this recipe so you'll have enough dressing for the whole bowl.

4. Replace the roasted beets with my Maple Spiced Roasted Carrots (page 228).

5. This bliss bowl is also delicious with a dollop of Roasted Eggplant Baba Ganoush (page 172), Pink Beet Hummus (page 168), or Golden Roasted Carrot Hummus (page 171) if you have any handy.

Serves 4 as a main or 8 as a side

Super-Stuffed Sweet Potatoes with Chickpea Chili

Vegan * Gluten-free * Grain-free * Nut-free Option * Refined Sugar-free

This stuffed sweet potato is a delicious stand-alone main or side dish. I flavour a chickpea chili with warm spices like smoked paprika, cumin, chili powder, and red chili flakes and stuff it into a piping hot sweet potato. A dollop of coconut yogurt or a scoop of my Creamy Avocado Mousse to top is the perfect partner to this spicy dish. Both my husband and I adore this dish—me because it is wholesome and nutritious, and Mitch because it is hearty and sticks with you.

1. Make the Baked Sweet Potatoes: Preheat the oven to 400°F (200°C). Line a baking sheet with parchment paper.
2. Using a fork, poke a few holes in the sweet potatoes. Brush the potatoes with the olive oil and place on the prepared baking sheet. Bake until cooked through, 35 to 45 minutes. To check doneness, insert a fork into the potato. It should easily slide through with no resistance.
3. Meanwhile, Make the Chickpea Chili: Heat the olive oil in a large pot over medium heat. Add the garlic, onion, and salt and cook, stirring often, until the onion has softened, about 10 minutes. Add the bell pepper and cook until slightly softened, about 5 minutes. Add the tomato paste, chili powder, cumin, paprika, chili flakes, and a pinch of black pepper. Stir to combine.
4. Pour in the diced tomatoes, chickpeas, tamari, and maple syrup and stir together. Bring to a simmer over medium-high heat and cook until the liquid has reduced significantly, 15 to 20 minutes.
5. Stir in the walnuts, and add the spinach and lime juice. Cover with a lid and let the spinach wilt for 3 to 5 minutes, then stir to combine.
6. Slice the baked sweet potatoes open lengthwise and stuff generously with the Chickpea Chili. Add a dollop of coconut yogurt and sprinkle with black pepper and chili flakes.

STORAGE

Store the Chickpea Chili and sweet potatoes separately in airtight containers in the refrigerator for up to 4 days. The Chickpea Chili can also be frozen for 2 months. If frozen, thaw before reheating.

BAKED SWEET POTATOES

4 small sweet potatoes, scrubbed
1 tablespoon olive oil

CHICKPEA CHILI

2 tablespoons olive oil
3 cloves garlic, finely chopped
1 yellow onion, finely chopped
½ teaspoon fine sea salt
1 red bell pepper, finely chopped
1 tablespoon tomato paste
1 teaspoon chili powder
1 teaspoon ground cumin
1 teaspoon smoked paprika
¼ teaspoon red chili flakes,
    more for garnish
Freshly ground black pepper,
    more for garnish
1 can (14 ounces/400 mL) diced tomatoes,
    drained
1 can (14 ounces/400 mL) chickpeas,
    drained and rinsed (see Tip)
1 tablespoon gluten-free tamari
2 teaspoons pure maple syrup
½ cup chopped raw walnuts
3 cups tightly packed baby spinach
2 tablespoons lime juice
Plain coconut yogurt or Creamy Avocado
    Mousse (page 175), for topping

Serves 4

Roasted Cauliflower with Pesto and Tahini Drizzle

Vegan * Gluten-free * Grain-free * Soy-free * No Added Sugar * Refined Sugar-free

ROASTED CAULIFLOWER

1 large head cauliflower (3 pounds/1.35 kg), cut into florets

¼ cup olive oil

¼ teaspoon fine sea salt

PESTO SAUCE

2 cups tightly packed fresh basil leaves

⅓ cup pine nuts

2 cloves garlic

1 tablespoon nutritional yeast

1 tablespoon lemon juice

¼ teaspoon fine sea salt

⅓ cup olive oil

TAHINI DRIZZLE

2 tablespoons tahini

2 tablespoons water

2 teaspoons lemon juice

Pinch of fine sea salt

¼ cup pomegranate seeds, for garnish

STORAGE

1. Store the Pesto Sauce in an airtight container in the refrigerator for up to 2 days or in the freezer for up to 6 months. Bring to room temperature.

2. Store the Tahini Drizzle in an airtight container in the refrigerator for up to 5 days. Bring to room temperature. Add a splash of water to thin, if desired.

This is definitely one of my favourite recipes in this cookbook. Roasted cauliflower is one of life's simple pleasures. I love the crispy golden floret tips and the melt-in-your-mouth interior, all beautifully elevated with bright and tangy basil pesto and a creamy tahini drizzle. I add a little sweetness and crunch with fresh pomegranate seeds to sprinkle, for a winning dish that turns simple cauliflower into an addictive side dish.

1. Make the Roasted Cauliflower: Preheat the oven to 400°F (200°C). Line a baking sheet with parchment paper.

2. In a large bowl, toss the cauliflower florets with the olive oil and salt. Evenly spread the cauliflower on the prepared baking sheet. (You might need 2 baking sheets if the cauliflower is overcrowded.) Bake until fork-tender and golden brown around the edges, 35 to 40 minutes. Stir at the 20-minute mark for even baking. Transfer the cauliflower to an oven-safe serving platter or casserole dish. Keep the oven on.

3. Meanwhile, Make the Pesto Sauce: In a food processor, combine the basil, pine nuts, and garlic. Pulse a few times to chop. Add the nutritional yeast, lemon juice, and salt and pulse again to incorporate. With the food processor on low speed, drizzle in the olive oil and continue blending until the pesto is combined but still has some texture.

4. Make the Tahini Drizzle: In a small bowl, whisk together the tahini, water, lemon juice, and salt.

5. Top the roasted cauliflower with the Pesto Sauce and Tahini Drizzle. Carefully cover with foil and place back in the oven for 6 to 8 minutes to warm everything for serving. Remove from the oven and sprinkle with the pomegranate seeds.

DO AHEAD

The Pesto Sauce can be prepared up to 2 days in advance (see Storage). The Tahini Drizzle can be prepared up to 5 days in advance (see Storage).

Moroccan Stuffed Eggplant with French Lentils and Parmesan

Vegan ✳ Gluten-free ✳ Grain-free ✳ Soy-free ✳ Refined Sugar-free

This stuffed eggplant is warm, filling, and flavourful. It is Moroccan-inspired, using such spices as cumin, paprika, and cilantro to flavour the rice and lentil stuffing. The eggplants are roasted until supple and tender, then stuffed with that hearty filling and sprinkled with nutty vegan parmesan cheese. A healthy dish that you can serve as a side or as a stand-alone main. I particularly love it served alongside salad, like my Herby Quinoa Tabbouleh Salad (page 208) or Shaved Brussels Sprouts Salad with Coconut Bacon, Pomegranate, and Parmesan (page 215).

2 tablespoons Sprinkle-on-Everything Parmesan (page 167)

3 baby eggplants

1 tablespoon olive oil

Pinch of fine sea salt

SPICED LENTIL FILLING

2 tablespoons olive oil

1 small yellow onion, finely chopped

2 cloves garlic, finely chopped

½ cup cooked brown rice

½ cup dried French green lentils (du Puy lentils)

½ teaspoon ground cumin

¼ teaspoon dried cilantro

¼ teaspoon cinnamon

¼ teaspoon smoked paprika

Pinch of red chili flakes

2 teaspoons lemon juice

2 teaspoons pure maple syrup

½ cup canned diced tomatoes, drained

¼ teaspoon fine sea salt

Pinch of freshly ground black pepper

1 tablespoon finely chopped fresh flat-leaf parsley, for garnish (optional)

1. Make the Sprinkle-on-Everything Parmesan.

2. Prepare and bake the eggplant shells: Preheat the oven to 375°F (190°C). Slice the eggplants in half lengthwise and, using a spoon or sharp knife, scoop out the flesh, leaving ½-inch-thick shells. Chop the flesh and reserve for the Spiced Lentil Filling (step 4).

3. Brush the inside of the eggplants with olive oil, sprinkle with salt, and tuck them snugly, flesh side up, into an 8 x 11-inch baking dish. Bake until golden and fork-tender, 30 to 35 minutes.

4. Make the Spiced Lentil Filling: Heat the olive oil in a large deep skillet over medium heat. Add the onion, garlic, and reserved eggplant flesh. Cook over medium heat, stirring often, until the mixture has softened, about 10 minutes. Add the brown rice, lentils, cumin, cilantro, cinnamon, paprika, chili flakes, lemon juice, and maple syrup. Stir to combine. Pour in the diced tomatoes and season with salt and pepper. Keep warm over low heat while the eggplants finish baking.

5. Stuff the baked eggplants with the lentil filling and top with the Sprinkle-on-Everything Parmesan. Return the stuffed eggplants to the oven for 10 to 15 minutes to lightly toast the parmesan. Sprinkle with the parsley (if using).

STORAGE

Store the stuffed eggplants in an airtight container in the refrigerator for up 3 days.

DO AHEAD

The Sprinkle-on-Everything Parmesan can be made well in advance. Store in an airtight container in the refrigerator for up to 1 month.

Serves 4

Ultra-Cozy Sweet Potato, Chickpea, and Spinach Curry

Vegan * Gluten-free * Nut-free * Soy-free * No Added Sugar Option * Refined Sugar-free

2 medium sweet potatoes, peeled and
    cut into 1-inch cubes (4 cups)

1 can (14 ounces/400 mL) chickpeas,
    drained and rinsed (see Tip)

1 teaspoon cinnamon

1 teaspoon ground cumin

1 teaspoon curry powder

1 teaspoon ground turmeric

¼ cup + 1 tablespoon avocado oil, divided

1 yellow onion, finely chopped

3 cloves garlic, finely chopped

½ teaspoon fine sea salt

1 tablespoon peeled and grated fresh ginger

1 can (14 ounces/400 mL) full-fat
    coconut milk

½ cup vegetable broth, more as needed

1 tablespoon pure maple syrup

4 cups tightly packed baby spinach

2 tablespoons lime juice

¼ to ½ teaspoon red chili flakes (optional)

3 cups cooked basmati rice, for serving

TIPS

1. If you prefer to cook chickpeas from
scratch, you will need to soak and cook
½ cup dried chickpeas to get 1½ cups
cooked (the equivalent of 1 can).

2. The sweet potato can be replaced
with ½ medium butternut squash
(about 4 cups peeled and cut into
1-inch cubes).

This Indian-inspired curry bowl is made with creamy coconut milk, warm spices like turmeric and cumin, and roasted veggies. I love making up a big batch on Sundays for a nourishing bowl to enjoy for dinner with delicious leftovers for lunch during the workweek. Feel free to double the recipe. Enjoy this curry on a bed of warm basmati rice, and top with a sprinkle of red chili flakes if you like it spicy.

1. Preheat the oven to 400°F (200°C). Line a baking sheet with parchment paper.

2. In a large bowl, combine the sweet potatoes and chickpeas. Sprinkle with the cinnamon, cumin, curry powder, and turmeric. Drizzle with ¼ cup of the avocado oil and mix to combine.

3. Transfer the sweet potato and chickpea mixture to the prepared baking sheet and spread out evenly. Roast until lightly golden, about 30 minutes.

4. In a large pot, heat the remaining 1 tablespoon avocado oil over medium heat. Add the onion, garlic, and salt and cook until the onions are softened, about 10 minutes. Add the ginger, coconut milk, vegetable broth, and maple syrup. Bring to a low simmer over medium-low heat. Stir in the roasted sweet potatoes and chickpeas. Cover with a lid and simmer until the sweet potatoes are very tender, 10 to 15 minutes.

5. Add the spinach and lime juice, cover, and let the spinach wilt for 3 to 5 minutes. Stir everything to combine. Taste, and add chili flakes to taste if you enjoy spicy curry. Add more salt to enhance flavours and more lime juice to brighten, if desired. Thin with a splash more vegetable broth if needed. Serve the curry with the basmati rice.

STORAGE

Store the curry in an airtight container in the refrigerator for up to 5 days or in the freezer for up to 3 months. If frozen, thaw before reheating.

SUGAR-FREE

Omit the maple syrup.

Serves 4 to 6

Crispy Peanut Tofu Bowl with Roasted Broccolini

Vegan ✳ Gluten-free ✳ Refined Sugar-free

This tofu bowl is a family favourite to enjoy mid-week. It is so easy to throw together, never disappoints, and makes delicious next-day leftovers. I love an Asian-inspired stir-fry bowl, and this one is a showstopper. It is protein-packed with crispy tofu and oven-roasted broccolini. Serve over a bed of hearty brown rice, drizzle with the luscious creamy and umami peanut sauce, and top with crunchy peanuts to finish. Of all the countless dinner recipes I create, this is the one when my husband, Mitch, always says, "Please make this again!" between mouthfuls.

1. Press the Tofu: Drain and rinse the tofu blocks and wrap each in a clean kitchen towel. Arrange the tofu blocks side by side on the countertop. Place a large cutting board securely on top, followed by a heavy cast-iron skillet or heavy pot. Let the weight of the pot "press" the excess water out of the tofu for 15 minutes.

2. Meanwhile, Make the Peanut Sauce: In a small bowl, whisk together the warm water and miso. Add the peanut butter, tamari, sesame oil, lime juice, garlic, ginger, maple syrup, and chili flakes. Whisk well to combine.

3. Prepare the Crispy Tofu and Roasted Broccolini: Place the oven racks in the upper and lower thirds of the oven. Preheat the oven to 400°F (200°C). Line 2 baking sheets with parchment paper.

4. Cut the tofu into bite-size cubes and toss into a small bowl. Drizzle with the avocado oil and sprinkle with the arrowroot powder, garlic powder, salt, and pepper. Using a spatula, gently stir the tofu to coat with the seasoning. Evenly spread the tofu cubes on one of the prepared baking sheets.

5. In a large bowl, drizzle the broccolini with the avocado oil. Sprinkle with the salt and toss to combine. Evenly spread the broccolini on the second baking sheet.

CRISPY TOFU

2 blocks (12 ounces/350 g each) extra-firm tofu
¼ cup avocado oil
¼ cup arrowroot powder
¾ teaspoon garlic powder
¾ teaspoon fine sea salt
Pinch of freshly ground black pepper

PEANUT SAUCE

3 tablespoons warm water
2 teaspoons white miso
¼ cup + 1 tablespoon natural peanut butter
¼ cup gluten-free tamari
1 tablespoon sesame oil or avocado oil
1 tablespoon lime juice
1 clove garlic, finely chopped
1 teaspoon peeled and grated fresh ginger
1 teaspoon pure maple syrup
Pinch of red chili flakes

ROASTED BROCCOLINI

1½ pounds (675 g) broccolini or broccoli florets (9 cups)
¼ cup avocado oil
¼ teaspoon fine sea salt

FOR SERVING

3 cups cooked brown basmati rice
⅓ cup chopped unsalted roasted peanuts

Recipe continues

STORAGE

Store leftover tofu and broccolini in separate airtight containers in the refrigerator for up to 3 days.

DO AHEAD

The Peanut Sauce can be prepared up to 3 days in advance. Store in an airtight container in the refrigerator. Bring to room temperature before using for drizzle consistency. Add a splash of water to thin, if desired.

6. Slide the tofu into the oven on the upper rack and bake for 10 minutes, then slide the broccolini into the oven on the lower rack and continue to bake for 15 minutes, or until the tofu is lightly golden and sizzling and the broccolini is lightly charred and crispy on the ends.

7. Transfer the baked tofu to a medium bowl, drizzle with 6 tablespoons of the Peanut Sauce, and gently toss to combine.

8. Divide the rice among bowls and top with the roasted broccolini and tofu. Drizzle with more Peanut Sauce and sprinkle with chopped peanuts.

Serves 6 to 8

Mushroom Bourguignon with Buttery Mashed Potatoes

Vegan ✳ Gluten-free ✳ Nut-free ✳ Refined Sugar-free

In my dream scenario, it is a cold Friday evening and I have just come in from a brisk walk. Meanwhile, my husband, Mitch, is cooking up a big batch of this mushroom bourguignon in the kitchen, accompanied by a bottle of fine red wine. The air is rich with the savoury scent of aromatic veggies. This recipe certainly makes a dreamy date-night dinner, especially during the colder months. Mushrooms, carrot, and shallots are simmered in a bold broth sauce with bay leaves and thyme and served over creamy mashed potatoes. It is a soulful and indulgent meal to toast a hard week's work and the relaxing weekend ahead.

1. Make the Bourguignon: In a small bowl, cover the shallots with boiling water and let soak for 3 minutes. Drain and rinse. (This makes them easier to peel.) Peel the skin off the shallots and discard. Cut small shallots in half lengthwise and bigger shallots into quarters.

2. Heat 2 tablespoons of the vegan butter in a large pot over medium heat. Add half of the mushrooms, increase the heat to medium-high, and cook, stirring occasionally, until the mushrooms are lightly browned, about 6 minutes. Transfer the mushrooms to a medium bowl.

3. Repeat with another 2 tablespoons of the vegan butter and the remaining mushrooms. Transfer the mushrooms to the bowl with the first batch of mushrooms.

4. In the same pot over medium heat, melt the remaining 2 tablespoons vegan butter. Add the shallots, carrots, garlic, and salt. Cook, stirring often, until the vegetables start to soften, about 10 minutes. Add the tomato paste and flour and stir to incorporate. Pour in the red wine, vegetable broth, tamari, and maple syrup. Then add the mushrooms. Stir to combine.

BOURGUIGNON

12 shallots

6 tablespoons vegan butter, divided

1 pound (450 g) cremini mushrooms, roughly chopped

2 large carrots, peeled and roughly chopped

3 cloves garlic, finely chopped

¼ teaspoon fine sea salt

1 tablespoon tomato paste

2 tablespoons gluten-free all-purpose flour

1 cup dry full-bodied red wine

2 cups vegetable broth

1½ tablespoons gluten-free tamari

1 tablespoon pure maple syrup

6 sprigs fresh thyme, tied together with twine, more for garnish

2 bay leaves

MASHED POTATOES

3 pounds (1.35 kg) white potatoes, cut into chunks

½ cup vegan butter

½ cup unsweetened almond milk

¼ to ½ cup plain coconut yogurt

¾ teaspoon fine sea salt

¼ teaspoon freshly ground black pepper

Recipe continues

Store the bourguignon and mashed
potatoes separately in airtight containers
in the refrigerator for up to 4 days.
The bourguignon can be stored in the
freezer for up to 3 months. If frozen,
thaw before reheating.

5. Toss in the thyme and bay leaves and bring the stew to a simmer
over medium-high heat. Cook until the sauce has thickened and
reduced and the veggies are cooked through, 20 to 30 minutes. Taste,
and add more salt or a splash more tamari, if needed. Remove the
thyme and bay leaves and discard. Cover with a lid and keep warm
over low heat until ready to eat.

6. Make the Mashed Potatoes: Bring a large pot of salted water to a boil
over medium-high heat. Add the potatoes and cook until fork-tender,
12 to 15 minutes. Drain the potatoes and return to the pot. Using a
potato masher or immersion blender, blend until fairly smooth.

7. In a small saucepan, heat the vegan butter and almond milk over
medium heat, whisking to combine. (Alternatively, you can use the
microwave for warming.) Fold the buttery milk into the potatoes.
Add ¼ cup of the coconut yogurt, salt, and pepper and fold again
to combine. Add up to ¼ cup more coconut yogurt if the mashed
potatoes taste too dry. Serve the buttery mashed potatoes topped
with the mushroom bourguignon. Garnish with thyme, if desired.

Serves 6

Balsamic Mushroom Risotto

Vegan ✳ Gluten-free ✳ Nut-free ✳ Soy-free ✳ No Added Sugar ✳ Refined Sugar-free

This mushroom risotto is a fan favourite on my blog. Regardless of their food preferences, everyone can fall in love with a luxurious bowl of rice! This risotto is a wonderful recipe to serve to friends and family, and it is also simple enough to enjoy on a weeknight. In my opinion, what makes it so rich and dreamy is the pan-fried balsamic mushrooms. Spoon them over the risotto or fold them right into the rice just before serving.

My husband, Mitch, and I served risotto at our wedding in Dordogne, France, and I created this recipe as a tribute to that special day and the joy of being reunited with our closest friends and family amongst love, good wine, and gorgeous food. I am thrilled that this risotto has become such a popular recipe on my blog, that people have enjoyed bringing it into their homes and building fond memories. I hope that it does the very same for you.

1. Make the Balsamic Mushrooms: In a large pot, melt the vegan butter over medium-high heat. Add the mushrooms and salt and cook, stirring occasionally, until brown and softened, 10 to 15 minutes. Reduce the heat to medium as the liquid from the mushrooms begins to evaporate. Pour in the balsamic vinegar and cook until there is little to no excess liquid, another 2 to 4 minutes. Scoop the mushrooms into a medium bowl and set aside.
2. Make the Risotto: In the same pot over medium heat, melt the vegan butter. Add the onion, garlic, and salt and cook, stirring often, until the onions are softened, about 10 minutes.

BALSAMIC MUSHROOMS

2 tablespoons vegan butter or coconut oil

1 pound (450 g) cremini mushrooms, thinly sliced

¼ teaspoon fine sea salt

4 teaspoons balsamic vinegar

RISOTTO

2 tablespoons vegan butter or coconut oil

1 yellow onion, finely chopped

3 cloves garlic, finely chopped

¼ teaspoon fine sea salt

1½ cups arborio rice

¾ cup dry white wine

4½ to 5 cups vegetable broth, more as needed

½ cup nutritional yeast

⅓ cup tightly packed curly or flat-leaf parsley leaves, chopped, more for serving

Pinch of freshly ground black pepper, for serving

Recipe continues

Store the risotto in an airtight container in the refrigerator for up to 4 days. Reheat over medium heat, stirring as it warms and thinning with a splash more vegetable broth, as needed.

You can substitute vegetable broth for the white wine. Add a squeeze of lemon juice to brighten the dish, if desired.

3. Add the rice to the pot and toast, stirring often, until the grains are lightly perfumed, 2 to 3 minutes. Pour in the white wine and let simmer and thicken, stirring often, about 3 minutes. Pour in 1 cup of the vegetable broth and continue cooking, stirring frequently, until the liquid is almost absorbed. Add the remaining 3½ to 4 cups of broth, a little at a time, stirring often, until the risotto thickens and the rice is soft and pleasantly chewy, 20 to 25 minutes. Remove from the heat. Sprinkle in the nutritional yeast and stir to combine.

4. Add the cooked mushrooms to the cooked risotto. (Alternatively, add half the mushrooms to the risotto and reserve the other half for topping.) Sprinkle with the parsley and stir to combine. If the risotto has become too thick, add a splash more broth to thin to desired consistency. Scoop the risotto into bowls and sprinkle with more parsley and pepper to taste.

Serves 4

Summer Rainbow Ratatouille

Vegan ✳ Gluten-free ✳ Grain-free ✳ Nut-free ✳ Soy-free ✳ No Added Sugar ✳ Refined Sugar-free ✳ One-pot

This ratatouille might look like an intimidating dish, but it's a simple veggie stew made with colourful tomato, zucchini, eggplant, summer squash, and fragrant herbs baked in a cast-iron skillet or casserole dish until soft and bubbling.

Ratatouille is a classic summer dish originating from Provence, in the South of France. Leave it to the French to make a simple stew so impressive! We absolutely love this French-inspired rainbow ratatouille for dinner, and often include it in our weekly rotation. I especially like to serve it with toasted baguette slathered with my vegan Blue Cheese (page 156) or topped with a dollop of Refreshing Ricotta Cheese (page 164).

1. Preheat the oven to 375°F (190°C).

2. Heat the olive oil in a 10-inch cast-iron skillet over medium heat. Add the red onion, garlic, and ¾ teaspoon of the salt. Cook, stirring often, until the onion has softened, about 10 minutes.

3. Add the bell pepper and cook, stirring occasionally, until softened, about 7 minutes. Pour in the crushed tomatoes and season with the herbes de Provence and 2 teaspoons of the thyme. Cook at a low simmer until the sauce has slightly thickened, 10 to 15 minutes. Add the basil and stir to combine. Remove from the heat.

4. Starting from the outer edge of the skillet and working your way to the middle, arrange the sliced veggies over the tomato sauce, snugly upright but slightly angled, and alternating the colours (zucchini, summer squash, eggplant, and tomato). Fan them apart slightly, if needed, to cover the entire pan with no large gaps. Sprinkle with the remaining 1 teaspoon thyme, remaining ¼ teaspoon salt, and the black pepper.

2 tablespoons olive oil

1 large red onion, finely chopped

4 cloves garlic, finely chopped

1 teaspoon fine sea salt, divided

1 red bell pepper, finely chopped

2 cans (28 ounces/800 mL each) crushed tomatoes

2 teaspoons herbes de Provence

3 teaspoons fresh thyme leaves, divided

½ cup tightly packed fresh basil leaves, chopped, more for garnish

1 green zucchini, sliced into ½-inch rounds

1 yellow summer squash, sliced into ½-inch rounds (or another green zucchini)

1 Japanese eggplant, sliced into ½-inch rounds

3 Roma tomatoes, sliced into ½-inch rounds

¼ teaspoon freshly ground black pepper

Fresh basil leaves, for garnish (optional)

Recipe continues

STORAGE

Store the ratatouille in an airtight container in the refrigerator for up to 5 days or in the freezer for up to 3 months. If frozen, thaw before reheating.

5. Cover the skillet with foil or an oven-safe lid and bake the ratatouille for 40 minutes. Remove the foil and continue cooking until the vegetables are very soft and the ratatouille is bubbling, another 20 to 30 minutes. Garnish with basil leaves just before serving, if desired.

TIPS

1. Try to buy all the veggies in a similar size, as it will be easier to arrange the slices over the sauce.

2. You can simplify this recipe by chopping the veggies into bite-size pieces. Mix the chopped veggies into the tomato sauce and gently simmer, covered, over medium heat, or in the oven, until very soft, 45 to 55 minutes.

3. You can also make the ratatouille in a large round or rectangular casserole dish. Prepare the sauce in a large skillet, transfer it to the casserole dish, and arrange the sliced veggies on top as instructed in step 4. If using a rectangular dish, arrange the sliced veggies in rows lengthwise.

4. Note that if you serve this with toasted baguette and my vegan cheeses, the recipe is no longer nut-free or gluten-free.

Serves 5 or 6

Spinach and Ricotta Stuffed Shells

Vegan * Nut-free * No Added Sugar * Refined Sugar-free

These spinach and ricotta stuffed shells make for a winning dish, combining all our favourite flavours with a creamy herb filling, bright and tangy tomato sauce, and cheesy vegan parmesan to sprinkle. Stuffed shells are so fun to prepare and truly make a simple pasta dish look and taste so gourmet! This is a quick recipe to make mid-week, yet divine enough to enjoy for entertaining.

1. Prepare the Sprinkle-on-Everything Parmesan and Refreshing Ricotta Cheese.

2. Preheat the oven to 350°F (180°C).

3. Bring a large pot of salted water to a boil. When the water is boiling, add the pasta shells and cook, stirring gently, until almost al dente, 8 to 9 minutes. (The shells should be slightly undercooked, as they will continue to cook in the oven.) Drain the pasta and rinse under cold running water. Off the heat, return the pasta to the pot, drizzle with the olive oil, and gently mix with a spatula. Cover with the lid and set aside.

4. In a small non-stick skillet over medium-high heat, cook the spinach, stirring often, until almost all the water has evaporated, about 7 minutes. Transfer to a medium bowl.

5. Add the ricotta to the spinach and gently stir with a spatula to combine.

6. To assemble, pour 1½ cups of the tomato sauce into an 8 x 11-inch rectangular baking dish and gently tilt the pan to spread the sauce in an even layer.

7. Stuff each pasta shell with about 2 tablespoons of the spinach ricotta mixture and place them filling side up in the pan to fit snugly. Pour the remaining 1 cup tomato sauce into the nooks and crannies between the stuffed shells. Cover with foil and bake for 20 minutes. Remove the foil and bake until the tomato sauce is bubbling, another 10 to 15 minutes. Garnish with chopped parsley and pine nuts, if desired. Sprinkle generously with a few tablespoons of Sprinkle-on-Everything Parmesan and serve the rest on the side.

⅓ cup Sprinkle-on-Everything Parmesan (page 167), for garnish

1 batch Refreshing Ricotta Cheese (page 164)

7 ounces (200 g) jumbo pasta shells (20 to 22 shells)

1 tablespoon olive oil

4 cups (12 ounces/300 g) thawed frozen chopped spinach

2½ cups tomato sauce, divided

GARNISHES

2 tablespoons finely chopped fresh flat-leaf parsley

1 to 2 tablespoons pine nuts (optional)

STORAGE

Store the stuffed shells in an airtight container in the refrigerator for up to 3 days.

DO AHEAD

1. The Sprinkle-on-Everything Parmesan can be made well in advance. Store in an airtight container in the refrigerator for up to 1 month.

2. The Refreshing Ricotta Cheese can be made up to 5 days in advance. Store in an airtight container in the refrigerator.

NUT-FREE

Omit the pine nuts.

Serves 4 ✳ Requires: soak time

Cauliflower au Gratin

Vegan ✳ Gluten-free Option ✳ Soy-free ✳ No Added Sugar ✳ Refined Sugar-free

¼ cup Sprinkle-on-Everything Parmesan (page 167)

½ cup raw cashews

1 large head cauliflower (3½ pounds/1.6 kg), cut into florets

1¾ cups unsweetened almond milk

¼ cup nutritional yeast

2 cloves garlic

2 tablespoons tahini

1 tablespoon Dijon mustard

¾ teaspoon fine sea salt

¼ teaspoon onion powder

¼ teaspoon freshly ground black pepper

Pinch of sweet paprika

5 tablespoons vegan butter, divided

3 tablespoons all-purpose flour

2 tablespoons bread crumbs

2 tablespoons finely chopped fresh flat-leaf parsley, for garnish

STORAGE

Store the cauliflower au gratin in an airtight container in the refrigerator for up to 3 days.

GLUTEN-FREE

Replace the bread crumbs and flour with gluten-free versions.

DO AHEAD

The Sprinkle-on-Everything Parmesan can be made well in advance. Store in an airtight container in the refrigerator for up to 1 month.

Made with a creamy vegan béchamel sauce infused with cheesy flavour, and sprinkled with vegan parmesan and bread crumbs, this piping hot cauliflower gratin is a little lighter than traditional potatoes au gratin yet equally comforting. We love to enjoy this comforting dish in the cooler months. It is so easy to eat the whole casserole, so don't count on leftovers and expect some fork-fighting over the final florets.

1. Make the Sprinkle-on-Everything Parmesan.

2. Place the cashews in a small bowl and cover with boiling water. Soak for 1 hour, then drain. (Alternatively, soak the cashews in room-temperature water to cover for at least 6 hours or overnight, then drain.)

3. Preheat the oven to 375°F (190°C).

4. Bring a large pot of water to a boil over medium-high heat. Add the cauliflower florets and boil for 5 minutes. Drain and set aside.

5. In a high-speed blender, combine the cashews, almond milk, nutritional yeast, garlic, tahini, mustard, salt, onion powder, pepper, and paprika. Blend on high speed until the béchamel sauce is smooth, about 1 minute.

6. Melt 3 tablespoons of the vegan butter in a small saucepan over low heat. Add a splash of the béchamel sauce, then add the flour and whisk to combine. Increase the heat to medium and slowly pour in the remaining sauce while whisking. Bring to a low simmer while whisking until the sauce has thickened, about 5 minutes.

7. Pour one-third of the béchamel sauce into an 8 x 11-inch oval baking dish. Gently swirl the dish to evenly coat the bottom. Spread the cauliflower florets over the sauce and drizzle with the remaining béchamel sauce.

8. Melt the remaining 2 tablespoons vegan butter. In a small bowl, combine the Sprinkle-on-Everything Parmesan and bread crumbs. Drizzle with the vegan butter and stir to combine. Sprinkle the mixture evenly over the cauliflower. Bake until golden and bubbling, 25 to 35 minutes. Garnish with the parsley.

TIPS

1. The shape of the casserole dish does not matter. Be sure to choose a dish that holds the cauliflower snugly.

2. The béchamel sauce should be smooth, which is achieved by continuous whisking. If you find it clumpy, pour the sauce into your blender and blend until smooth.

DO AHEAD
The miso gravy can be made up
to 2 days in advance. Store in an
airtight container in the refrigerator.
When ready to use, warm in a small
saucepan. Whisk until smooth and
add a splash of broth or water to thin,
if desired.

Serves 4

Baked Potatoes with Mushrooms, Spinach, and Gravy

Vegan * Gluten-free * Grain-free * Nut-free * No Added Sugar * Refined Sugar-free

Baked potatoes are comfort food at its finest, especially when stuffed with mushrooms and spinach and drizzled with vegan gravy. This dish comes together effortlessly for a simple dinner that is wholesome and filling. Enjoy it as a main or side dish.

1. Make the Baked Potatoes: Preheat the oven to 425°F (220°C). Line a baking sheet with parchment paper.

2. Using a fork, poke a few holes in the potatoes. Brush the potatoes with the avocado oil and place on the prepared baking sheet. Sprinkle with salt and pepper. Bake for 40 to 50 minutes, until a fork inserted into the centre of the potato easily slides through with no resistance.

3. Meanwhile, Make the Miso Gravy: In a small saucepan, stir together the miso, tamari, and onion powder to make a paste. Add the vegan butter and ½ cup of the vegetable broth and whisk over medium-high heat until smooth, 5 minutes. Pour in ½ cup more broth, then add the nutritional yeast and arrowroot powder, and again whisk until smooth. Add the remaining ½ cup broth, reduce the heat to medium, and simmer until thickened and smooth, about 10 minutes. Cover with a lid and keep warm until ready to use. Whisk again to smoothen before serving.

4. Make the Mushroom Spinach Topping: In a medium skillet, heat the avocado oil over medium heat. Add the garlic, mushrooms, and salt and cook, stirring occasionally, until the mushrooms have softened and browned, 10 to 12 minutes.

5. In a small bowl, whisk together the almond butter and balsamic vinegar. (If it is more like a paste, add a splash of water to thin for drizzle consistency.) Pour it over the mushrooms and cook for 2 to 3 more minutes, until the liquid has absorbed into the medley a little. Add the baby spinach and drizzle with the lemon juice. Cook until the spinach is wilted, 2 to 3 minutes.

6. Slice the baked potatoes open lengthwise and top with the mushroom and spinach mixture. Pour the miso gravy overtop. Sprinkle with sesame seeds, if desired.

BAKED POTATOES

4 russet potatoes

1 tablespoon avocado oil

Pinch each of fine sea salt and freshly ground black pepper

MISO GRAVY

1 tablespoon white miso

1 tablespoon gluten-free tamari

½ teaspoon onion powder

2 tablespoons vegan butter

1½ cups vegetable broth, divided

2 tablespoons nutritional yeast

2 tablespoons arrowroot powder

MUSHROOM SPINACH TOPPING

1 tablespoon avocado oil

2 cloves garlic, finely chopped

8 ounces (225 g) cremini mushrooms, sliced

Pinch of fine sea salt

1 tablespoon natural almond butter

1 tablespoon balsamic vinegar

2½ cups baby spinach

1 tablespoon lemon juice

Sesame seeds, for sprinkling (optional)

STORAGE

Store the topped baked potatoes and miso gravy in separate airtight containers in the refrigerator for up to 2 days.

Darling Desserts

If you ask me, a meal is just not complete without a little something sweet at the end. These darling desserts will hit the spot at any occasion, from individually portioned desserts like Kryptonite Chocolate Lava Cakes (page 278) and Classic Crème Brûlée (page 293) to tarts so gorgeous they will drop jaws.

This chapter contains all types of delightful plant-based desserts, whether you prefer fruity, chocolatey, or creamy. It includes quick and easy recipes for when your sweet tooth strikes (my Raspberry Clafoutis, page 285, is great for this!). But whether quick and simple or a little more involved, the recipes in this chapter promise to be deliciously decadent no matter the time spent.

Serves 12 ✳ Requires: soak time + cool time + chill time

Lemon Tart

Vegan ✳ Gluten-free ✳ Soy-free ✳ Refined Sugar-free

This luscious lemon tart is a show-stopping dessert that is perfect to serve for celebrations. Made with a silky lemon curd filling that is bright, citrusy, creamy, and sweet, this tart melts in your mouth, yet is firm enough to hold its shape when sliced. The crust pairs perfectly with its oat, almond, and walnut base. It is lightly baked until golden for a nutty flavour and crispy texture.

Lemon tart was served at our wedding in the Dordogne region of France. Even though all the food was a smashing success, it's the lemon tart that my mum always raves about. I created this recipe in tribute to that tart, so that I can serve it to my mum for years to come.

1. Place the cashews in a small bowl and cover with boiling water. Soak for 1 hour, then drain. (Alternatively, soak the cashews in room-temperature water to cover for at least 6 hours or overnight, then drain.)

2. Make the Pastry Crust: Preheat the oven to 350°F (180°C).

3. In a food processor, pulse the oats until they reach a flour-like consistency. Transfer the oat flour to a small bowl.

4. Add the walnuts to the food processor and pulse into a fine meal. Add the oat flour, almond flour, coconut oil, maple syrup, and salt. Pulse until well combined, 15 to 30 seconds.

5. Transfer the dough to a 9-inch round tart pan with removable bottom and press it evenly into the bottom and up the sides. Using a fork, poke 10 to 12 holes in the base of the dough. (This will stop the base from lifting as it cooks. There's no need to use pie weights with this crust.) Place on a baking sheet and blind-bake until golden brown, about 10 minutes. Let the crust cool on a wire rack for at least 20 minutes.

1 cup raw cashews

CRUST

1 cup (133 g) gluten-free old-fashioned
    rolled oats
½ cup (60 g) raw walnuts
½ cup (50 g) almond flour
¼ cup (50 g) coconut oil, melted
2 tablespoons pure maple syrup
¼ teaspoon fine sea salt

LEMON FILLING

1 can (14 ounces/400 mL) full-fat
    coconut milk
Zest of 1 lemon
½ cup lemon juice
¼ cup pure maple syrup
⅛ to ¼ teaspoon ground turmeric,
    for colouring
Pinch of fine sea salt
1 teaspoon agar agar

GARNISHES (OPTIONAL)

1 lemon, thinly sliced
¼ cup fresh raspberries
1 tablespoon unsweetened coconut flakes

Recipe continues

Store the tart in the pan with the top covered with plastic wrap, or in a round airtight container, in the refrigerator for up to 1 week.

TIPS

1. I find that for covering the tart, plastic wrap works better than reusable wrap. Plastic wrap is easier to peel away from the filling without sticking.

2. If your filling cracks when it sets, it could be that you transferred the tart to the refrigerator before the filling had completely cooled to room temperature. Alternatively, it's possible that the filling was overheated and got a bit too thick. The ideal consistency is a pourable custard. However, cracks are totally okay. It tastes just the same with or without cracks!

3. See Pantry Staples (page 17) for information about agar agar powder and where to buy.

DO AHEAD

The crust can be assembled 1 day in advance. Press the dough into the tart pan, cover with plastic wrap, and refrigerate for up to 24 hours. Bring to room temperature and bake as directed.

6. Meanwhile, Make the Lemon Filling: In a high-speed blender, combine the drained cashews, coconut milk, lemon zest, lemon juice, maple syrup, ⅛ teaspoon of the turmeric, and salt. Blend on medium-high speed until smooth and combined. Add up to ⅛ teaspoon more turmeric for colouring, if desired. (Note that the colour will deepen when the filling is heated.) Add the agar agar and blend on low speed until combined, 15 to 20 seconds.

7. Pour the filling into a medium saucepan. Over medium heat, stir often with a spatula until the mixture has thickened to a pourable custard consistency (just before it reaches boiling) and there is a bit of resistance, 7 to 10 minutes. Working quickly, pour the filling into the blind-baked tart shell. It will begin to thicken immediately. If the filling is uneven, gently jostle the tart back and fork on the counter to smooth the top. Pop any air bubbles with a toothpick.

8. Let the tart cool completely in the pan on a wire rack at room temperature. Then cover with plastic wrap (it's okay if it touches the filling) and chill in the refrigerator for at least 3 hours, preferably overnight. To serve, gently remove the sides of the pan. If desired, garnish the tart with thinly sliced lemon rounds, fresh raspberries, and a sprinkle of coconut flakes.

Serves 6 ✳ Requires: chill time

Pear Tarte Tatin

Vegan ✳ Nut-free ✳ Soy-free

This rustic tarte Tatin is such an impressive dessert, with pears cooked in a homemade caramel sauce resting atop a sweet, golden pastry crust. A tarte Tatin is made similar to an upside-down cake, starting with the caramel in a cast-iron pan, then adding the fruits and pastry crust. Once baked, it is flipped over to expose the beautifully caramelized pears in all their glory. This recipe is a bit more involved than other desserts, but well worth the effort! Expect sweet and buttery caramel flavour, supple pears, and a crispy pastry base ready for devouring.

1. Prepare the Pastry Crust: In a food processor, combine the flour, cane sugar, and salt. Cut the vegan butter into small chunks and add to the bowl. Pulse a few times to lightly mix the ingredients, then add the water and pulse a few times more to form a crumbly dough. (You can also combine all the ingredients in a large bowl, except the water, and massage with your hands to form a crumbly dough. Add the water and massage to form a shaggy dough). Do not over-knead the dough (see Tip). Transfer the dough to a work surface. Using your hands, form the dough into a ball.

2. Invert a 9-inch cast-iron skillet onto a piece of parchment paper and trace around the skillet with a pencil. Flip the parchment over and lightly sprinkle it with flour. Using a rolling pin, roll out the dough to fit the circle. (It's okay if it's not a perfect circle.) Lightly sprinkle the dough with flour if the rolling pin is sticking to it. (An 8-inch or 10-inch cast-iron skillet as works well. Roll out the dough to the size of your skillet.)

3. Slide the parchment onto a large plate, cover the dough with reusable wrap or another sheet of parchment paper, and refrigerate for 1 hour.

4. Make the Topping: Preheat the oven to 375°F (190°C). Place a baking sheet on the bottom rack to catch any filling that bubbles over the skillet.

PASTRY CRUST

1 cup (130 g) all-purpose flour

¼ cup (54 g) organic cane sugar

Pinch of fine sea salt

½ cup (4 ounces/115 g) vegan butter, cold (see Tip)

1 tablespoon cold water

TOPPING

4 ripe small Bartlett pears

1 tablespoon lemon juice

¼ teaspoon cinnamon

Pinch of ground nutmeg

½ cup (107 g) granulated sugar (see Tip)

3 tablespoons vegan butter

Vegan vanilla ice cream, for serving

STORAGE

Store the tart, covered with a pie cover or plastic wrap, at room temperature for up to 2 days.

DO AHEAD

The pastry dough can be prepared up to 2 days in advance. Cover with reusable wrap and store in the refrigerator until ready to use.

Recipe continues

1. The pastry dough can be prepared by hand or in a food processor. I like to use the food processor to ensure the ingredients are evenly distributed. Do not over-knead the dough. Pulse or massage the ingredients together until just combined, and then form together with your hands.

2. Different vegan butters have different water contents. If your pastry dough is too crumbly as you roll, it is too dry. Bring the dough back together, rinse your hands with water, and lightly flick over the dough to add a few water droplets. Work the water in gently and roll again. If the dough gets too warm, cover with reusable wrap and transfer it to the refrigerator to let it chill. Once chilled, it should roll more easily.

3. I recommend using a softer vegan butter for this recipe, such as Earth Balance, for a more flexible pastry dough. See Pantry Staples (page 17) for more information about this vegan butter and other recommendations for successful vegan baking.

4. Granulated sugar is not always vegan. To make your own granulated sugar, add ½ cup organic cane sugar to a high-speed blender and pulse a few times. Measure out ½ cup of the fine sugar for this recipe and keep the rest for another use. (You should only have a little extra.)

5. Choose pears that are small and with a stubby tip for easier arranging. If the tips are too long, it might be difficult to arrange snugly in a perfect fan. You can always trim the tips slightly to fit better.

5. Peel the pears and cut in half lengthwise. Scoop out the core. Transfer the pear halves to a medium bowl. Drizzle with the lemon juice and sprinkle with the cinnamon and nutmeg. Using your hands, gently turn the pears to evenly coat them with the lemon juice and spices, and let sit for at least 10 minutes at room temperature. Leave one pear half intact, and cut the remaining halves into 2 wedges each.

6. Spread the granulated sugar in the cast-iron skillet and place over medium heat. When the sugar starts to melt (about 6 to 8 minutes), reduce the heat to low. Cook the sugar, gently nudging any dry bits into the melted bits with a spatula, until the sugar is completely melted and turns a deep golden brown, about 4 more minutes. (Sugar is vulnerable to burning quickly, so keep a close watch. It should not smoke or smell burnt. If it does, discard and start over.) Add the vegan butter and whisk well to combine. Remove from the heat.

7. Remove the pastry dough from the refrigerator. Let it sit at room temperature for a few minutes. It will be easier to work with.

8. Working quickly and carefully, as the caramel is extremely hot, arrange the pear slices in the skillet: Start by placing the single pear half cut side up in the centre of the pan. Snugly fan the pear wedges around the skillet like a flower, with the narrow tip of the pears facing the centre. Make sure the pears are snug in the skillet, as they will shrink while they cook.

9. Peel the parchment paper from the pastry dough and drape the pastry over the skillet. If needed, use a fork to gently tuck the edges of the dough inside the edge of the skillet to fit flush inside. Transfer the skillet to the oven and reduce the temperature to 350°F (180°C). Bake until the crust is golden, 30 to 40 minutes.

10. Remove the skillet from the oven and let it sit for 5 minutes. Place a large rimmed platter over the skillet. Using oven mitts, hold the skillet and platter together tightly and invert, allowing the tart to release and settle onto the platter. Let stand for 15 seconds, then lift off the skillet. If any of the pears have fallen out of place, simply rearrange them. Use a spatula to gather any liquid from the pan and drizzle it over the tart. (Wash the cast-iron skillet immediately so that the caramel doesn't stick to the pan.) Let the tart cool to room temperature. Slice and serve with your favourite vegan vanilla ice cream.

Sweet Cherry Frangipane Tart

Vegan ✳ Soy-free

This cherry frangipane tart is sweet, fruity, and nutty, with its crispy, buttery tart crust and rich almond filling. The combination of flaky pastry and velvety smooth filling is a pleasurable marriage. This is an indulgent dessert to impress, and certainly one of my favourites in this cookbook. I shared this tart with my family, and my then one-year-old niece, Charlie, absolutely loved it, every mouthful accompanied with a big "Mmm!" and a sweet cheeky grin. I truly cherish the memory.

1. Prepare the Pastry Crust: In a food processor, combine the all-purpose flour, cane sugar, and salt. Cut the vegan butter into small chunks and add to the bowl. Pulse a few times to lightly mix the ingredients. Add the water and vanilla and pulse a few more times to form a crumbly dough. (You can also combine all the ingredients in a large bowl, except the water, and massage with your hands to form a crumbly dough. Add the water and massage to form a shaggy dough.) Do not over-knead the dough (see Tip).

2. Transfer the dough to a work surface. Using your hands, form the dough into a ball. Lightly dust the work surface with flour. Using a rolling pin, roll out the dough into a circle ⅛ inch thick and 12 inches wide. Lightly sprinkle the dough with flour if the rolling pin is sticking to it.

3. Roll the dough around the rolling pin. Gently lift the dough and unroll over an 11-inch round tart pan with removable bottom. Press the dough into the bottom and up the sides of the pan. For a clean edge, use a knife to trim off excess dough. Patch any cracks with the excess dough. Refrigerate the tart shell for 1 hour.

4. Preheat the oven to 425°F (220°C).

5. Poke 10 to 12 holes in the base of the crust using a fork. (This will stop the base from lifting as it cooks. There's no need to use pie weights with this crust.) Place on a baking sheet and blind-bake the tart shell until lightly golden, about 15 minutes. Let cool. Reduce the oven temperature to 375°F (190°C).

PASTRY CRUST

2 cups (260 g) all-purpose flour

⅓ cup (72 g) organic cane sugar

¼ teaspoon sea salt

½ cup (4 ounces/115 g) vegan butter, cold (see Tip)

¼ cup cold water

1 teaspoon pure vanilla extract

FILLING

1¼ cups (125 g) almond flour

¼ cup (32 g) all-purpose flour

½ cup (4 ounces/115 g) vegan butter, soft (see Tip)

½ cup pure maple syrup

⅓ cup (90 g) plain coconut yogurt

1 tablespoon arrowroot powder

1 teaspoon baking powder

1 teaspoon pure vanilla extract

½ teaspoon pure almond extract

Zest of 1 lemon

1½ cups (300 g) cherries, pitted and halved

⅓ cup (30 g) slivered almonds

Organic icing sugar, for dusting (optional)

Recipe continues

Store the tart in the pan, covered with plastic wrap, or in a round airtight container, in the refrigerator for up to 5 days.

DO AHEAD
The pastry dough can be prepared up to 2 days in advance. Cover with reusable wrap and store in the refrigerator until ready to use.

6. Make the Filling: In a medium bowl, combine the almond flour, all-purpose flour, vegan butter, maple syrup, coconut yogurt, arrowroot powder, baking powder, vanilla extract, almond extract, and lemon zest. Stir together until smooth and creamy.

7. Pour the filling into the blind-baked tart shell and smooth the top with a spatula. Press the cherries into the batter, cut side up, to create a spiral pattern. Sprinkle with slivered almonds.

8. Bake the tart until the top is lightly golden and the filling is semi-firm to the touch, about 30 minutes. Let the tart cool in the pan on a wire rack for 15 minutes before removing the sides of the pan. Serve warm or at room temperature. Dust with icing sugar before serving, if desired.

TIPS

1. The pastry dough can be prepared by hand or in a food processor. I like to use the food processor to ensure the ingredients are evenly distributed. Do not over-knead the dough. Pulse or massage the ingredients together until just combined, and then form together with your hands.

2. Different vegan butters have different water contents. If your pastry is too crumbly as you roll, it's too dry. Bring the dough back together, rinse your hands with water, and lightly flick over the dough to add a few water droplets. Work the water in gently and roll again. If the dough gets too warm, transfer to the refrigerator to let it chill. Once chilled, it should roll more easily.

3. I recommend using a softer vegan butter for this recipe, such as Earth Balance, for a more flexible pastry dough. See Pantry Staples (page 17) for more information about this vegan butter and other recommendations for successful vegan baking.

4. It's helpful to roll out the pastry dough on parchment paper so it doesn't stick to the countertop.

French Apple Tart

Vegan * Nut-free * Soy-free

This classic apple tart is one that I think of as so traditionally French. Whether you are a master baker or an everyday home cook, everyone should know how to make this signature recipe. Think of this apple tart as the French version of apple pie—a flaky, buttery short crust as the base, a sweet-tart filling of stewed apples, and an exposed top (instead of closed) with a delicate fan of apple slices. Serve as is or with a dollop of Chantilly (page 298) or vegan vanilla ice cream.

1. Prepare the Pastry Crust: In a food processor, combine the flour, cane sugar, and salt. Cut the vegan butter into cubes and add to the bowl. Pulse a few times to lightly mix the ingredients. Add 2 tablespoons of the water and pulse a few more times to form a crumbly dough. Pinch some dough together; if it sticks together when pinched then it's ready for the next step. If the dough is too crumbly, add up to 1 tablespoon more water and pulse again. (You can also combine all the ingredients in a large bowl, except the water, and massage with your hands to form a crumbly dough. Add the water and massage to form a shaggy dough.) Do not over-knead the dough (see Tip).

2. Transfer the dough to a work surface. Using your hands, form the dough into a disc. Cover with reusable wrap and chill in the refrigerator for 1 hour.

3. Meanwhile, preheat the oven to 425°F (220°C).

4. Make the Apple Filling: Peel and core the apples and cut into small chunks. Toss the apples into a medium saucepan. Add the coconut sugar, water, lemon juice, cinnamon, and salt. Stir together to combine and bring to a simmer over medium heat. Cover with a lid and cook until the apples are fork-tender, 20 to 30 minutes. Transfer to a high-speed blender and blend on medium speed until smooth, about 1 minute. Taste, and add more coconut sugar if desired for sweetness; blend again until smooth.

PASTRY CRUST

1½ cups (195 g) all-purpose flour

¼ cup (54 g) organic cane sugar

¼ teaspoon fine sea salt

½ cup (4 ounces/115 g) vegan butter, cold
    (see Tip)

2 to 3 tablespoons cold water

APPLE FILLING

4 small Golden Delicious apples

¼ cup (35 g) coconut sugar,
    more if needed

3 tablespoons water

1 tablespoon lemon juice

1 teaspoon cinnamon

Pinch of fine sea salt

TOPPING

2 to 3 small Golden Delicious apples

2 tablespoons vegan butter, cold, cubed

1 to 2 teaspoons organic cane sugar

2 tablespoons apricot jam

1 teaspoon water

Recipe continues

Store the apple tart, covered with a glass pie cover or plastic wrap, at room temperature for up to 3 days.

TIPS

1. The pastry dough can be prepared by hand or in a food processor. I like to use the food processor to ensure the ingredients are evenly distributed. Do not over-knead the dough. Pulse or massage the ingredients together until just combined, and then form together with your hands.

2. Different vegan butters have different water contents. If your crust is too crumbly as you roll, it's too dry. Bring the dough back together, rinse your hands with water, and lightly flick over the dough to add a few water droplets. Work the water in gently and roll again. If the dough gets too warm, transfer to the refrigerator to let it chill. Once chilled, it should roll more easily.

3. I recommend using a softer vegan butter for this recipe, such as Earth Balance, for a more flexible pastry dough. See Pantry Staples (page 17) for more information about this vegan butter and other recommendations for successful vegan baking.

4. It's helpful to roll out the pastry dough on parchment paper so it doesn't stick to the countertop.

5. Lightly dust a work surface with flour. Using a rolling pin, roll out the dough into a circle 10 inches wide. Lightly sprinkle the dough with flour if the rolling pin is sticking to it.

6. Roll the dough around the rolling pin. Gently lift the dough and unroll over a 9-inch tart pan with removable bottom. Press the dough into the bottom and up the sides of the pan. For a clean edge, use a knife to trim off excess dough. Patch any cracks with the excess dough. Poke a few holes in the base of the pie using a fork. (This will stop the base from lifting as it cooks. There's no need to use pie weights with this crust.) Blind-bake until lightly golden, about 15 minutes. Let the crust cool completely on a wire rack. Reduce the oven temperature to 350°F (180°C).

7. Prepare the Topping and Assemble: Peel and core the apples and thinly slice ¼ inch thick.

8. Pour the Apple Filling into the tart shell and smooth the top with a spatula. Arrange the apple slices on top of the filling, fanning them out around the outer edge of the tart to make a complete circle. (It is helpful to use apple slices of even length.) Fill the inner circle with broken and smaller apple slices to level the tart, then fan out another smaller circle of apple slices in the opposite direction.

9. Evenly distribute the cubed vegan butter over the tart. Lightly sprinkle with the cane sugar. Bake until golden brown and the apples are soft but not mushy, 30 to 40 minutes. Let cool slightly on a wire rack.

10. In a small bowl, stir together the apricot jam and water. Microwave for a few seconds to melt, then whisk well. (Alternatively, stir together in a small saucepan over medium heat until melted.) Brush the tart with the jam to create a nice shine. Let the tart cool completely before removing the sides and slicing.

DO AHEAD

The pastry dough can be prepared up to 2 days in advance. Cover with reusable wrap and store in the refrigerator until ready to use.

Level-Up Chocolate Mousse Tart

Vegan ✳ Gluten-free

This chocolate mousse tart is a level up from my gorgeous Mousse au Chocolat. As we know, mousse au chocolat is divine on its own. It is rich, decadent, and oh so chocolatey. But slathering it into a salty-sweet chocolate almond crust takes it to the next level for the royal flush of desserts. Contrary to how tasty and eye-catching this dessert is, it is incredibly easy to prepare. The mousse can be made well in advance, so all that's required is a ten-minute baked crust to create an impressive dessert tart (see Tip).

1. Make the Mousse au Chocolat. Cover with a kitchen towel and store in the refrigerator until ready to use.

2. Make the Crust: Preheat the oven to 350°F (180°C).

3. In a food processor, pulse the oats until they reach a flour-like consistency. Add the almond flour, cocoa powder, and salt and pulse a few times to mix. Pour in the melted coconut oil and maple syrup and pulse until a crumbly dough forms.

4. Tip the dough into a 9-inch tart pan with removable bottom. Press the dough into the bottom and up the sides of the pan. Using a fork, poke 10 to 12 holes in the base. (This will stop the pie base from lifting as it cooks. There's no need to use pie weights with this crust.) Blind-bake until lightly brown, 10 to 12 minutes. Let cool completely on a wire rack, at least 20 minutes.

5. Scoop the Mousse au Chocolat into the cooled tart shell and spread evenly with the back of a spoon. Optional to reserve ¼ cup of the mousse du chocolate for piping. Chill in the refrigerator for at least 2 hours or overnight. (If storing overnight, cover gently with plastic wrap; it's okay if it touches the filling.) Before serving, decorate the tart with raspberries and pomegranate seeds and pipe the reserved Mousse au Chocolat using a star tip, if desired.

TIP

I find that for covering the tart, plastic wrap works better than reusable wrap. Plastic wrap is easier to peel away from the filling without sticking.

1 batch Mousse au Chocolat (page 281)

CRUST

1 cup (133 g) gluten-free old-fashioned rolled oats

1 cup (100 g) almond flour

2 tablespoons cocoa powder

½ teaspoon fine sea salt

¼ cup (48 g) coconut oil, melted

2 tablespoons pure maple syrup

TOPPINGS (OPTIONAL)

1 cup raspberries

¼ cup pomegranate seeds

STORAGE

Store the tart in a round airtight container or cake tin in the refrigerator for up to 1 week or in the freezer for up to 2 months. If frozen, thaw for 30 to 40 minutes before serving for easier slicing and optimal taste.

DO AHEAD

1. The Mousse au Chocolat can be made up to 1 week in advance. Store in an airtight container in the refrigerator.

2. The crust can be assembled 1 day in advance. Press the dough into the tart pan, cover with plastic wrap, and refrigerate for up to 24 hours. Bring to room temperature and bake as directed.

Makes 4

Kryptonite Chocolate Lava Cakes

Vegan ✳ Soy-free

½ cup unsweetened almond milk

½ teaspoon apple cider vinegar

½ cup (65 g) all-purpose flour

½ cup (45 g) cocoa powder,
　　more for the ramekins

½ cup (50 g) organic icing sugar,
　　more for dusting

½ cup (92 g) dairy-free semi-sweet
　　chocolate chips

½ cup (4 ounces/115 g) vegan butter,
　　cut into chunks, more for the ramekins

1 teaspoon pure vanilla extract

FOR SERVING (OPTIONAL)

½ cup fresh raspberries

Vegan vanilla ice cream

TIPS

1. This recipe can easily be halved for the perfect date-night dessert for two.

2. Instead of ramekins, you can use 6 cups of a muffin tin. Make sure to grease the tin very well. Reduce the bake time to 10 to 12 minutes. Flip onto a baking sheet and carefully transfer to plates.

3. These lava cakes are deliciously decadent served on their own. They are *extra* decadent served with a scoop of vegan vanilla ice cream or Chantilly (page 298). They are also delicious served with fresh raspberries.

This popular French dessert is a chocolate lover's kryptonite! It is gorgeously rich and indulgent. Expect a flawless marriage of chocolate cake and soufflé with its cakey exterior and a liquid chocolate centre. It is mesmerizing to watch the hot chocolate spill like lava as you cut the cake open. I love to make these molten lava cakes when we are craving a chocolate fix. In addition, it is one of the easiest desserts to make. It is quick and straightforward, and its individual cups make it the perfect size.

1. Preheat the oven to 350°F (180°C). Butter four 4-ounce ramekins. Lightly sprinkle the bottom and sides with cocoa powder. Tap out the excess cocoa powder. Line a baking sheet with parchment paper and set the ramekins on top.

2. In a small bowl, whisk together the almond milk and apple cider vinegar. This is your buttermilk. Set aside.

3. Into a separate small bowl, sift the flour, cocoa powder, and icing sugar. Set aside.

4. In a medium saucepan, bring 2 inches of water to a low simmer over low heat. Place a medium heatproof bowl on top of the pot, making sure the bottom of the bowl is not touching the water. Add the chocolate chips and vegan butter and melt, stirring often, until completely smooth. Remove from the heat. (Alternatively, you can melt the chocolate in the microwave in 30-second intervals.) Pour in the vanilla and stir to combine.

5. Sprinkle the dry ingredients over the melted chocolate, then add the buttermilk and whisk well until smooth and glossy. Divide the batter equally among the prepared ramekins.

6. Bake until the edges look firm and cakey, but the centres look slightly soft and batter-like, 12 to 14 minutes. Let the cakes cool for 1 minute. Working one at a time, place a dessert plate over a ramekin. Using oven mitts, hold the ramekin and plate together tightly and invert. Let sit for 30 seconds, then carefully remove the hot ramekin. Sprinkle the cakes with icing sugar. Garnish the plate with a few fresh raspberries and a scoop of vegan vanilla ice cream, if desired. Serve immediately.

Serves 6 to 8 * Requires: chill time

Mousse au Chocolat

Vegan * Gluten-free * Grain-free * Oil-free Option * Raw/No-bake

This chocolate mousse is thick, rich, and velvety. The recipe uses silken tofu, which is a stellar ingredient in desserts as it gives a creamy and luscious texture. Its mild flavour also allows for other ingredients to shine—in this recipe, chocolate! This is one of my husband, Mitch's, all-time favourite desserts and one that convinced him, in those early transition days, that we could still enjoy our favourite recipes on a plant-based diet.

1. In a small saucepan, bring 2 inches of water to a low simmer over low heat. Place a small heatproof glass bowl on top of the pot, making sure the bottom of the bowl is not touching the water. Add the dark chocolate and coconut oil and melt the chocolate, stirring often, until completely smooth. Keep over low heat until ready to use. (Alternatively, you can melt the chocolate in the microwave in 30-second intervals. Optional to reserve a chunk of the chocolate and cut it into 1 to 2 tablespoons of fine shavings for garnish.)
2. Transfer the silken tofu to a nut milk bag (or a thin kitchen towel, gathering the corners to form a small sack). Squeeze the bag with your hands to remove most of the water. (You should not have to squeeze too hard to release the water. Once it becomes difficult to squeeze, you can stop.)
3. Transfer the squeezed tofu to a food processor. Add the maple syrup, cocoa powder, vanilla extract, salt, and the melted chocolate. Pour in 4 tablespoons of the almond milk and blend together until smooth. Add more almond milk, a little at a time, if the consistency is too thick. It should be puddingy. It will thicken slightly as it chills.
4. Scoop the mousse into a medium bowl and cover with reusable wrap. Chill in the refrigerator for at least 2 hours. To serve, scoop into small bowls or glass cups and sprinkle with flaky sea salt and reserved chocolate shavings, if desired.

OIL-FREE

Omit the coconut oil when melting the chocolate. The mousse will not be quite as silky smooth, but it will still be near perfect!

2 bars (7 ounces/200 g each), 70% dark chocolate, broken into chunks

1 teaspoon coconut oil

2 blocks (12 ounces/340 g each) silken tofu

¼ cup + 2 tablespoons pure maple syrup

¼ cup cocoa powder

2 teaspoons pure vanilla extract

½ teaspoon fine sea salt

4 to 6 tablespoons unsweetened almond milk, more as needed

Flaky sea salt, for sprinkling

DO AHEAD

The chocolate mousse can be made up to 1 week in advance. Store in the refrigerator in an airtight container.

TIPS

1. Squeezing the tofu to remove excess water will result in a thicker mousse. You might have to squeeze the tofu in two batches, especially if using a kitchen towel.
2. You can make this mousse in a high-speed blender instead of a food processor. It might require more almond milk for blending. Use the tamper while blending on medium speed for the best result. If you do not have a tamper, stop the blender from time to time and stir with a wooden spoon to help the blending process.

Makes about 22 truffles * Requires: chill time

Chocolate Peanut Butter Truffles

Vegan * Gluten-free * Soy-free * Raw/No-bake

It still amazes me how gorgeously decadent and delicious these chocolate peanut butter truffles are, when the ingredients are so simple and wholesome. This is a truffle that I feel good about indulging in. Although they may look fancy, it is simple to achieve that regal chocolate-box look with a few candied sprinkles or some melted chocolate to drizzle.

1. In a food processor, pulse the oats until they reach a flour-like consistency. Add the dates and pulse into smaller pieces. Then add the peanut butter, maple syrup, cinnamon, and salt. Pulse to a smooth and doughy consistency.

2. Line a large cutting board or baking sheet with parchment paper. Spoon out about 22 even portions of the dough and roll each one between your hands into 1½-inch balls. Place the balls on the prepared baking sheet. Place in the refrigerator for 30 minutes or in the freezer for 15 minutes, until cold and firm.

3. In a small saucepan, bring 2 inches of water to a low simmer over low heat. Place a small heatproof glass bowl on top of the pot, making sure the bottom of the bowl is not touching the water. Add the chocolate chunks and coconut oil and melt, stirring often, until completely smooth. (Alternatively, you can melt the chocolate in the microwave in 30-second intervals.)

4. Remove the truffles from the refrigerator (or freezer) and roll them, one at a time, in the melted chocolate, using a spoon to manoeuvre the ball to coat it entirely in chocolate, then return to the baking sheet. While the chocolate is still wet, sprinkle the top of the truffle with candied sprinkles (if using). If the melted chocolate starts to stiffen, reheat it. Reserve remaining melted chocolate for drizzling, if desired.

5. Place the truffles in the refrigerator for 10 minutes or in the freezer for 5 minutes, until the chocolate has fully hardened.

6. If drizzling with chocolate, reheat the remaining melted chocolate. Spoon and drizzle the chocolate over the truffles in a zigzag pattern. Place the truffles back in the refrigerator for 10 minutes or in the freezer for 5 minutes to harden.

½ cup gluten-free old-fashioned rolled oats

⅔ cup tightly packed Medjool dates (about 12 dates), pitted

1 cup natural peanut butter

¼ cup pure maple syrup

1½ teaspoons cinnamon

½ teaspoon fine sea salt

1 bar (8 ounces/225 g) dairy-free semi-sweet chocolate, cut into chunks

2 teaspoons coconut oil

1 to 2 tablespoons candied sprinkles (optional)

STORAGE

Store the truffles in an airtight container in the refrigerator for up to 10 days or in the freezer for up to 2 months. If frozen, thaw for 20 minutes before serving.

Serves 6

Raspberry Clafoutis

Vegan * Gluten-free Option * Refined Sugar-free

These clafoutis are a lifesaver for when you need a last-minute dessert. The batter blends quickly and bakes effortlessly for a French-inspired dessert ready in under forty minutes. The flavours are creamy and custardy, lightly sweet and fruity. In addition, for the little effort required, it is an astonishingly beautiful dessert to look at! You can count on this back-pocket dessert recipe.

1. Preheat the oven to 350°F (180°C). Lightly grease a 7½ x 2-inch round baking dish (such as a brie baking dish) or a 6- or 7-inch pie plate with coconut oil.

2. In a high-speed blender, combine the silken tofu, flour, arrowroot powder, almond milk, maple syrup, coconut oil, lemon zest, vanilla, almond extract (if using), and salt. Blend until smooth and creamy, stopping to scrape down the sides if needed.

3. Scatter ½ cup of the raspberries in the baking dish. Pour the creamy batter over the raspberries to fill the baking dish. Decorate the top of the batter with the remaining ½ cup raspberries.

4. Bake until beautifully puffed and golden, about 35 minutes. Let cool slightly, about 10 minutes. Dust with icing sugar, if desired, and serve warm.

1 block (12 ounces/340 g) silken tofu

1 cup (130 g) all-purpose flour

1 tablespoon arrowroot powder

½ cup unsweetened almond milk

⅓ cup pure maple syrup

1 tablespoon coconut oil, more for the pan

1 tablespoon lemon zest

1 teaspoon pure vanilla extract

½ teaspoon pure almond extract (optional)

¼ teaspoon fine sea salt

1 cup (340 g) fresh or frozen raspberries, divided

1 tablespoon organic icing sugar, for dusting (optional)

STORAGE

Store the clafoutis, covered with reusable wrap, in the refrigerator for up to 3 days.

TIP

Raspberries can be replaced with fruits of your choice. Traditionally, clafoutis are made with pitted cherries, but pear, apple, and plum, chopped into bite-size pieces, are also popular.

GLUTEN-FREE

Replace the all-purpose flour with rice flour or gluten-free baking flour.

Serves 6

Just Peachy Crumble

Vegan　✳　Gluten-free Option　✳　Soy-free

PEACH FILLING

2 pounds (900 g) ripe peaches
　　(about 9 medium), sliced

¼ cup organic cane sugar

1 tablespoon arrowroot powder

1 tablespoon lemon juice

1 teaspoon pure vanilla extract

½ teaspoon cinnamon

¼ teaspoon ground ginger

CRUMBLE TOPPING

¾ cup gluten-free old-fashioned rolled oats

½ cup all-purpose flour

¼ cup slivered almonds

½ cup dark brown sugar

¼ teaspoon cinnamon

¼ teaspoon fine sea salt

⅓ cup vegan butter or coconut oil, melted

Vegan vanilla ice cream or coconut yogurt,
　　for serving

STORAGE

Store the peach crumble in an airtight
container in the refrigerator for up to
5 days.

DO AHEAD

The crumble topping can be made up to
2 weeks in advance. Store in an airtight
container in the refrigerator. Bring to
room temperature before using.

This no-fail crumble is warm and cozy, with bubbling sweet peaches under a crisp oaty topping. Crumbles have been one of my favourite desserts since childhood. We were never deprived of a weekly "forgotten-fruit crumble"—a crumble made of all the fruits we hadn't eaten that week. They are easy to make, relatively quick, and healthy and luscious. This version's saucy stewed peaches and crispy crumble topping is a glorious combo to enjoy during summer weekends at the cottage with friends and family.

1. Preheat the oven to 375°F (190°C).

2. Prepare the Peach Filling: In a large bowl, combine the peaches, cane sugar, arrowroot powder, lemon juice, vanilla, cinnamon, and ginger. Stir together well to coat the peaches and let sit for 10 minutes, gently stirring occasionally to distribute the juices.

3. Prepare the Crumble Topping: In a medium bowl, combine the oats, flour, almonds, brown sugar, cinnamon, and salt. Pour in the melted vegan butter and stir to combine.

4. Scrape the peach filling and the juices into an 8-inch square baking dish. Sprinkle the crumble topping evenly over the filling. Bake until the crumble topping is golden and the peach filling is bubbling up the sides, 50 to 60 minutes. Let cool slightly. Serve warm or cold with your favourite vegan vanilla ice cream or coconut yogurt.

TIP

The riper your peaches, the sweeter and juicier your crumble will be. I like to use peaches that are slightly past their prime, with wrinkly skins. Don't throw them away—they make for a perfect peach crumble. Hence the name "forgotten-fruit crumble."

GLUTEN-FREE

Replace the all-purpose flour with gluten-free baking flour.

Winter Poached Pears with Spiced Syrup

Vegan ✳ Gluten-free ✳ Grain-free Option ✳ Nut-free Option ✳ Oil-free ✳ Soy-free ✳ One-pot

These poached pears are full of signature winter spice from cinnamon, ginger, cloves, and star anise. You will be surprised just how gorgeous a pot of pears boiled in sugar water becomes! Once the pears are soft and tender, the spiced liquid is boiled down to a luxurious syrup for pouring. I love to make this recipe during the holidays for a very simple dessert that is warming and sophisticated. Serve the pears with a dollop of coconut yogurt or vegan vanilla ice cream and my Maple Pecan Granola for a touch of crunch. They are also delicious served on top of my Creamy Chia Pudding (page 47).

1. Make the Maple Pecan Granola, if using.
2. In a large pot, combine the water, cane sugar, and agave. Bring to a simmer over high heat, stirring until the sugar and agave are melted and combined. Add the vanilla bean, cinnamon stick, star anise, clove, ginger, and salt.
3. Submerge the pears in the liquid and simmer, with the lid off, turning the pears occasionally until they are fork-tender, 15 to 20 minutes. Using a slotted spoon, transfer the pears to a plate.
4. Continue simmering the liquid over high heat. After 10 minutes, scoop out and discard the vanilla bean, cinnamon stick, star anise, clove, and ginger slices. Continue simmering until the liquid is syrupy and reduced by more than half, 20 to 30 minutes. (Lower the heat to medium as it starts to thicken after about 20 minutes of boiling.)
5. Place a small hand sifter over a small jug and pour the syrup into the jug, catching any small pieces of spices that may have broken off. Let the syrup cool slightly and thicken further, about 10 minutes.
6. Serve the poached pears with a dollop of Chantilly, coconut yogurt, or your favourite vegan vanilla ice cream. Drizzle lightly with the spiced syrup and sprinkle with Maple Pecan Granola for some crunch, if desired.

Maple Pecan Granola (page 44),
    for serving (optional)
6 cups water
½ cup organic cane sugar
6 tablespoons agave
1 vanilla bean, split
1 (3-inch) cinnamon stick
1 star anise
1 whole clove
1 (3-inch) piece fresh ginger, peeled
    and sliced
Pinch of fine sea salt
4 Bosc pears, peeled

Chantilly (page 298), plain coconut yogurt,
    or vegan vanilla ice cream,
    for serving

NUT-FREE AND GRAIN-FREE
Serve without the Maple Pecan Granola.

Serves 4 or 5 ✳ Requires: chill time

Blueberry Ginger Galette

Vegan ✳ Soy-free

Vegan or not, everyone loves a fruity galette. This one is bursting with juicy blueberries with a hint of ginger, surrounded by a sweet, rustic, crispy crust. Finish a summer BBQ or cottage weekend with a slice of this gorgeous galette. I love to serve it with a big dollop of vegan vanilla ice cream or Chantilly (page 298) on the side.

1. Make the Pastry Crust: In a food processor, combine the flour, cane sugar, salt, and cinnamon. Cut the vegan butter into small chunks and add to the bowl. Pulse a few times to lightly mix the ingredients. Add the water and pulse a few more times to form a crumbly dough. (You can also combine all the ingredients, except the water, in a large bowl, and massage with your hands to form a crumbly dough. Add the water and massage to form a shaggy dough). Do not over-knead the dough (see Tip).

2. Turn the dough out onto a work surface. Using your hands, knead the dough until smooth. Form into a disc, cover with reusable wrap, and chill in the refrigerator for at least 1 hour.

3. Prepare the Filling: Toss the blueberries into a medium bowl. Sprinkle with the cane sugar, arrowroot powder, ginger, and lime juice. Stir together to combine, cover, and store in the refrigerator until ready to use.

4. Preheat the oven to 375°F (190°C).

5. Cut a sheet of parchment paper to fit a baking sheet and lay it on a work surface. Lightly sprinkle the parchment with flour. Using a rolling pin, roll out the dough on the parchment into a 13-inch circle, ⅛ inch thick. Turn the parchment as you roll to create a more even circle, rolling from the centre of the disc outwards. It's okay if the edges are not perfect. It adds to the rustic look of the galette. Slide the parchment with the dough onto the baking sheet.

PASTRY CRUST

1½ cups (195 g) all-purpose flour

4 teaspoons organic cane sugar

½ teaspoon fine sea salt

¼ teaspoon cinnamon

½ cup (4 ounces/115 g) vegan butter, cold (see Tip)

¼ cup cold water

1 to 2 tablespoons unsweetened almond milk, for brushing

1 to 2 teaspoons demerara sugar or coarse sugar, for sprinkling

FILLING

3 cups fresh or frozen blueberries

2 tablespoons organic cane sugar

1 tablespoon arrowroot powder

1 tablespoon peeled and grated fresh ginger

1 tablespoon lime juice

Vegan vanilla ice cream or Chantilly (page 298), for serving (optional)

Recipe continues

Store the galette in an airtight container at room temperature for up to 3 days.

DO AHEAD

The pastry dough can be prepared up to 2 days in advance. Cover with reusable wrap and stash in the refrigerator until ready to use.

6. Scrape the prepared blueberries into the centre of the dough, leaving a 2-inch border. Fold the sides of the dough up and over the filling, overlapping slightly, making an edge of about 2 inches. Pinch the dough together as needed to seal any holes or cracks. Brush the dough lightly with almond milk and sprinkle with demerara sugar. Bake until the crust is golden brown and the filling is bubbling, about 40 minutes. Let slightly cool for at least 20 minutes. Serve warm or at room temperature with vegan vanilla ice cream or a dollop of Chantilly, if desired.

TIPS

1. The pastry dough can be prepared by hand or in a food processor. I like to use the food processor to ensure the ingredients are evenly distributed. Do not over-knead the dough. Pulse or massage the ingredients together until just combined, and then form together with your hands.

2. Different vegan butters have different water contents. If your crust is too crumbly as you roll, it's too dry. Bring the dough back together, rinse your hands with water, and lightly flick over the dough to add a few water droplets. Work the water in gently and roll again. If the dough gets too warm, transfer to the refrigerator to let it chill. Once chilled, it should roll more easily.

3. I recommend using a softer vegan butter for this recipe, such as Earth Balance, for a more flexible pastry dough. See Pantry Staples (page 17) for more information about this vegan butter and other recommendations for successful vegan baking.

4. It's helpful to roll out the pastry dough on parchment paper so it doesn't stick to the countertop.

Makes 3 or 4 ramekins ✳ Requires: cool time + chill time

Classic Crème Brûlée

Vegan ✳ Gluten-free ✳ Grain-free ✳ Oil-free ✳ Soy-free ✳ Raw/No-bake

I bet you never thought you could make a crème brûlée vegan! Well, my friends, this one is just as creamy and custardy as you remember, and still topped with a thin layer of that classic crackle caramelized sugar, which is music to the ears. This is a gorgeous sweet treat to serve at gatherings, as it's so impressive, simple to make, and can be made the day before. Be sure to torch the sugar just before serving for optimal crackle texture.

1. In a high-speed blender, combine the coconut milk, almond milk, lemon zest, maple syrup, arrowroot powder, vanilla, nutritional yeast, agar agar, salt, and turmeric (if using). Blend on medium-low speed until smooth and combined.

2. Pour the custard into a medium saucepan. Heat over medium-high heat, stirring often with a spatula, until the mixture has thickened slightly to a custard consistency (just before it reaches boiling) and there is a bit of resistance, 7 to 10 minutes.

3. Divide the custard evenly among three 6-ounce ramekins or four 4-ounce ramekins, filling them three-quarters full. Let cool completely, uncovered, at room temperature for 1½ to 2 hours. Cover each ramekin with plastic wrap and chill in the refrigerator for 3 to 4 hours or overnight.

4. When ready to serve, lightly sprinkle the tops with a thin layer of sugar. Using a kitchen torch, caramelize the sugar until it turns deep golden brown. (It is helpful to hold the torch far enough back so that the tip of the flame melts the sugar.) Serve immediately.

1 can (14 ounces/400 mL) full-fat coconut milk

⅓ cup unsweetened almond milk

Zest of 1 lemon

3 tablespoons pure maple syrup

2 tablespoons arrowroot powder

1 tablespoon pure vanilla extract

2 teaspoons nutritional yeast

¾ teaspoon agar agar

Pinch of fine sea salt

Pinch of ground turmeric, for colouring (optional)

2 to 3 tablespoons organic cane sugar

Recipe continues

DO AHEAD

The crème brûlée can be made up to 24 hours in advance. Keep refrigerated, covered with plastic wrap, until ready to serve. Sprinkle with sugar and brûlée the top just before serving.

TIPS

1. The crème brûlée must be completely cooled before refrigerating, as condensation can affect its texture. You can cool the crème brûlée uncovered in the refrigerator for a few hours, then cover in plastic wrap once you are certain it is completely cool.

2. For covering the crème brûlée, I prefer plastic wrap rather than reusable wrap because it does not stick to the custard if it touches. If using reusable wrap, ensure there is enough space so the wrap does not touch the custard.

3. A kitchen torch achieves the best crackly caramel topping, but if you do not have one, you can use the broiler. Place an oven rack in the highest position and set the oven to broil. Lightly sprinkle the top of each crème brûlée with a thin layer of sugar. Place on a baking sheet, transfer to the oven with the door ajar, and broil until the sugar is golden brown and bubbling, 3 to 5 minutes. (This may melt the crème brûlée's interior slightly. You can refrigerate for 30 to 45 minutes to firm up before serving.)

4. See Pantry Staples (page 17) for information about agar agar powder and where to buy.

Makes four 4-ounce ramekins * Requires: cool time + chill time

Crème Caramel

Vegan * Gluten-free * Grain-free * Oil-free * Soy-free

Similar to my Crème Brûlée (page 293), this recipe is sweet, creamy, custardy, and puddingy. It is all too easy to devour this delightful dessert. What sets this recipe apart from my Crème Brûlée is the thin layer of maple caramel sauce instead of a crunchy top. This recipe is simple to make and does not require any special gadgets.

1. Make the Caramel: In a small saucepan, combine the sugar, maple syrup, and apple cider vinegar. Whisk together over medium-high heat and bring the mixture just to a simmer. Reduce the heat to medium-low and let simmer until dark golden brown and slightly thickened, 2 to 3 minutes. Divide the caramel evenly into four 4-ounce ramekins, gently tilting the ramekins to spread the caramel evenly in the bottom. Let cool completely, about 15 minutes.

2. Make the Custard: In a high-speed blender, combine the coconut milk, almond milk, maple syrup, arrowroot powder, vanilla, nutritional yeast, agar agar, and salt. Blend on medium-low speed until smooth and combined.

3. Pour the custard into a medium saucepan. Heat over medium-high heat, stirring often with a spatula, until the mixture has thickened slightly to a custard consistency (just before it reaches boiling) and there is a bit of resistance, 7 to 10 minutes.

4. Divide the custard evenly among the ramekins. Let cool completely, uncovered, at room temperature for 1½ to 2 hours. Cover each ramekin with plastic wrap and chill in the refrigerator for at least 6 hours or overnight.

5. When ready to serve, run a sharp knife around the edge of each ramekin to loosen the custard. Invert each custard onto a small plate. Gently shake the ramekin to release the custard. Remove the ramekin, garnish with mint leaves, if desired, and serve.

DO AHEAD

This crème caramel can be made up to 24 hours in advance. Keep refrigerated, covered with plastic wrap, until ready to serve.

CARAMEL

3 tablespoons organic cane sugar

1 tablespoon pure maple syrup

¼ teaspoon apple cider vinegar

CUSTARD

1 can (14 ounces/400 mL) full-fat coconut milk

⅓ cup unsweetened almond milk

3 tablespoons pure maple syrup

2 tablespoons arrowroot powder

1 tablespoon pure vanilla extract

2 teaspoons nutritional yeast

¾ teaspoon agar agar

Pinch of fine sea salt

Fresh mint leaves, for garnish (optional)

TIPS

1. The crème caramel must be completely cooled before refrigerating, as condensation can affect its texture. Store uncovered in the refrigerator for a few hours until completely cooled, then cover in plastic wrap.

2. For covering the crème caramel, I prefer plastic wrap rather than reusable wrap because it does not stick to the custard if it touches. If using reusable wrap, ensure there is enough space so that the wrap does not touch the custard.

3. See Pantry Staples (page 17) for information about agar agar powder and where to buy.

Makes 2 cups

Chantilly

Vegan ＊ Gluten-free ＊ Grain-free ＊ Nut-free ＊ Oil-free ＊ Soy-free ＊ Raw/No-bake ＊ One-bowl

½ cup aquafaba (liquid from
    canned chickpeas)
1 teaspoon pure vanilla extract
¼ teaspoon cream of tartar
3 to 4 tablespoons organic icing sugar

TIPS
1. Chantilly collapses over time, so it
is best to make it just before serving.
If you plan to use later, keep chilled in
the refrigerator and re-whip for a few
minutes before serving. You cannot
over-mix this recipe.
2. Reserve the chickpea liquid from
recipes that call for canned chickpeas.
Store in an airtight container in the
refrigerator for up to 5 days or in the
freezer for up to 2 months. If frozen,
thaw before using.

This sweet, creamy, light, and fluffy Chantilly is made using aquafaba, the liquid in canned chickpeas! This wondrous discovery from the vegan community makes it so easy to whip up in just minutes your own whipped cream that is as light as a cloud and oh so delicious.

Use this Chantilly to top your favourite sweets and desserts. Scoop it on my Chocolat Chaud (page 90) or Wally's Chocolate Coffee Freakshake (page 93) or serve it with my Chocolate Almond Torte (page 140), Winter Poached Pears with Spiced Syrup (page 289), French Apple Tart (page 273), Kryptonite Chocolate Lava Cakes (page 278), and Blueberry Ginger Galette (page 291).

1. In a stand mixer fitted with the whisk attachment, combine the aquafaba, vanilla, and cream of tartar. (Alternatively, you can use a glass or metal bowl and a hand mixer.) Begin whipping on low speed and gradually increase to high speed while gradually adding 3 tablespoons of the icing sugar. Whip until firm, stiff peaks form, about 7 minutes (10 to 12 minutes if using a hand mixer). Add up to 1 tablespoon more icing sugar to sweeten, if needed, and continue whipping until combined. Serve immediately.

A Note from Hannah

The saying "You are exactly where you need to be" has never felt more certain than it has while I was writing this cookbook. Before moving home to Canada from France, my husband and I hummed and hawed about whether it was the right move. Were we ready to say goodbye to the life we had built together in France? There were so many things we were going to miss! Our beautiful apartment with its Juliet balcony, the cobblestoned streets, daily farmers' markets, and boulangeries at every corner. Heck, we could even bring our sweet dog, Penny, into restaurants! It seemed absurd to give up a lovely life we had taken comfort in.

Yet deep down there was a strong yearning, a voice inside saying, "It's time to come home now." I will forever be grateful to that little voice that guided us back to Canada, for the next year and a half would prove to be the most rewarding and most challenging of my life.

Upon returning home, my *Two Spoons* blog flourished. In a few months, my Instagram and blog following soared, and partnerships with beloved brands came flooding into my inbox. Somehow, little old me was making a name for myself in the plant-based community, and my recipes were becoming ever more popular. I was able to transition *Two Spoons* to my full-time job and truly live my passion for making delicious plant-based recipes worth sharing.

Six months after moving home, I was offered the opportunity of a lifetime—to write this cookbook. Things were unfolding in ways that I had only ever dreamed of. In addition, that deep yearning—the voice that said "It's time to come home"—felt all the more sure.

At the same time that my business was soaring, however, my personal life started to unravel. The year 2020 marked the start of the COVID-19 pandemic, which left the world reeling in isolation and confusion. There is no doubt that we all felt the weight of it. In addition, Mitch and

I had planned to start a family when we moved home. Unfortunately, this was not happening as quickly as we had hoped, and six months later, my anxiety surfaced.

#Tryingtoconcieve took over our lives, and the rollercoaster of hope and disappointment was a never-ending journey. The idea of having a baby began to feel utterly impossible after so many months of trying. And then, my one-month-old nephew, Max, suddenly passed away, which shook our family to the core. It seemed like even when you could have a baby, you still could not really have them. Just a few weeks later, Mitch and I were medically diagnosed with infertility, and my anxiety cascaded into depression.

My close family and friends, who were aware of our struggle, would ask, "Is it hard to write a cookbook with all of this going on?" The truth is, it was my saving grace. This book was my light source, which brought me true joy in creating something to love during a time that would have otherwise been too heavy to hold. The kitchen became a place to lose myself in joy and passion. My book became a safe space amidst all the noise, where I could quietly feel that deep yearning again: "You are exactly where you need to be."

I have never felt as sure of these words as I do today, or as resilient, as I make my final remarks for my baby of a book, then move my hand down to my baby bump that is starting to take form.

We do not always get to choose what life throws at us, but we do get to choose how we react to it. In struggle, there is learning to be had, and beauty to be revealed. I chose to pour my beauty into these recipes as my guide for joy. Fond memories of what-once-was were stored away to be treasured, and beautiful new ones were created. I hope this resonates through the pages.

All my love,
Hannah

Acknowledgements

I must begin by thanking YOU, kind readers and followers of *Two Spoons*. It wouldn't be possible to do what I love, creating plant-based recipes worth sharing, without your support. Thank you for choosing this book, visiting my blog, sharing my recipes with your friends and family. I wish I could thank each and every one of you individually, because your contribution has had a profound impact on the trajectory of my life. Thank you from the bottom of my heart.

To my husband, Mitch: Thank you for your unwavering support and for giving me the title of "best cook you know!" Cooking is my love language, and it brings me so much joy to make recipes for you and our growing family. You have been my biggest cheerleader from the very beginning. Thank you for seeing my light on the days when I couldn't find it. And thank you for getting only *slightly* annoyed when I set the oven mitts on fire while developing my Pear Tarte Tatin recipe for this cookbook. I will eventually get around to buying a new pair…

To my mum and dad: Mum, thank you for running over at the drop of a hat with kitchen and styling accessories. I am so grateful for your constant support in my creativity, and I have you to thank for it. Dad, thank you for eating all my recipe-testing rejects. There have been many, and you've taken it like a champ.

To my talented friend Lauren Miller, who is responsible for much of the lifestyle photography and the cover photo in this book: You believed in this project before I even had a cookbook deal, and I'm so happy to have taken this journey with you by my side. Thank you for bringing my visions to life and for telling my story through your art. And to my beloved and gifted friend Craig George, who is responsible for the Paris photography in this book. Thank you for capturing pieces of our life in France. I cherish them fondly, and it's a great honour to share them.

Thank you to my wonderful editor, Andrea Magyar, who I respect and admire so much. You saw the vision for this book and gave me the opportunity to create it with your gifted team. I am a better writer and recipe developer because of you. A big thank you to everyone at Penguin Random House Canada who contributed to creating this book. There are many hands that touched it, and I am so grateful for your contributions.

A million thank yous to my recipe testers (and friends)! I'm publishing this book with confidence knowing just how much you enjoyed these recipes. I'm so appreciative of your honesty and feedback. To name a few who went above and beyond: Krystal (who cooked every recipe from the book—sometimes twice!), Matthew, and Erin. Thank you, my sweet friends.

And finally, to my fellow Canadian food bloggers: Angela Liddon, Erin Ireland, Joy McCarthy, Laura Wright, Lauren Toyota, and Sam Turnbull, to name just a few. I'm a forever fan of your work, and you've all inspired me in more ways than you'll ever know. Thank you for lighting my path and sparking the flame to pursue my own dreams. It's an honour and privilege to be among you.

Index